Making a Meal of It

Jui-shan Chang

Making a Meal of It

Sex in Chinese and Western Cultural Settings

Outskirts Press, Inc.
Denver, Colorado

Making a Meal of It
Sex in Chinese and Western Cultural Settings

V5.0

Outskirts Press, Inc.
http://www.outskirtspress.com

ISBN: 978-978-1-4327-6821-8

Library of Congress Control Number: 2011920714

PRINTED IN THE UNITED STATES OF AMERICA

Contents

List of Tables

Acknowledgments

The contents of this book represent my academic journey of studying sexuality as a sociologist. I wish to thank all the institutions which had accompanied and supported me: the University of Michigan, the East-West Centre in Hawaii, the University of Tasmania, the University of Iowa and the University of Melbourne. These institutions stimulated me in different ways as well as nurtured my intellectual growth in this long journey.

I wish to thank all funding agencies for financing all the major research projects in my journey: the Hewlett Foundation, Population Council, the Pacific Cultural Foundation, the Australian Research Council and the Chiang Ching-Kuo (CCK) Foundation for International Scholarly Exchange. In addition to money, another necessary condition is people. I wish to thank all respondents and interviewees who had kindly participated in my research projects conducted over the last two decades.

I also wish to thank Prints India, Sage and Elsvier who have permitted my earlier works published by them to be reframed, revised and incorporated in this book.

Chapter 2 contains revisions from parts of:

> Chang, Jui-shan. (1996). Negotiating Sexual Permissiveness in a Contemporary Chinese Setting: Young People in Taipei. *International Journal of Sociology of the Family*. 26(1):13–36.

Chapter 3 contains revisions from parts of:

Chang, Jui-shan. (2004). Refashioning Womanhood in 1990s' Taiwan: An Analysis of Taiwanese Edition of *Cosmopolitan* magazine. *Modern China* 30(3):361–397.

Chapter 7 contains revisions from parts of two articles:

Chang, Jui-shan. (2000). Familial Values, Gender Politics and Meanings of Infidelity: A Cross-Cultural Comparison of Extra-Marital Affairs. In Miller, R. & Browning, S. (Eds.), *With This Ring: Divorce, Intimacy, and Cohabitation from a Multi-Cultural Perspective* (pp. 185–218). JAI Press.

Chang, Jui-shan. (1999). Scripting Extra-Marital Affairs: Marital Mores, Gender Politics and Infidelity in Taiwan. *Modern China* 25(1):69–99.

I also wish to acknowledge that parts of Chapter 1 and Chapter 6 contain revisions from two articles in which I (the author) own the copyright:

Chang, Jui-shan. (1994). Change and Persistence: Autonomy of Dating, Engagement and Premarital Sex among Women in Taiwan. *Australian and New Zealand Journal of Sociology* 30(2):132–48.

Chang, Jui-shan. (2000). Agony-Resolution Pathways: How American Men Are Perceived by Women in the Agony Column of *Cosmopolitan*. *Journal of Men's Studies* 8(3):285–308.

I wish to thank my good friend Richard Volpato. He was a colleague when I was teaching at the Department of Sociology at the University of Tasmania. His wide reading, lively mind, Italian heritage and theological reflection always expanded my horizons about cross-cultural insights. Although we have moved on to other institutions, the collegial relationship, the friendship and the intellectual companionship have continued. He has read all the drafts contained in this book, mostly when the arguments were still being formed. My appreciation toward Richard is beyond the words of "thank you," but I still wish to express that here.

Finally, I wish to thank my immediate and dispersed family members. My 27-year-old son (Yu-chiao Hsueh) had accompanied me when he was a small child not just during numerous late nights in the computer centre at the University of Michigan but also during all the travelling across different continents in my academic pursuit.

My husband (Ya-seng Hsueh) had to be separated from me on two different continents on and off for two decades due to competing work commitments, but his love, support, patience and care toward me have remained so real and transcended the space, time and harsh tests in our lives.

My three brothers (Jui-fan, Jui-te and Jui-chun) are in Taiwan, but their love, encouragement and support have kept my hopes alive.

My parents (Chih-ming and Tao-ying) passed away this past year. They exemplify love, self-contentment and devotion to family, friends, community and society. They will linger in my heart for the rest of my life as loving humans and a source of inspiration. This book is dedicated to them.

Preface
Journeys

Kinsey ...

For several years I have wanted to write about the path I have taken in carrying out sociological sex research over 20 years. The opportunity to present this journey in book form permits me to be reflective about the major twists and turns in this journey—both personal and intellectual. Just as I first embarked on this reflection in 2004, a movie was showing called *Kinsey*. What a coincidence! It is about a pioneer in sex research. The movie documents Alfred Kinsey's transition from a zoologist to a sexologist, studying diverse male and then female sexual behaviours in 1950s' America, and, of course, the relation between his research and his personal life.

One of the major contributions of Kinsey's survey findings was that many "ordinary" Americans did not need to feel guilty, embarrassed or anxious about some of their "abnormal" sexual practices. This movie provided not just a sort of "genre" for my intended writing at that time, but more important, this coincidence has given me confidence to document my engagement with this complex area of human life: after all, something valuable could be documented and debated, even though as a sociologist my name and influence in the field and society is relatively insignificant, particularly compared to someone like Kinsey!

I grew up in Taiwan. I graduated from National Taiwan University and the University of Michigan, majoring in sociology. I began researching sexuality in 1980s' Taiwan at a time when a "quiet" sexual revolution started happening. I then extended my research to Hong Kong and mainland China to explore what, if anything, was sexually in common among the three Chinese societies that went beyond variations on an individual, community or regional level.

In the 1990s, I extended the comparison into Western cultural settings. This way, whatever was sexually common among Chinese societies and could be called "Chinese sexuality" would leap out at me once I compared what I had studied with non-Chinese societies. From all this emerged a cross-cultural research program into what I call the "embedded meanings of sex" in the Chinese and Western cultural settings.

The embedded meaning of sex in each of the two cultural settings would be harder to be made visible without framing sex under the wider cultural configurations of human nature, sex, self, family, manhood/womanhood/personhood and individual transcendence, as well as comparing with "the other" via contrasting the wider cultural configurations of these aspects of human condition defined by the two world religions, Confucianism and Christianity. The youthful puzzlement with sexuality, informed by sociology and cross-cultural comparison, has ended up in a large canvas upon which I can develop ideas about sexuality.

Kinsey's methodology in studying sex had stuck to survey data using statistical analysis. My methodological journey had a similar beginning, namely a positivistic quantitative methodology with hypothesis testing, using survey data with advanced statistical modelling (particularly event history analysis). I was then at the University of Michigan.

After I started my academic career in Australia, I got closer to the data itself, rather than to statistical summaries. Using various data visualisations, I realised that more nuances could be verbalised than might be captured in statistical models. This opened up into interpretative qualitative methodology in which I analysed diverse forms of data: from focus groups, in-depth interviews and cultural artefacts (such as newspaper reports, movies, popular women's magazines, Confucian classics and the Christian scriptures). From all of this, and from the "bottom up," as it were, I could generate insights and interpretations that could capture deeper meanings about sexuality than was possible in the Kinsey-style approach.

Kinsey's observation about how many Americans were ignorant about sex knowledge and sexual techniques (including a problematic first-sex consummation between husband and wife) and how this "commonsense" sex knowledge was primarily derived from religion and morality, rather than scientific findings, motivated and committed him to scientific research into the sexual practices of Americans.

While finding the number and range of Americans that had had to go through a lot (of nonsense!) in their sexual journeys in diverse orientations, Kinsey had also acknowledged and actualised the "diverse" aspect of his own sexuality. According to a known Kinsey scale to measure sexual orientation (0 defined as "exclusively heterosexual" and 6 as "exclusively homosexual"), Kinsey's own scores sometimes fluctuated between 0 and 6. Various unconventional sexual episodes between him, his wife and a third party (a man) had caused him pain. His personal experience in sexuality would have no doubt made his sex research more relevant, not only to 1940s' and '50s' Americans but also to himself.

Not just Kinsey, for many academics, generally, research and personal lives tend to be intertwined in some way(s). I remember one famous American family sociologist confessing to me in a taxi on our way to a family conference in Taichung, Taiwan, "I've divorced, so I study divorce. It is the advantage of being a sociologist—when we have problems, we study them!" In my case, I am interested in studying so-called life-course transitions, which (to me, at least) have generated a range of problems, excitements, puzzlements, surprises, disappointments, hope, regression, progression, mistakes, enlightenments, muddle-headedness, wisdom, hurts and love. Beyond my (particularly) life, ultimately, learning to be a man or a woman and achieving self-transcendence, or at least, self-reflection, at a particular time, space and sociocultural context in life's rich journey remains, I think, central to the (general) human condition.

East Meets West

When I went to Ann Arbor, Michigan, in 1983, I certainly experienced cultural shock, particularly at how my American classmates expressed and asserted themselves. Initially, I thought and hoped that once my spoken English got better, I could express myself better in seminars. After one year, I did open my mouth in seminars, but I found it more challenging and awkward to express *my* own view than to express sociological knowledge as a sort of third-party entity. I became close friends with a few Americans. Some of them have remained my good friends for more than 20 years. Through the first several years, I noticed the "exoticness" in my friends gradually fading, and I learned that humans are human, regardless of cultures. In a way, this realisation helped me to learn to express myself in academic as well as social settings.

However, such clear but "adjustable" East-West duality in my life in Michigan was challenged again when I moved to Honolulu and worked at the East-West Centre. The majority of people I had interacted with there were Orientals. Somehow, I felt that the communication between me as an Oriental and the Orientals in Hawaii had not been as natural and easy as I had imagined (compared to the communication between me and my Western friends in Michigan). I seemed more Western than the Orientals in Hawaii.

In (July) 1993, the natural beauty of Hobart made me accept an offer to teach at the University of Tasmania and decline an offer from another university in New York City. My exposure to aspects of Australian culture (in terms of the spirit of collective mateship and "a fair go") in Tasmania, as well as aspects of British culture (in terms of the consciousness of class and status) and the reserved manner of my migrant academic colleagues from England allowed me to experience the diversity within the West and the Western culture. I was perceived by English colleagues as "too American" (outspoken, assertive and straightforward) and perceived by Australian colleagues as "too individualistic." All felt a bit disappointed that I was not the sort of Chinese woman they had expected.

In 1996, I returned to America teaching at the University of Iowa. I experienced living in America differently again, with my newfound understandings about certain aspects of Australian and British contexts. This time, I understood that there was diversity within Western culture, and I did not try to fit Western culture into a single model, "the" American way, which I had imagined as "the" Western way before. I suppose that in the eyes of my American colleagues, I was more "exotic"—being Chinese, American and Australian!

In 1997, I came to Melbourne, starting the Sociology Program with two other sociologists at the University of Melbourne. My experience and understanding of the "West" had been further expanded. My appreciation of/sensitivity to cultural nuances have certainly become more sophisticated by living in Melbourne, a truly multicultural context, with many migrants from Southern Europe, particularly Italy and Greece. I learned from my Italian friends that familism is strong in the Italian culture and in the Mediterranean societies generally, but I found that there remains something "Western" among these familial souls compared to the familial Chinese with whom I am familiar. The validation of being an Italian man or woman seems beyond fulfilling the familial roles.

In 2009, I started my training to become a psychotherapist and have seen clients in supervised placements. Most of my clients have been Anglo-Celtic adults who tend to have ultimate concerns about self-identity, desire and existential issues. Regardless of their gender, socioeconomic status, age, life stage, marital status or the trigger(s) to bring them to therapy, there are common issues raised, such as "Who am *I*?" "What do *I* really want?" or "What is the purpose of *my* life?" Such identity and existential issues are urgent for people in their 20s who struggle with deficits in actualising their sense of independence as an individual adult. These issues are also urgent for people in their 30s and 40s who wish somehow to transcend their multiple roles/responsibilities in relation to their work and family. They also seem particularly urgent for people in their 50s and beyond with grown-up children who have "done their bit" for the family but who are struggling in redefining/repositioning themselves in terms of exploring who they are, what they want for themselves (rather than for everyone else in the family), and whom they could be becoming.

In contrast, the validation of being a man/woman/person primarily through familial roles remains fundamental for most Chinese people. Perhaps this is why some in the field of Chinese studies argue that many Chinese people don't have a "self" or have a "self" that is primarily defined by relations and roles.

In 2007, I had conducted in-depth interviews with cultural elites,[1] 12 in Beijing and five in Hong Kong, aged from late 20s to mid-50s. They all articulated a common core ideal of harmony (which I call as "the habit of a Chinese heart") and a most generic ethical norm—piety (submitting to, and fulfilling duties for, roles). All elites perceived the essence of roles as meaningful, and to them, "the meaning of life" is closely tied to fulfilling duties or actualising roles, starting from family (in a vertical direction, including parents and children) and being extended to work, community or society.

After more than two decades of experiencing and "learning" to be a world citizen in these various Western cultural contexts, I feel that I have gradually developed a "self" and have been able to express and act on my own views and arguments in my thinking, writing, teaching, social and personal life (as well as even in departmental politics). While expressing "my voice," I also feel that the underlying "me" still has a "self" more connected with familial roles and relations than an individualistic and/or individualized orientation. On one level, it is "Chinese," but my "Chineseness" is different from being Chinese in other contemporary Chinese societies (including in my homeland, Taiwan).

On another level, while I remain different from "the other" in Western societies, I have been able to appreciate and become "the other" as well as developing a "self" in my own way, grounded in my biography in cross-cultural experiences with numerous trial-and-errors and gains from deep pain. This "self" emerged in the West, despite being grounded in Chinese cultural ideals and a family structure. Certain incidents, situations and moments have provoked me to reflect and raise a question, "Am I *merely* equal to the sum of my familial roles?" However, this question seems to be only situational or momentary to me, rather than being fundamental as to my Western friends or clients in Melbourne.

In my younger days in Taiwan, I had started to be, and have always been, interested in culture(s), particularly when Chinese culture contrasts with "the other" culture (i.e., Western culture). Perhaps if there were no contrasts between cultures, I would not have been interested in culture or fascinated by differences between cultures. Such contrast started from popular songs.

I have been exposed to rock 'n' roll since primary school, when my oldest brother started listening to it. I didn't know what the songs'

English lyrics were, but I was able to taste the different "flavours" between the two: the intense melody and the (up) "beats" excited me, while the soft and sweet Chinese songs, like a river flow, calmed me down. Somehow, both love songs seemed to be expressing love, but in different ways.

The Chinese songs expressed love in a reserved but deep way with descriptions about scenes, while the Western songs seemed direct and intense with a strong "I" in them. Even "love" felt different between the two: the Chinese "love" sounded implicit, delicate and melancholy, while the Western "love" sounded explicit, romantic and lustful.

At age 14, I wrote and published my very first short story in a newspaper after I listened to the Rolling Stones' "As Tears Go By." Although I did not capture the lyrics, a singer's expressive voice aroused my affective feeling toward my second brother, Jui-te, with whom I shared similar academic interests. I wrote that story about a bond between a brother and a sister with a Chinese familial theme. I felt the same way when I was exposed to, and contrasted, paintings and novels from the two cultural modes—I was fascinated by the "other" culture.

I have learned from social studies in high school that family is the primary institution in the Chinese society, and familism is the core of Chinese culture. Given that family is also the primary institution in Western society, I wonder why the "self" is presented and represented in popular songs, novels and paintings so much more visibly and powerfully than in the Chinese cultural artefacts. Why is "love" represented so differently? Do different representations mean that "love" has different meanings in the two cultures? How about sex? Why do Western songs and movies dare to present the lustful aspect of sexuality? What does sex mean? Does sex mean the same in the two cultures? What is the relation between sex, sexuality and manhood/womanhood? What do a man, a woman and a decent person mean in each of the two cultural settings?

Have I found answers for any of the "innocent" questions I posed in my youth? This book, based on my two-decade sociological research, hopes to provide some clues, or insights, which could lead to further research, debates or reflections among numerous individuals and families in Chinese and Western cultural settings.

NOTES

1. Among my 12 interviewees in Beijing (four women), there were:

   - one in cultural policy (a director of a cultural development foundation);
   - five "cultural mediators," including a principal and a (female) director of moral/ethics education of an elite school, a director of students' affairs of an elite university, and an editor of a major magazine on current socioeconomic issues in China; and
   - six "cultural innovators," including one critical intellectual on current education reform and implementing the reform via a NGO in China, a (female) environmental advocate who is also an entrepreneur in the finance industry, a (female) editor for a major imported women's magazine, a (female) academic in Chinese film critique, an artist, a critical intellectual/blogger who owns an elite bookshop, and a critical thinker/innovator on Chinese philosophy.

   Among my five interviewees in Hong Kong, there were:

   - one in cultural policy (a director of a cultural policy research centre in a major university);
   - two "cultural mediators": including the owner of the most influential news corporation and an editor for a major newspaper; and
   - two "cultural innovators": including one artist/art critique, and one female academic in cultural studies and an advocate in heritage preservation.

Introduction

This book presents my original sociological research in *framing* sex with issues regarding self-identity, manhood/womanhood/personhood, marriage and family under the common impacts of modernisation between different contemporary Chinese societies (Taiwan, Hong Kong and mainland China) that have been through different systems of political economy and colonial experiences, as well as between the Chinese and Western societies that have been grounded in different civilisations.

This book addresses the Chinese-style of modernity, particularly starting from the historical turning points of changing sexual mores, marriage, family, self, life-course transitions and manhood/womanhood under rapid socioeconomic transformation and cultural change. It documents my two-decade sociological research and original arguments regarding these aspects of Chinese modernity.

Through my comparative research into Chinese and Western sexuality, I have critiqued the application of Kinsey-type sex (survey) research to Chinese societies. My main argument regarding Chinese sexuality (versus Western sexuality) is presented in Chapter 8. This is because without building upon some of my earlier works as presented from the seven preceding chapters, the specific approach and the major argument I have particularly proposed in Chapter 8 cannot have been developed. I have argued that, with the loosening premarital sexual mores in Chinese societies in the rapid process of modernisation (including exposure to contemporary Western ideas and values), particularly after the mid-1990s, it might appear there is a "convergence" toward behaviours of the secular West.

My cross-cultural comparative research indicates that, despite the diversity that exists within each of the Chinese or Western settings, the metaphors and embedded meanings of sex actually remain different. Each cultural setting has its own distinct "home base" metaphor and embedded meaning of sex: where sex functions likes a "meal" for "sustenance" in Chinese cultural settings versus it being part of a "game" for individual recognition and validation as a man or a woman in Western cultural settings. This contrast would be harder to emerge unless we do cross-cultural comparisons *and* frame sexual behaviors with issues regarding self, manhood/womanhood/personhood, marriage and family.

This book argues and illustrates that the modernisation argument (to put it simply, the more "modern" a society becomes, the more permissive the sexual mores become) is indeed inadequate when it focuses only on trends, particularly those trends which are "converging" to the West, and fails to ground the trends in the traditions and histories of specific societies. This inadequacy is due to making "truncated" comparisons between societies, particularly societies rooted in different cultural traditions.

In our fascination with our "neighbours" in this global village, we run the risk of imagining that we are all becoming alike, without asking where our neighbours came from or indeed where they might be going!

Parallel to my life journey, which I have sketched in the preface, the chapters in this book highlight the twists and turns in my intellectual journey. More important, they demonstrate a cumulative development not just in sociological approaches of researching sex but also in shifting theoretical paradigms in studying the impacts of modernisation on different cultures and societies—from modernisation theory into the multiple modernities.

The insights of sex, self, manhood/womanhood, marriage and family presented in this book can particularly critique the conventional modernisation paradigm that equates modernity with Western modernity. Furthermore, these insights can enrich the newly emerging paradigm of multiple modernities (notably Eisenstadt, 2000, 2003), given that this new paradigm has been primarily built upon the studies of varieties in democratic and capitalistic institutions, rather than in family institutions in the contemporary societies across different civilisations on the globe.

The journey presented in this book starts from the post-World War II Taiwan. Why did I start from Taiwan in this stream of comparative studies of sex and exploring what being modern means when sex is framed with the areas of self-identity, manhood/womanhood, marriage and family and its implications for the paradigm of multiple modernities?

Taiwan in the 1960s was a "laboratory" for studying Chinese society and culture, notably argued by Professor Chen Shao-hsin in 1966 (Chen, 1966), a distinguished cultural anthropologist at that time. Since the late 1970s, there has been a movement toward political independence in Taiwan, but I would argue that such a "lab" status of studying the impacts of modernisation on Confucian Chinese culture remains even today.

The pro-independence Democratic Progressive Party entered the multiparty platform in 1991 after martial law was lifted in 1987. It had won presidential elections for eight years (2000–2008) and particularly promoted a Taiwanese political and cultural identity in past decades. However, the newly emerging "Taiwanised" identity promoted by the pro-independence movement emphasises more on Taiwan's geography, history, politics and a culture influenced by multiple cultural/colonial sources than "de-Sinologizing" its traditional Chinese family structure and values.

This "lab" status derives from Taiwan's particular political and economic situation during the 1950s to the 1990s. Although Taiwan had been under Japanese colony for five decades in the first half of the twentieth century, the Confucian tradition, in spite of being implanted by politics, privileged Taiwan with this "lab" status. The Nationalist Party had intensively implanted an orthodox Confucian cultural tradition in Taiwan.

After the party lost the civil war to the Communist Party in the mainland and fled to Taiwan in 1949, Confucian classics were a compulsory part of the curriculum at every level of education (from primary school to university) and tested in national entrance exams to higher education, public services and all other civil exams. In the same period, Hong Kong remained a British colony and mainland China went through the major 10-year Cultural Revolution. Furthermore, both Taiwan and Hong Kong started the process of modernisation in the 1960s, while mainland started it almost two decades later. Therefore, Taiwan has been the first contemporary Chinese society with orthodox Confucian values and nationalist political ideology to start modernisation.

To study how modernisation has affected Confucian values and different cohorts of Chinese people's life-course transitions from the early stage of modernisation of the 1950s and onward, Taiwan is indeed an unusual, if not the only, "lab" for such research.

Overall, this entire intellectual journey has been like using a "grounded theory" approach with a process of analytic induction. Grounded in the most appropriate data, research strategy and the theoretical paradigm for the questions proposed at the time, each chapter of this book made an "extra" elaboration regarding the topic—further questions posed, more constructs unfolded, deeper insights revealed and my argument expanded.

This intellectual journey starts from positivistic quantitative sociology in a premarital, normative Taiwanese cultural context in the 1980s. At that time, after Taiwan had undergone rapid modernisation in the 1960s and 1970s, one of the effects of the two-decades of social change was on young women's transition to adulthood, including finishing schooling, leaving home, nonfamilial work and living experience, autonomy in dating and the transition to the first sexual experience. Sophisticated survey data were required to study trends and changes in these crucial events occurring during life-course transition to adulthood across two decades of different birth cohorts. The sophistication lies in enhancing the capacity of a cross-sectional survey to collect time-specific data over each individual's life course.

An instrument called an "event history calendar" was used to collect information of the age of each major life event that occurred. When I collected such data along with a major 1986 islandwide KAP (knowledge, attitude and behaviour) survey of 5,000 Taiwanese women, I felt that I was part of this social change, given that my personal transition to adulthood was also occurring during the period of time I was studying. Chapter 1 demonstrates how I used a life-course approach, with the advanced quantitative methodology of "event history analysis" that I learned at the University of Michigan, to study the newly emerging social phenomenon of increasing premarital sex for women who had grown up in 1950s'–1980s' Taiwan and to frame their first sexual experience with other major life events in their transition to adulthood.

After the study on the level of behaviour via survey data, my intellectual journey extended into the exploration on the level of meaning regarding how young men and women perceived and negotiated premarital sexual permissiveness in 1990s' Taiwan.

Chapter 2 presents my approach shifted from using a positivistic quantitative survey into interpretative qualitative methodology using a grounded theory approach with focus groups. I conducted focus groups among Taipei young people in 1994. When I taught at the

University of Tasmania, to my surprise, the interpretative paradigm also involved cutting-edge technology. I learnt how to transcribe my focus group data in videotapes by listening attentively to the tapes, and used digital recording equipment to tag segments of videos and to transcribe back and forth by tracing those tags. Only then did I feel I could venture a thorough interpretation.

When the bigger (academic and social) environment was shifting from the modernisation paradigm to postmodernisation and globalisation, my intellectual journey went into the dynamics between globalism and localism. I became particularly fascinated by the way the "global"/"Western" can be used as a means to achieve the "local"/"Chinese" ends for contemporary Chinese women to construct a modern womanhood with a more fulfilled career, relationships, marriage, family and sexuality.

When I taught at the University of Melbourne, my further exploration in qualitative sociology was moving into the level of discourse represented in popular culture.

Chapter 3 presents a discourse analysis of how globalism and localism interacted in the arena represented by the 1990s' Taiwanese edition of *Cosmopolitan* magazine. I remember for six months I maintained huge spreadsheets of coded "Agony Aunt" columns and *Cosmo* materials in bed with me as my bedtime stories, perhaps allowing me to spot patterns when at times I couldn't fall asleep.

Chapters 1 to 3 set out my investigation of how modernisation has impacted sexual perceptions, attitudes and behaviours as well as popular discourse regarding modern womanhood across different cohorts of people who had grown up during the first three decades of modernisation in Taiwan.

I then questioned if there was something which could be called "Chinese sexuality" and recognised that I wouldn't know it unless I engaged in comparative research with two levels of comparison required. The first level was to compare the findings and insights obtained from my studies in Taiwan with those from studies of other contemporary Chinese societies, primarily those of Hong Kong and China, which also have been under rapid modernisation in recent decades. The second level was to extend the comparison from "between Chinese societies" to "between Chinese and non-Chinese societies." My intellectual journey had turned into comparative sociology with two levels of comparative studies.

Chapters 4 and 5 present my studies on the first level of comparison, i.e., between the three contemporary Chinese societies. I made my first trip to mainland China and Hong Kong in 1994. These trips were historical for me, having grown up in Taiwan where direct communication between mainland China and Taiwan had been banned for four decades. Everything I saw there was interesting and worthwhile to me as a Chinese person from Taiwan and as a researcher in Chinese studies. I probed every single conversation in my focus group discussions and in-depth interviews as well as in my every conversation with anyone in Shanghai! My local host, Professor Liu Dalin at Shanghai University, with a reputation of "the Kinsey in China," helped in many ways, including suggesting that I wear a jacket outside of my colourful sundress that would be more in keeping with local expectations.

Chapter 4 provides an overview and identifies different pathways of liberalising premarital sexual mores between these contemporary Chinese societies from the 1950s to the mid-1990s, and it explores, after the mid-1990s, what direction these changes in sexual mores appeared to take with implications for the modernisation argument.

Chapter 5 explores issues pertinent to the overall trend of loosening sexual mores in contemporary China, Hong Kong and Taiwan and studies whether these changes in premarital sexual behaviour reflect an underlying attitudinal trend toward secular Western permissiveness. In particular, it explores whether young people growing up in the most modernised major cities are "loosening up" relative to core traditional values and what "traditional" values are perceived and lived by these young people in the three Chinese societies.

I conducted in-depth interviews of highly educated young Chinese growing up in the major cities of these three societies in 2005. The study revealed that loosening premarital sexual mores has not resulted in these highly educated urban youths becoming less "Chinese" with regard to core values of familism.

Before presenting my studies on the second level of comparison, i.e., extending the comparison to non-Chinese societies, primarily to Western cultural settings, Chapter 6 provides a prelude into the level of contemporary discourse about sex, gender and relationship issues prevalent and represented in popular culture in the secular West.

In parallel to the analysis in Chapter 3 of the Taiwanese edition of *Cosmopolitan* magazine, Chapter 6 analyses the American edition of *Cosmopolitan* magazine. The Taiwanese and American editions of *Cosmopolitan* (*Cosmo*) magazines offer a way of exploring different themes in these two cultural settings. Chapter 3 presents a discourse analysis of refashioning womanhood. In particular, it is focused on the theme of how globalism and localism were intermeshed and represented by the 1990s' Taiwan *Cosmo*. This is the strength of utilising this specific magazine at that time period to explore such a theme, because the content of the Taiwanese *Cosmo* was being gradually localised in terms of using a higher proportion of locally written articles as against translated articles from the *Cosmopolitan* headquarters throughout the 1990s.

In contrast, Chapter 6 has its focus on the "Agony Aunt" columns in the 1990s' American edition of *Cosmopolitan*. This secular advisory system represented in advice columns provides me with a data set with a unique structure (composed the agony presented in real lives of the women who write in, and the specific advice given by the

Agony Aunt). Chapter 6 analyses such texts or representations and constructs theoretical typologies of "Agony-Resolution Pathways" to reveal the nature of gender politics and modern agony and solutions underlined by individualism.

Through the work presented in this chapter, I got into men's studies after a long period of studying women's issues, because I realised that gender issues require study into, and understanding of, both genders. This adventure, thus, started from a cross-gender approach, how American men are perceived by women in the "Agony Aunt" columns of *Cosmopolitan*.

Following the understanding about the condition of gender politics, its agony and resolution in the secular West represented in popular culture, Chapters 7 and 8 present my comparative studies between Chinese and Western cultural settings.

Chapter 7 probes the topic of sexuality further by studying sexual transgression. While witnessing and being fascinated by how marriages worked or didn't work in the Western cultural settings, from statistical figures and representations in popular culture and anecdotal stories, I realised that studying the "nonnormative" extramarital sex can be more illuminating than the study of "normative" marital sex—simply because transgression marks out and crosses social boundaries and reveals deeper meanings. I found myself on many occasions in an "agony aunt" role with people in such predicaments who assumed that I might have useful advice to offer.

Chapter 7 explores extramarital transgressions, using ethnographic content analysis of real stories in newspaper reports in the 1990s, with typology construction regarding the boundary of family and the meanings of (in)fidelity, love and sex in Chinese and Western cultural settings.

In the later part of my journey of conducting comparative studies between Chinese and Western cultural settings in the 2000s, my approach has deepened. This is because the pervasive differences between the Chinese and Western cultures have driven me to trace each of their "roots"—the aspect of cultural origins represented in the classics of Confucianism and the Christian Bible. In 2002, I reread the Confucian classics with a specific lens (unlike the way I had memorised these texts for exams from primary school to university in Taiwan). In 2003, I started to learn to read the Bible, both English and Chinese editions. I read through the whole Bible, reading certain parts three times, inserting yellow stickers on many pages. Most of my colleagues and students in Melbourne were amazed by this, because none of them had gone through the Bible even once.

The last chapter of this book, Chapter 8, presents how I did my "genealogical" research by digging into the "roots" of the two world religions. Most important, this work has challenged the adequacy of much research into sexual practices in different societies, which has reported a ubiquitous trend toward permissiveness due to modernisation and globalisation. Such Kinsey-inspired research compares rates of specific sexual practices across different societies, presuming that sexual behaviours have the same meanings everywhere.

This work proposes a cross-cultural sociological approach to locate sexual practices at a more fundamental level—namely, the embedded meaning of sex. The "embedded meaning of sex" can more clearly emerge through cross-cultural contrasts of different definitions and configurations regarding human nature, sex, self, human relations, marriage, family and the recognition and validation of being a man, a woman or a "decent" human being. Without cross-cultural contrasts on these deeper configurations defined by different world religions, the embedded meanings of sex would be harder to be made visible, because people in the same culture would take for granted what sex means within that culture.

Cross-cultural contrasts can show the different possibilities, and people in specific cultures have a distinct "home base" regarding their embedded meaning of sex that operates. Different metaphors and the embedded meaning of sex *emerge* from such cross-cultural contrasts: "meal" for "sustenance" in Chinese contexts versus "game" for "individual recognition, validation and completion" in Western contexts. In Chinese contexts, sex is not who you are but what you do—"who you are" is primarily tied to familial roles; in Western contexts, sex is not what you do but who you are.

Finally, "Concluding Remarks" highlights the implications derived from the research and findings presented in this book. Theoretically, the findings of my research in sex, self, manhood/womanhood, marriage and family in Chinese and Western cultural settings can critique the conventional modernisation paradigm and enrich the new paradigm of multiple modernities. Methodologically, this book presents a variety of innovative research strategies to upgrade the Kinsey-style surveys in studying sex.

As for practical implications for the future, I have developed the notion of a "transcultural wisdom bank"—the collection of the "set" of possible solutions from different cultures or societies to *recurrent* problems that are common to the human condition, and which no one culture has (ever) managed to solve completely.

With respect to my cross-cultural research of the embedded meanings of sex, a "wisdom bank" about the metaphors of sex, meanings of sex, sexual norms and sanctions, the relationships between sex, love, marriage and family, and self becomes possible—taking wisdom from this bank, individuals will be less likely to be "stuck" in their own definitions of and issues about sex (particularly if they do not work!).

Afterword

I completed the research of this book in 2007 as a sociologist. Since then, I have been exploring my career and personal journeys from academia, to industry, and to psychotherapy and psychoanalysis. These initiatives were adventurous searching—to understand my being, and to explore who I can be becoming. At the same time, it seems that these adventures have never taken me too far away, because these adventures have not involved "breaks away" but rather "repositioning" myself in relation to a position which is defined by my families (family of origin, and a dispersed and then reunited nuclear family of my own), as well as a Confucian ideal of being an intellectual who not only connects to the wider society/world but also feels obligated to reflect, document and share how I make sense of certain issues and aspects of human conditions.

This book presents my journeys. More important, it presents the turning points, pathways and the processes of a "quiet" sexual revolution occurring in contemporary Chinese societies making their historical transformations into modernity in a globalised world. Although this sexual revolution may have started with being "quiet," as presented in this book, the understanding and implications can actually open up new possibilities to anyone. After all, framing sex with manhood, womanhood, personhood, relationships and family is a core part of human conditions. Thus, it should never be too late for me to share my thinking presented in this book despite the fact that this book may not contain the most updated data.

Part 1:

1950s'–1980s' Taiwan

Chapter 1

A Quiet Sexual Revolution

The influence of social change on family life was a central issue in the social sciences in the twentieth century (Ogburn and Tibbets, 1933; Goode, 1970; Caldwell, 1982; Thornton, 2005). Social scientists have long correlated industrialisation, urbanisation, educational expansion and economic growth with changes in family and demographic behaviour (Goode, 1970, 1982; Ogburn and Nimkoff, 1976; Hareven, 1982; Thornton and Fricke, 1987). A phenomenon of increasing premarital sex was emerging in 1980s' Taiwan, accompanied with the taking off of industrialisation, urbanisation and cultural change in the 1960s and 1970s. This chapter examines and interprets the transition to sexual experience among ever-married women born between 1936 and 1960 who had completed the transition to adulthood during the 1950s–1980s in Taiwan, a society which has been characterised historically as familistic and which had experienced rapid socioeconomic transformation during those decades of the early phases of modernisation.

There are two reasons why this chapter emphasises only the women's side of the story regarding this quiet revolution. One is that historically men in Chinese culture have always had more sexual freedom. Traditionally, the husband-wife relationship was to produce children, but only men had "alternative" sexual outlets (i.e., concubines and prostitutes). This double standard regarding chastity persisted in 1980s' Taiwan—it remained tolerable for men to have sex outside the marital context. Therefore, given the constant permissiveness of men's sexuality, the real change for the "loosening up" in this quiet sexual revolution in Taiwan was more likely to be from women than men.

The other reason for the focus on women in this study is that, given the fact that both men and women were exposed to this new courtship system and a changing sociocultural environment in 1980s' Taiwan, the new autonomy which individuals gained from education, working outside of the home and living away from home brought more changes to women's lives than to those of men. This, in turn, had an impact on young couples' (particularly young women's) transition to sexual experiences.

According to traditional Chinese norms, sexual intercourse is permitted only in marriage and is considered "adult behaviour." This is evident in a Chinese saying: "Before getting married, one is always a child!" However, a 1980 islandwide survey of married women in Taiwan found that half of the wives in the age group of 20–24 years in Taiwan said they had had sexual intercourse with their future husbands before marriage. Furthermore, the youngest age group of wives interviewed, 20- to 24-year-olds, were nearly 60 percent more likely to have had premarital sexual intercourse with their future husbands than the 25- to 29-year-old wives, and nearly 2.5 times as likely as the wives aged 30 to 34 (Cernada et al., 1986). These statistics provides prima facie evidence of changes in traditional norms from the 1960s to the 1980s.

The dramatic increase in sexual intimacy before marriage in Taiwan was described as "a very quiet sexual revolution" in the 1980s (Rindfuss and Morgan, 1983) and attributed to a shift from arranged marriages toward romantic marriages and changes to dating behaviour and the courtship process (Thornton et al., 1989). However, it can be argued that the apparent increase in the proportion of Taiwanese women[1] engaging in premarital sexual relations before the 1980s is not an indicator that a sexual revolution was occurring as a result of socioeconomic changes and Westernisation, but rather it is a presentation of preexisting values hitherto imperfectly understood. This interpretation depends on how the term or concept of "marriage" has been defined in Chinese culture.

In Chinese culture, "getting married" is a process that starts much earlier than the wedding day, but the term "being married" means that someone has completed the whole marriage process (i.e., has had the wedding ceremony). Therefore, the term "premarital sex" used in this chapter, which is measured in the Western way (i.e., sex occurring before the wedding day), actually refers to, or should be cultural-specifically identified as sex before the finalised step or the completion of the marriage process.

In the following sections, I first discuss in detail the sociocultural and theoretical background to that thesis regarding the change and persistence of Taiwanese women's transition to sexual experiences from the 1950s to the 1980s. Then I use a life-course approach with data gathered from a 1986 islandwide survey to examine that thesis by incorporating both trend analysis and multivariate analyses.

Theoretical Framework

Virginity Value in Chinese Tradition

Traditional Confucianism proscribes romantic love lest it threaten the parent-child tie, which is seen as the basic structural basis of the Chinese family. "Courtship" practices could not therefore operate. The husband-wife relationship was a utilitarian one, to produce children. The importance of female chastity before and after marriage has long been stressed in Chinese culture as a requisite for orderly family life regarding inheritance and the undisturbed continuation of the lineage. To ensure chastity, Confucianists advocated the complete separation of the sexes (Gulik, 1974). Historically, the virtuous woman was called *lienü*. The importance of chastity for defining female virtue increased sharply during the Neo-Confucian Era, starting from the Sung (AD 960–1279) dynasty. In the periods Yuan (AD 1299–1368) and Ming (AD 1369–1644), female chastity became virtually the only qualification for *lienü* (Chiao, 1969). In those periods, a woman had to remain chaste at all costs.

Change and Persistence

Particular periods in history have, as Mannheim (1952) notes, a distinctive "spirit of the time." From the 1950s to the 1980s, as a result of rapid socioeconomic transformation and cultural change, Taiwan had become an urban and industrial society with widespread education and extensive contacts with the outside world. Many nonfamilial ideas and values had been added to preexisting Chinese familial ideals during this process of rapid socioeconomic transformation. Individuals were likely to be exposed to these nonfamilial ideals either through their personal participation in nonfamilial activities (such as schooling, labour force participation and living outside of the parental home), or through the mass media, friends, relatives or the community without having direct personal nonfamilial experiences. In addition, many Western ideas and values (including those of democracy, freedom, egalitarianism, romantic love and the dating culture) had been imported or copied directly from Western role models. In general, younger cohorts of women in 1980s' Taiwan had grown up in a period of a greater infusion of nonfamilial and Western ideals, and in a more rapidly changing socioeconomic structure than was the case for women who grew up prior to the 1960s.

Since the 1960s, this new socioeconomic structure has modified young Taiwanese women's entry into adulthood. From the 1960s to the 1980s, participation in nonfamilial institutions had exposed young women not only to the ideas and influences of a nonfamilial context, but also to more opportunities for interactions with the opposite sex, and had enabled a level of autonomy not evident in their past experiences at home. As a result, increased premarital sexual intimacy had become likely.

Nonetheless, in 1980s' Taiwan, many traditional institutions persisted. The patrilineal system, filial piety and continuity of the family line continued to be diffused across generations and was still emphasised. The double standard regarding premarital chastity persisted. Further, contraception was officially only available for married women, and legalised abortion was accessible to married women only with spousal consent. Moreover, even if the decrease in parental control over the choice of marital partners seemed great, the meaning of engagement and marriage remained a "contract" between the two families, rather than between two young people. While weddings in Taiwan had been "Westernised" in terms of the principal actors now travelling by car (rather than sedan chair) and the bride wearing a white wedding gown (instead of a red one), the structure of marriage remained very much within the Chinese tradition, and the procedure followed the traditional "Six Rites" (Wolf, 1972; Cohen, 1976; Hu, 1982).

The "Six Rites" make clear that in Chinese culture marriage is a *process*. Freedman has summarised the "Six Rites" as follows: inquiries are made in a girl's family by the go-between of a family seeking a bride; genealogical and horoscopic data are sought by the go-between; the girl's horoscope is matched with the boy's; the betrothal is clinched by the transfer of gifts; the date of the wedding (that is, the transfer of the bride) is fixed; the bride is moved (Freedman, 1970).

Among Taiwanese people, the time when the betrothal is finalised by the transfer of gifts and publicised to the close relatives of both sides of the families is called *xiaoding* (small engagement), and the time when the date of the wedding (that is, the transfer of the bride) is fixed and publicised to a larger group of people, *dading* (big engagement). The boy's family brings to the girl's family a small proportion of *pinjin* (the bride price) on the day of the small engagement and brings a large proportion of the bride price on the day of the big engagement. Taiwanese define "officially getting engaged" as occurring with the first event of engagement, which is *xiaoding*.

Therefore, the *xiaoding* is the first official step in what is essentially a process. It establishes the official bond of affinity between the two families. This bond of affinity between the two families can rarely be broken: "After betrothal a marriage exists that traditionally can be broken only by death or a negotiated rupture; but if one of the two parties dies, the marriage may still be carried to the second stage by the surviving girl proceeding as a widow to take her place in the boy's house or the surviving boy going through the final rites of marriage with the dead girl" (Freedman, 1970, p. 290). The wedding ceremony and the transfer of the bride represent the finalising of this marriage process.

In 1980s' Taiwan, romantic love and a dating culture that impacted this unique marriage system made sex occur earlier within this process. In the Western sense, sex occurring at any time in the process before the actual wedding ceremony would be identified or coded as "premarital sex," but in Taiwanese eyes, this so-called premarital sex was actually occurring in what they saw as a marital context.

Life-Course Perspective

As part of a life-course perspective, transitional events should be viewed in a social context. In one sense, the life-course perspective emphasises that status transitions only take on meaning when they are placed in a social context defined as the significant moments in "the persistent organic interdependency of the cohort-specific life history" (Ryder, 1965, p. 290). In another sense, a life-course perspective implies that certain status transitions can best be understood when they are related to other status transitions which usually follow or closely precede the entrance to these statuses (Modell et al., 1978, p. 121), as in a sort of causal chain.

Therefore, theoretically, the transition to sexual experience is viewed in a social context in this study by means of two strategies. One strategy is to consider the experiences of different birth cohorts, because rapid social change can produce unique cohort-related constellations of influence (Riley, 1976; Elder, 1979). The other strategy is to place the transition to sexual experience for women in Taiwan in the context of the marriage process and other life events in the passage to adulthood, such as finishing school, participating in the labour force, living away from home, dating, being engaged and getting married. This is because early life experiences are expected to influence later events or transitions and also because, as was discussed before, in Chinese culture, the transition to sexual experience for women in 1980s' Taiwan should be viewed within the context of transition to adulthood, which was culturally defined by marriage.

A Thesis regarding Premarital Sex for Women in 1980s' Taiwan

Based on the preceding discussion, I hypothesise that, in the 1980s' sociocultural setting in Taiwan, premarital sex for a woman most likely occurred in a marital context (i.e., within the context of courtship leading to marriage or when she was being readied for her marriage). At that time, "a marital context" for a Taiwanese woman might have included two situations. One situation was that a woman had been engaged. The other situation was that a woman had not had the "official" engagement ceremony (e.g., *xiaoding, dading*), but she has made this commitment, with the consent and great involvement of her parents and those of her partner, to a real marriage plan. Either of these two situations "almost" guaranteed the young couple to be married. Therefore, the positive impact of this marital context (i.e., being engaged or "before" engaged) on the likelihood of engaging in premarital sex can be expected.

Furthermore, I hypothesise that this positive impact of "a marital context" on premarital sex was crucially conditioned by the mechanism of autonomy in dating for women in 1980s' Taiwan. Traditionally, marriages were arranged by families, not by individuals, and young couples did not expect to see each other until the day of the wedding. Even if some couples did meet before engagement, they usually could not get to know each other well due to the lack of dating. So, practically, even an engaged couple was not likely to have premarital sex. In 1980s' Taiwan, parental approval was still required most of the time, but the young couple began to play a more active part and to have opportunities to independently meet and to extensively date before marriage. In this situation of having autonomy in dating, premarital sex became a greater possibility and, I argue, more likely. To test this thesis, survey data were used.

The Survey Data

The Survey

The data for this research were taken from a random sample of ever-married women aged 20 to 49 interviewed as part of a 1986 island-wide knowledge, attitude and practice (KAP) survey of fertility and family planning in Taiwan. Sample size was approximately 5,000 and the response rate was 86 percent. This survey was a collaborative project between the Institute for Social Research at the University of

Michigan and the Taiwan Provincial Family Planning Institute. I had participated in every phase of this project. My research questions were formulated and included as part of this KAP survey questionnaire.

Information on each respondent's transition to adulthood was gathered by means of a face-to-face interview with an "event history calendar." The calendar was used to collect information on school attendance, amount of schooling, work experience before marriage, living arrangements while working before marriage, dating experience, first sexual experience with the future husband, engagement, marriage and first pregnancy. The information regarding first premarital sexual experience with someone other than the future husband was gathered by asking the respondent to anonymously fill out a self-administered questionnaire. This self-administered questionnaire was designed to deal with the issues of privacy and embarrassment. The topic of personal experience of premarital sex was still very sensitive in 1980s' Taiwan—particularly for women.[2] Therefore, underreporting the incidence of premarital sex in this society at that time can be expected. On the other hand, the number reporting premarital sex in the 1986 KAP survey may be taken as representing the *minimum* level of the incidence of premarital sex for Taiwanese women.

Methods

With this kind of data, it became feasible to test the thesis that the increased autonomy of dating increased premarital sex particularly within a "marital context" in 1980s' Taiwan. Given the life-course perspective used, I first analyse the historical trends in Taiwanese women's transition to sexual experience through the use of trend analysis in which cohorts are viewed as groups "following each other" through history. Second, I use multivariate analyses to explore the specific effects of autonomy of dating and engagement on premarital sex for women in 1980s' Taiwan. In order to test for these specific effects, the multivariate analyses will need to include controls for early life experiences, such as education and nonfamilial work/living experiences—as these have been found to be in some ways associated with premarital sex for women in Taiwan (Chang, 1996).

Trend Analysis

Trend analysis classifies the women interviewed by their *birth cohorts* and then compares the cohorts' experiences in their transition to adulthood, which includes such "events" as dating, engagement, marriage and first sexual encounter. If there were historical changes, the proportional distributions and the age distributions of specific events would vary across different cohorts.

The sample for the trend analysis is limited to women born between 1935 and 1960. Women born between 1961 and 1965 are excluded from the analysis, because the selectivity of marriage makes the sample of these ever-married women unrepresentative of women of the younger cohort, 1960–1965.[3]

Multivariate Analysis

The strategy of the multivariate data analysis used can be divided into two parts, based on two types of data.

One type of multivariate analysis is event history analysis and relies on time-specific dynamic models across the period of most marriageable ages (15 to 28) of each woman's life course, using age-specific "event history" data. In general, event history analysis is a dynamic method of incorporating time-varying explanatory variables to account for how an individual changes or develops over the life course. In this context, variables such as the birth cohort of the respondent, education and nonfamilial work and living experiences and "being engaged" can be tested to see if they affect the likelihood of the first premarital sex encounter occurring at a specific age. In this chapter, for the age-specific models, analysis is limited to women who were still virgins by each specific age being studied across ages 15 to 28 over their life courses. Women who had had premarital sexual relations or had married before the specific age being studied are censored for each analysis across ages 15 to 28.

The other type of multivariate analysis is cross-sectional analysis and relies on non-time-specific regression models, using non-age-specific data. Here, even the cross-sectional analysis in this chapter contains a timing element. I first look at sexual intercourse before engagement, and then, for those with no preengagement sex, I examine sexual experience after engagement but before the wedding day.

The sample for the multivariate data analysis is limited to women born after the Second World War, i.e., the "young generation" in 1980s' Taiwan. This is because the autonomous experiences of schooling, nonfamilial employment and living arrangements were features of passage to adulthood for women in the young generation more than they were for women in the old generation.

Presentation of Results

The discernment of historical trends from the cross-sectional survey, while also paying due regard to the determinants of individuals' age-specific sexual behaviours, requires the kinds of analyses described above. In order to present the results of such work, it is useful to see each of the following tables as "peeling away" different levels of a complex process. The first table describes historical trends which can be read by comparing the proportion distributions *across* different five-year birth cohorts. Distributional discrepancies suggest historical shifts.

The following two tables (1-2 and 1-3) then compare various regression models in which more explanatory variables of premarital sex are controlled. The fourth table reveals the key role of "engagement" in affecting the likelihood of premarital sex. Finally, the last two tables (1-5 and 1-6) involve regressions which are age-specific, that is, the extent to which "being engaged" affects the likelihood of first premarital sexual encounters by controlling for birth cohort, education and nonfamilial work and living experiences.

In looking at these tables (1-4, 1-5 and 1-6), it is important to remember that the age-specific regressions relate to each specific age at which first sexual encounters occurred. All of the regressions involve logits, which is a specific transformation of the dichotomous dependent variable (i.e., "yes" or "no" to premarital sex), which overcome the problems that occur in using ordinary least-square regression on such a dependant variable.

Cohort Trends in Women's Transition to Sexual Experience

Within the theoretical framework, an increase in premarital sex is expected to be associated with trends toward romantic love and dating. Also, an increase in premarital sex is hypothesised to occur within the context of courtship leading to marriage in 1980s' Taiwan. This hypothesis is first tested by a trend analysis. Table 1-1 summarises the historical trends in the process of dating, premarital sex, and marriage for women who grew up and made a transition to adulthood between the 1950s and 1980s in Taiwan.

Table 1-1: Transition to Adulthood for Taiwanese Women, by 5-Year Birth Cohort of 1936–1960

	Cohort 36–40	Cohort 41–45	Cohort 46–50	Cohort 51–55	Cohort 56–60
Autonomy When Dating Future Husband					
no dating with future husband before marriage	62.6	51.2	35.9	18.7	10
asked parental permission before dating	29.8	37.9	50.7	60.8	62
did not ask parental permission before dating	7.6	10.9	13.4	20.5	28
TOTAL (%)	100	100	100	100	100
N	473	588	785	1022	923
Transition to Sexual Experience					
(for women with the experience of engagement only)[ab]					
first sex with someone else	2.2	0.5	0.8	1.6	1.7
first sex with future husband before engagement	4.4	4.3	5.9	10.3	19.4
first sex with future husband after engagement	2.9	7.9	9.2	12.7	16.9
first sex after marriage	90.5	87.3	84.1	75.4	62
TOTAL (%)	100	100	100	100	100
N	455	557	761	993	897
Experience of Having a Publicised Engagement Ceremony					
Yes	91.6	92.4	94.9	95.1	94.6
No	8.4	7.6	5.1	4.9	5.4
TOTAL (%)	100	100	100	100	100
N	479	595	788	1030	931

Age at First Premarital Sex *(for women with premarital sex only)*[b]						
	–15	2.9	0	3	0.9	0
	16–18	20.6	25.8	10.1	12.7	11.8
	19–20	20.6	19.4	30.3	19.8	26.6
	21–22	32.4	30.6	21.2	25.9	29.9
	23–25	23.5	24.2	35.4	40.7	31.7
	TOTAL (%)	100	100	100	100	100
	N	34	62	99	212	304
	Mean	21.1	22.4	22	22	21.7
	Median	21	21	22	22	22
Age at First Sex[c]						
	–18	7.8	9.6	9.8	8.4	7.9
	19–20	18.5	16.8	16.8	13.4	15.6
	21–22	29.4	27.7	22.2	20.9	22.3
	23–25	29.2	29.5	29.1	33.5	34.4
	26–	15.1	16.5	22.1	23.8	19.8
	TOTAL (%)	100	100.1	100	100	100
	N	449	553	756	983	885
	Mean	22.5	22.6	22.7	23.2	22.8
	Median	22	22	22	23	23
Age at First Marriage[d]						
	–18	6.9	9.1	9.4	7.7	7.4
	19–20	18.2	16.7	17.6	12.6	12
	21–22	28.2	26.7	22.7	20.6	22.7
	23–25	30.5	30.2	29.1	34.1	36.4
	26–	16.2	17.3	21.2	25	21.5
	TOTAL (%)	100	100	100	100	100
	N	478	592	788	1030	931
	Mean	22.5	22.7	22.9	23.8	23.1
	Median	22	22	23	23	23

a. Here, "with the experience of engagement" is defined as "the experience of having the public engagement ceremony."

b. "Premarital sex"is defined as "sex occurring before the completion of the marriage system or sex before the wedding day."

c. For women with the experience of premarital sex, age at first sex is defined as the age when the first premarital sex occurred.

d. For women without the experience of premarital sex, age at first sex is defined as the age of their first marriage.

As expected, the more direct involvement of young people in the mate selection process was accompanied by greater autonomy of dating with the future spouse in the courtship process. The data indicate that the percentage of women who said that no dating with their future husband occurred before marriage decreased remarkably from 62.6 percent for the birth cohort of 1936–1940 to 10 percent for the cohort of 1956–1960. Furthermore, the substantial increase in women saying that they did not ask parental permission before dating their future husbands, from 7.6 percent for the birth cohort of 1936–1940 to 28.1 percent for 1956–1960, implies greater personal autonomy in the dating period for the younger cohorts of women (see Table 1-1). At the same time, also as expected, within this dating system, Chinese parents retained a powerful influence and involvement. Even among women of the most recent cohort in the 1986 survey with the greatest autonomy of dating, 62 percent reported that they had asked parental permission before dating.

As for the transition to sexual experience in the overall courtship and marital contexts, greater autonomy of mate selection and dating was, as expected, accompanied by increased premarital sexual intimacy for women in Taiwan. Table 1-1 shows that the incidence of premarital sexual intercourse substantially increased overall from 9.5 percent for the birth cohort of 1936–1940 to 38 percent for the birth cohort of 1956–1960. Furthermore, this trend toward increasing premarital sex occurred both before engagement and after engagement between the 1950s to the 1980s in Taiwan. This trend implies that, for the younger cohorts, the timing of women's first sexual experience tended to be ahead of schedule relative to the wedding day, or sometimes even earlier than the engagement ceremony. However, at the same time, the timing of most of the first sexual experience was actually *not far* ahead of schedule, as evidenced by the fact that most women had sex only with their future husbands. Only 1.4 percent of women reported that they had had premarital sexual relations with someone other than their future husbands, and there was no large or consistent cohort trend toward this phenomenon (Table 1-1).

As for the marital process, overall, 93.7 percent of the women had gone through the public ceremony of engagement. Table 1-1 shows that the prevalence of having a public engagement ceremony had not changed over cohorts. In regards to the timing of the first sexual experience and marriage,[4] a delayed timing at these two transition events is found in the 1986 survey data. For the delayed timing at marriage, data show that the percentage of women who married at age 23 and above increased from 46.6 percent for the 1936–1940 cohort to 59.1 percent for the 1951–1955 cohort, and the percentage started to decrease very slightly to 57.9 percent for the 1956–1960 cohort due to marriage selectivity of birth cohort truncation bias. Likewise, the percentage of women experiencing sex for the first time at age 23 and above had the same timing pattern (Table 1-1). Therefore, the increased incidence of premarital sex was not accompanied by an "early" timing of having the first sexual experience. Instead, the timing of having the first sexual experience was delayed for Taiwanese women as a result of the rising age at marriage. All of the median ages at these two events increased from 22 to 23 over successive cohorts. As for the group of women who had premarital sex, the median age at the first premarital sexual experience increased from 21 to 22 over cohorts (Table 1-1).

These findings, that most women had sex only with their future husbands and that the age at the first sexual experience and marriage were delayed, are consistent with the hypothesis that premarital sexual relations for Taiwanese women (even preengagement sex in the cohorts of 1951–1955 and 1956–1960) was still associated to some extent with marriage rather than in relationships not leading to marriage. In general, "the person I have sex with should be the person I get married to" still seemed to be a deeply rooted idea in women's minds in 1980s' Taiwan.

"Autonomy of Dating" and Premarital Sex

Given that the aggregate level data demonstrate the concurrent trends toward autonomy of dating and premarital sex, then the various individual-level multivariate logistic regression models[5] are used to examine the specific impact of autonomy of dating on the likelihood of engaging in premarital sex for women in 1980s' Taiwan.

The results of cross-sectional analysis for the relationship between autonomy of dating and premarital sex are presented in Table 1-2 and Table 1-3. The logistic regression coefficients in Model 1 in both tables show that the impact of autonomy of dating is very strong on both first premarital sex occurring before engagement and first premarital sex occurring after engagement. After controlling for education and nonfamilial work/living experiences (in Model 3), the regression coefficients of autonomy of dating decrease very slightly (compared to those in Model 1). In other words, regardless of educational levels and nonfamilial work/living experiences, women who dated their future husbands were significantly more likely to have premarital sex with them than women who did not date. So, dating was crucial for a young couple becoming acquainted and sexually intimate.

Moreover, all of the regression coefficients of "high" autonomy of dating are larger than those of "low" autonomy of dating in all the models in both Table 1-2 and Table 1-3. This pattern demonstrates that among women who dated their future husbands, women who did not ask parental permission before dating were more likely to have premarital sex than women who asked parental permission. This implies that not only dating but also the level of autonomy in dating strongly determined the likelihood of engaging in premarital sex both before and after engagement for women in 1980s' Taiwan.

Table 1-2: Estimates for Multivariate Logit Models for the Likelihood of Having First Premarital Sex with the Future Husband before Engagement for Taiwanese Women of Birth Cohort 1946–1960

Explanatory Variables	Model 1 parameter	(S.E.)	Model 2 parameter	(S.E.)	Model 3 parameter	(S.E.)
Intercept	8.43***	(0.76)	9.96***	(0.93)	10.19***	(0.95)
Cohort	0.12***	(0.02)	0.13***	(0.02)	0.12***	(0.02)
Primary school	-	-	1.34**	(0.53)	1.20*	(0.53)
Junior high school	–	-	1.23*	(0.54)	1.03*	(0.55)
High school	-	-	0.82	(0.54)	0.68	(0.55)
Junior Col/Univ & above	-	-	0.59	(0.58)	0.47	(0.59)
Nonfamilial work experience	-	-	-	(0.11)	0.18	(0.11)
Nonfamilial living experience	-	-	-	(0.13)	0.18	(0.13)
Autonomy of dating (low)	1.20***	(0.28)	1.24***	(0.28)	1.14***	(0.28)
Autonomy of dating (high)	2.04***	(0.29)	2.11***	(0.29)	1.99***	(0.29)
Sample size	2482		2482		2427	
Log likelihood difference[a]	176.84		200.47		202.5	
Fraction explained[b]	0.7		0.71		0.71	
D.F.	3		7		9	
P-Value	0		0		0	

Note: *: p< 0.05; **: p< 0.01; ***: p< 0.001

a. Parameters are estimated for two models: the full model, which includes the explanatory variables; and the null model, which includes only the constant term. The value of -2*Log(Likelihood) is computed for both models. The difference between these two values is a statistic with an approximate chi-square distribution when the sample size is large. It is a test of all the independent variables combined.

b. "Fraction explained" is defined as exp((log(likelihood))/n) for each model, where n is the number of cases.

Dependent Variable:

Having First Premarital Sex with the Future Husband before Engagement, given that women had the experience of an engagement:
No (0), Yes (1)

Explanatory Variables:

Birth Cohort: 1946–1960
Educational Levels:
- Primary school: No formal schooling (0), primary school (1)
- Junior high school: No formal schooling (0), junior high school (1)
- High school: No formal schooling (0), high school (1)
- Junior college or university and above: No formal schooling (0), junior college or university and above (1)

Nonfamilial work experience (the most autonomous work experience before marriage):
- No work experience or working for the family without pay (1)
- Working for money at home (2)
- Working for money outside the home (3)

Nonfamilial living experience before marriage: No (0), Yes (1)
Autonomy of dating (two dummy variables):
- Low: No dating with the future husband before marriage (0)
  - Asked parents' permission before dating with the future husband before marriage (1)
- High: No dating with the future husband before marriage (0)
  - Did not ask parents' permission before dating with the future husband (1)

Table 1-3: Estimates for Multivariate Logit Models for the Likelihood of Having First Premarital Sex with the Future Husband after Engagement for Taiwanese Women of Birth Cohort 1946–1960

Explanatory Variables	Model 1 parameter	(S.E.)	Model 2 parameter	(S.E.)	Model 3 parameter	(S.E.)	Model 4 parameter	(S.E.)
Intercept	6.50***	0.72	6.78***	0.78	6.27***	0.76	7.00***	0.81
Cohort	0.08***	0.02	0.09***	0.02	0.07***	0.02	0.09***	0.02
Primary school	-	-	0.03	0.31	0.22	0.33	0.09	0.33
Junior high school	-	-	0.24	0.34	0.06	0.36	-0.12	0.37
High school	-	-	0.29	0.34	0.04	0.35	-0.15	0.36
Junior col/Univ & above	-	-	0.6	0.39	-0.26	0.4	-0.49	0.41
Nonfamilial work experience	-	-	-	-	-0.02	0.1	-0.04	0.1
Nonfamilial living experience	-	-	-	-	0.18	0.14	0.2	0.14
Autonomy of dating (low)	1.40***	0.26	1.50***	0.26	1.34***	0.24	1.44***	0.26
Autonomy of dating (high)	1.85***	0.28	1.99***	0.28	1.83***	0.26	1.96***	0.29
Length of engagement	0.05***	0.02	0.05***	0.01	-	-	0.05***	0.01
Sample size	2116	2116	2100	1955				
Log likelihood difference[a]	49.36	52.71	112.53	137.56				
Fraction explained[b]	0.65	0.65	0.66	0.67				
D.F.	3	7	9	10				
P-Value	0	0	0	0				

Note: *: p< 0.05; **: p< 0.01; ***; p< 0.001

a. See footnote a in Table 1-2.

b. See footnote b in Table 1-2.

Dependent Variable:

Having First Premarital Sex with the Future Husband after Engagement, given that women had the experience of engagement and had not had premarital sex before engagement: No (0), Yes (1)

Explanatory Variables:

Length of engagement: in months

See the definitions for the rest of the explanatory variables in the footnote in Table 1-2.

Engagement and Premarital Sex

In 1980s' Taiwan, most young couples had opportunities to meet and to date extensively during the courtship process. Once they became engaged—the first official step of the marriage process and the establishment of a contract between two families—the positive impact of engagement on the likelihood of having sex during this period of engagement can be expected. Moreover, sexual relations, even pregnancy, for an engaged couple was supposed to make the contract between the two families more unbreakable. The age-specific data in this study confirm this strong impact of engagement on the likelihood of engaging in premarital sex for women in 1980s' Taiwan.

Table 1-4 shows that the proportions of those engaging in premarital sex were significantly higher for women who had been engaged than for women who had not been engaged across ages.[6] Moreover, all of the logistic regression coefficients of "engagement" in Table 1-5 and Table 1-6 are highly statistically significant. These models demonstrate that engagement had its own strong direct impact on the likelihood of engaging in premarital sex across ages of each Taiwanese woman's life course, even after controlling for the antecedent effects of school attendance, amount of schooling and nonfamilial work/living experiences.

Furthermore, it can be expected that the longer the duration of engagement, the greater the chance of engaging in premarital sex. This is demonstrated by the significant net effect of "length of engagement" on the likelihood of first premarital sex occurring after engagement. (See the significance of "length of engagement" in Model 4 at Table 1-3.) At the same time, we have to be aware that there might be a reverse relationship between length of engagement and the likelihood of premarital sex, because it is quite likely that engaging in premarital sex might shorten the length of engagement due to premarital pregnancy.

Table 1-4: Age-Specific Proportion of Having First Premarital Sex by Engagement Status for Birth Cohort 1946–1960*

	Being Engaged (Yes)			Being Engaged (No)		
Age	No. of women still virgin	No. of women having first premarital sex	Age-specific proportion having first premarital sex	No. of women still virgin	No. of women having first premarital sex	Age-specific proportion having first premarital sex
15	5	a	a	2423	3	0.001
16	7	a	a	2414	8	0.003
17	12	2	0.167	2390	20	0.008
18	31	9	0.29	2315	31	0.013
19	48	5	0.104	2187	46	0.021
20	70	18	0.257	2005	76	0.038
21	75	12	0.16	1780	65	0.037
22	86	19	0.221	1507	64	0.042
23	110	15	0.136	1215	75	0.062
24	99	13	0.131	911	55	0.06
25	85	9	0.106	646	38	0.059
26	75	11	0.147	434	20	0.046
27	42	0	0.000	263	7	0.027
28	32	2	0.063	164	10	0.061

*Data were collected in spring 1988. The cohort of 1960 was not included for the analysis of ages 26–28, and the cohort of 1959 was not included for ages 27–28.

a. In the early ages of 15 and 16, the number of women who had been engaged is too small (less than 10) so that the age-specific proportion having first premarital sex is not presented.

Table 1-5: Logit Regressions for the Age-Specific Likelihood of Having First Premarital Sex by Birth Cohort, School Attendance, Nonfamilial Work and Living Experiences, and Engagement Status for Taiwanese Women of Birth Cohort 1946–1960*

			Regression Coefficients				
Age	No. of women still virgin	No. of women virgin & finished school	Cohort	Finished school	Having both work and living exp	Having either work or living exp	Engagement
15	2428	1324	a	a	a	a	a
16	2421	1381	a	a	a	a	a
17	2402	1541	0.16**	1.66**	0.14	-0.87	3.04***
			(0.06)	(0.68)	(0.53)	(0.67)	(0.83)
18	2346	1626	0.11*	1.24*	0.11	0.44	3.20***
			(0.05)	(0.57)	(0.46)	(0.41)	(0.45)
19	2235	1604	0.06	1.38**	0.64*	0.15	1.53***
			(0.04)	(0.55)	(0.37)	(0.39)	(0.5)
20	2075	1708	0.14***	0.79*	0.70*	0.47	2.33***
			(0.03)	(0.42)	(0.32)	(0.31)	(0.32)
21	1855	1624	0.17***	1.47*	0.77*	0.25	1.78***
			(0.03)	(0.73)	(0.38)	(0.39)	(0.36)
22	1593	1411	0.12***	1.05*	0.29	-0.34	1.86***
			(0.03)	(0.61)	(0.33)	(0.34)	(0.3)
23	1325	1199	0.05*	1.94*	1.26**	1.04*	0.98***
			(0.03)	(1.01)	(0.46)	(0.45)	(0.31)
24	1010	927	0.14***	-0.15	0.44	0.04	0.82**
			(0.04)	(0.5)	(0.43)	(0.42)	(0.34)
25	731	695	0.07*	4.24	0.95	0.33	0.67*
			(-0.04)	(5.75)	(0.64)	(0.64)	(0.4)
26	518	490	b	b	b	b	b
27	305	296	b	b	b	b	b
28	196	192	b	b	b	b	b

Note: Standard errors are in parentheses. *: $p< 0.05$; **: $p< 0.01$; ***: $p< 0.001$

* Data were collected in spring 1986. The cohort of 1960 was not included in the analysis for ages 26–28, and the cohort of 1959 was not included for ages 27–28. Analysis is limited to women who had not had premarital sex or had not married by the listed age.

a. In the early ages of 15 and 16, the number of women who had been engaged is too small (less than 10) so that the estimates for these ages are not presented.
b. In later ages of 26 to 28, the number of women with no formal schooling remaining virgin and unmarried is too small (less than 7) so that the estimates for education variables are not presented.

Dependent Variable:	Having first premarital sex at a certain age, No (0), Yes (1), given that premarital sex or marriage had not already occurred.
Explanatory Variables:	Birth Cohort: 1946–1960
	Finished School: No (0), Yes (1)

Two dummy variables for having nonfamilial work and living experiences before a certain age being studied:

Having both nonfamilial work and nonfamilial living experiences:
None (0). Having both nonfamilial work and nonfamilial living experiences (1)
Having either nonfamilial work or nonfamilial living experience:
None (0). Having either nonfamilial work or nonfamilial living experience (1
Engagement Status: Not being engaged (0). Being Engaged (1

Table 1-6: Logit Regressions for the Age-Specific Likelihood of Having First Premarital Sex by Birth Cohort, Educational Level, Nonfamilial Work and Living Experiences, and Engagement Status for Taiwanese Women of Birth Cohort 1946–1960 Who Had Finished School[a]

Regression Coefficients

Age	No. of women still virgin	Cohort	Primary	Junior. High	High	Junior Col & Uni	Having both work & living experience	Having either work or living experience	Engage-ment
15	1324	b	b	b	b	-	b	b	b
16	1381	b	b	b	b	-	b	b	b
17	1541	0.18**	0.22	0.69	-3.94		0.14	-0.86	3.32***
		(0.07)	(1.06)	(1.12)	(16.88)		(0.54)	(0.69)	(0.89)
18	1626	0.12**	0.92	1.14	-3.14	-	-0.17	0.18	3.34***
		(0.05)	(0.84)	(0.86)	(10.53)		(0.47)	(0.43)	(0.48)
19	1604	0.04	4.03	4.14	4.24	0.07	0.72*	0.22	1.72***
		(0.04)	(3.78)	(3.8)	(3.83)	(23.85)	(0.40)	(0.42)	(0.51)
20	1708	0.18***	0.09	-0.04	-0.66	-4.21	0.48	0.37	2.29***
		(0.03)	(0.57)	(0.61)	(0.64)	(11.33)	(0.34)	(0.33)	(0.33)
21	1624	0.16***	0.87	1.33	0.83	1.32	0.68*	0.26	1.85***
		(0.04)	(1.04)	(1.06	(1.06)	(1.47)	(0.40)	(0.4)	(0.38)
22	1411	0.15***	-0.1	-1.15*	-0.49	-4.64	0.38	0.29	1.80***
		(0.03)	(0.58)	(0.68)	(0.61)	(6.02)	(0.35)	(0.36)	(0.31)
23	1199	0.05*	0.06	-0.27	0.02	-0.60	1.25**	0.99*	0.96***
		(0.03)	(0.76)	(0.81)	(0.78)	(0.96)	(0.47)	(0.46)	(0.31)
24	927	0.16***	0.55	-0.59	0.26	-0.50	0.43	-0.16	0.86**
		(0.04)	(1.06)	(1.12)	(1.07)	(1.20)	(0.45)	(0.45)	(0.35)
25	695	0.09*	0.31	-0.07	-0.25	-0.03	0.95	0.36	0.69*
		(0.05)	(1.1)	(1.14)	(1.12)	(1.15)	(0.64)	(0.65)	(0.41)
26	490	c	c	c	c	c	c	c	c
27	310	c	c	c	c	c	c	c	c
28	192	c	c	c	c	c	c	c	c

Note: Standard errors are in parentheses. *: p< 0.05; **: p< 0.01; ***: p< 0.001

a. See footnote a in Table 1-5.
b. In early ages of 15 and 16, the number of women with high school education who had finished school is too small (less than 10) and the number of women who had been engaged is too small (less than 10) so that the estimates for education and engagement are not presented.
c. See footnote c in Table 1-5.

Dependent Variable: Having first premarital sex at a certain age, No (0), Yes (1), given that premarital sex or marriage had not already occurred.

Explanatory Variables:
Educational Levels:
- Three dummy variables for ages 15–18:
  - Primary School: None (0), Primary School (1)
  - Junior High School: None (0), Junior High School (1)
  - High School: None (0), High School (1)
- Four dummy variables for ages 19–28:
  - Primary School: None (0), Primary School (1)
  - Junior High School: None (0), Junior High School (1)
  - High School: None (0), High School (1)
  - Junior College and University: None (0), Junior College and University (1)

Please see the definitions for the rest of the explanatory variables in the footnote in Table 1-5.

Summary and Discussion

Romantic love, dating and premarital sex can be seen as having been changing from the 1950s to the 1980s in Taiwan, but premarital sex in a marital context remained within the Chinese tradition. This chapter has used both time-specific and cross-sectional survey data to examine and support this thesis.

The Chinese term *dinghun* (including *xiaoding, dading,* etc.) has been translated as "engagement" in English. Engagement is almost unbreakable, so people regard an engaged couple as almost married. The Chinese term *jiehun* has been translated as "marriage" in English, but the marriage which is defined as beginning with the wedding ceremony in Western societies is different from the social transaction of *jiehun* in Chinese culture. I argue that Taiwanese marriage is more usefully conceptualised as a process involving a number of steps, none of which can be accurately translated as "marriage."

The engagement ceremony is the first "official" step in the marriage, while the wedding ceremony represents the final step of this process. Therefore, "premarital" sex occurring after engagement is in some ways regarded as "marital" sex for people in Taiwan.

Furthermore, in addition to defining the Chinese term *jiehun* as a process actually starting from *dinghun*, in 1980s' Taiwan, it is also useful to conceptualise *dinghun* in a broad sense as a process involving a number of steps, none of which can be correctly translated as "engagement." The engagement ceremony is to officially mark and complete the process of *dinghun*. The starting point of *dinghun* is rather imprecise. The engagement process may start from the time when a couple make their commitment to get married, or may start after the parents of the two families approve and set up the marriage plans for their children. The "subjectively" perceived timing of "being engaged" for the young couple themselves may be much earlier than the timing of their engagement ceremony. Therefore, premarital sex occurring at any time after a young couple makes this commitment, but before the actual engagement ceremony, could in some ways be also seen as premarital sex occurring in the context of engagement. In this situation, premarital sex would have been categorised as occurring before engagement in the data analysis, but in context may actually belong to the category of "after engagement" (i.e., a marital context).

In summary, the transformation of marital arrangements from arranged marriage toward the love match accompanied with the newly developed dating culture and the broader perceptions regarding the process of getting engaged and getting married can explain why the increase in so-called premarital sex (occurring either before engagement or after engagement) in this study was most likely to occur within a marital context for women in 1980s' Taiwan.

This "Chinese" pattern of premarital sexuality in Taiwan implies that the core cultural ideas on marriage and female chastity persisted in

1980s' Taiwan, despite the fact that women in the younger generation had more autonomous experiences in the transition to adulthood in terms of schooling, nonfamilial labour force participation and living away from parents. This finding is consistent with the finding I have published elsewhere (Chang, 1996). In that article, I found that, in a nonmarital context, Taiwanese women at the less marriageable young ages tended not to take advantage of living outside the parental home to engage in premarital sex, even if they recognised that their parents could not supervise their activities. Young women with nonfamilial jobs and living away from home might be still "living with" their traditional values as autonomous as it might seem in the 1980s.

In situations of rapid socioeconomic change, values may lag behind such change (Ogburn, 1964). People tend to respond to new situations on the basis of preexisting values. This may apply to many Taiwanese women in the 1986 survey working outside the home before marriage, and can explain value continuities in the context of new circumstances. Other studies also found that, in the 1960s and 1970s when Taiwan was industrialising, nonfamilial working was a new activity for women to achieve traditional goals, and filial piety continued to be one of the most important motivating forces (Hu, 1982; Kung, 1983; Greenhalgh, 1985). Since the family remained as an economic unit, parents had expectations for receiving the wages of their children. In particular, many Taiwanese still believed that daughters "will belong to other people after they marry out" so therefore, daughters should financially contribute as much as possible to the family before getting married. In that circumstance, wage earning provided these Taiwanese women with a new way of paying their debt and fulfilling obligations to their parents before marriage (Kung, 1983).

Therefore, for Taiwanese women who were born between 1946 and 1960, as they were growing up and in their transition to adulthood from the 1950s to the 1980s, the old values had conditioned the potential positive impact of nonfamilial work and living experiences on the incidence of engaging in premarital sex. The impact of exposure to new ideas and autonomy, which these young women gained from nonfamilial labour force participation and living outside the home during the early stage of modernisation in Taiwan, was apparently not great enough for them to engage in premarital sex in a nonmarital context.

NOTES

1. Throughout this book, the term "Taiwanese women" refers to women in contemporary Taiwanese society. Nowhere does "Taiwanese" have any ethnic connotation (e.g., distinguishing Taiwanese from Mainlanders).

2. The data on premarital sexual experience for Taiwanese women were collected by means of the following questions:

   "Before you were married, did you have sexual intercourse with your future husband?" (If yes and respondent had been engaged): "Did you have intercourse with your future husband before you were engaged?"

   "How old were you when you first had sexual intercourse with future husband?" (Chinese age)

   "Before you were married, did you have sexual intercourse with anyone other than your husband?"

   "How old were you when you first had intercourse with someone other than your husband before marriage?" (Chinese age)

   The data on "autonomy of dating" were defined by three categories: (1) "did not date the future husband before marriage" is defined as no autonomy of dating; (2) "asked parental permission before dating the future husband" is defined as low autonomy of dating; and (3) "did not ask parental permission before dating the future husband" is defined as high autonomy of dating. Based on this definition, the "autonomy of dating" was measured in the early stage of dating the future husband. The translation of the Chinese wording of the relevant question was "Did you get your parents' permission when you first began to date your future husband?" The answer "No" to this question is categorised as "high" autonomy.

As I have emphasised, the term "be married" in Chinese refers to someone who has completed the whole marriage process (i.e., has had the wedding ceremony). "Had been engaged" in Chinese means "has had the publicised engagement ceremony."

3. The problem of representativeness or selectivity results from birth cohort truncation bias. This is because the limitation of the sample to ever-married women restricts the universe to those who were married at the time of the interview. The percentage of each cohort that was ever married and eligible for the survey thus varies by their age at the survey. The earlier birth cohorts include a much-wider range of ages at marriage than the later birth cohorts. The later birth cohorts in the survey are limited only to women who married at a young age. This problem is particularly serious for the birth cohort 1961–1965, which was age 20–24 at the time of the 1986 interview. In 1985, 67 percent of Taiwanese women were still single by age 24 (Taiwan-Fukien Demographic Fact Book, Ministry of the Interior, 1985). In order to avoid the truncation bias of age at marriage or the problems of representativeness and selectivity, women born between 1961 and 1965 are excluded from the trend analysis.

4. Here, age at marriage is measured as age on the wedding day. The age used in this chapter refers to Chinese age (i.e., Western age plus one).

5. From now on, birth cohort will always be the control variable in all of the multivariate models. This is because the cohort trends in women's transition to sexual experience have been discussed in the section on trend analysis. The impact of birth

cohort in the models will not be discussed further for the remainder of this chapter.

6. This difference might be explained by a tendency for underreporting of such activities by those not engaged but actually participating in premarital sex. There are two considerations against such a view. First, the difference is too large to be attributed solely to underreporting. Second, given the self-administration of the questionnaire, such underreporting as is imputed is unlikely to be so large for one group since any strong cultural force against reporting premarital sex could be expected to lead to underreporting for the engaged group as well.

Part 2:

1990s' Taiwan

Chapter 2

Negotiating Sexual Permissiveness

As concluded in Chapter 1, the quiet "sexual revolution" was not a real revolution in Taiwan from the 1950s to the 1980s, because among Taiwanese women, premarital sex usually occurred only in relationships where marriage was already planned (i.e., in which the couple was engaged) or being seriously considered. This pattern implies that romantic love, dating and premarital sex were seen as changes in Taiwan, but that premarital sex in a marital context remained within the Chinese tradition. What about in the 1990s? Were the further socioeconomic development and cultural changes in the 1990s still conditioned by the Taiwanese old way of thinking, and the new behaviours still reflected their preexisting values?

Following up the momentum of modernisation which began in the 1960s, there was an acceleration of social, political and cultural changes originating from the political liberalisation which resulted from the abandonment of martial law in Taiwan in 1987. This political liberalisation had exposed even the "tabooed" ideas of the past to global ideals and the ideas. In the 1990s, the mass media highlighted the many ways that this further societal "liberalisation" and openness had "speeded up" the modification of Chinese people's thinking about and behaviour toward sexuality and marriage.

The speed of change and the complexities of response in 1990s' Taiwan, particularly in areas of sexual mores, were such as to reduce the relevance and longevity of survey data collected in earlier years. Those earlier studies had been quantitative and survey based, and were mainly focused on the aspect of behaviours. Less had been done on the way individuals in this rapidly changing society were interpreting these changes around them, and how such interpretations varied between men and women of different age groups and education backgrounds.

In 1990s' Taiwan, given the trend toward more sexual permissiveness, how was this "lived" by those who made the trend occur? This chapter is based on a qualitative focus group study I conducted in 1994 in Taipei, the capital city of Taiwan, to explore and interpret the changing sexual mores and the value of female virginity among never-married young people. The purpose of this study was to expand the understanding of this topic from the behaviours of "ordinary" Taiwanese in the 1980s (represented by the random samples from surveys) to the specific perceptions, attitudes, values and meanings of diverse groups of young men and women in Taipei who were leading the trends of sexual mores in the 1990s.

As discussed in Chapter 1, norms concerning marriage and family are a core part of the traditional Chinese culture with *zhencao* (virginity and chastity) being a crucial value regarding sexual mores. The questions posed for this chapter are: In 1990s' Taiwan, what were some of the underlying uncertainties experienced and/or dealt with by young people regarding sexual mores that result from social changes? How were the two genders responding? What did *zhencao* mean for each gender? To what extent did specific Chinese cultural elements filter and modify the way that global (mainly Western) activities and ideas affect sexual mores? Using focus group interviews of diverse groups of never-married young people in Taipei, a number of elaborations of sexual mores are revealed in which men and women of different ages and educational backgrounds show divergent responses and interpretations to these social changes in 1990s' Taiwan.

Methodology

Attitudes have long been studied through quantitative data collected by surveys that show the distribution of positions along attitude items. Such an approach assumes that attitudes are relatively stable. However, in the area of sexual mores in 1990s' Taiwan, attitudes were changing rapidly, so a set of items would have been difficult to formulate, and even if items were formulated, such items were likely insensitive to nuances and changes. Accordingly, it would be more appropriate to collect qualitative data to explore this area. Regarding qualitative data collection, individual depth interviews can run into difficulty, because personal matters so easily intrude into any probing, and the interviewee's sensitivity can produce embarrassment (Lee, 1993).

In contrast, a more appropriate method for my study is focus group, because once participants realise that the "focus" is on the group rather than the individual, they feel quite secure about presenting themselves and to being candid about sensitive topics. In addition, a "synergistic" effect of group dynamics and the flexibility of the interviews can facilitate and generate wider, deeper and more diverse information which is beyond the kind of data collected and accumulated by each separate individual in-depth interview (Fetterman, 1989; Steward and Shamdasani, 1990).

The data for this study were collected through six focus group interviews with never-married young people which I conducted in June and July of 1994 in Taipei. Eliminating married people was appropriate as a means of reducing the serious bias from self-selectiveness and the reciprocal effect from their own marital and sexual experiences.

The key variables for "coverage" were age, gender and education. Six focus groups were made up on the basis of gender (male vs. female), age (17 to below 20 vs. 20 and above) and education ("below university level" vs. "junior college graduate or university level" vs. "National Taiwan University education").[1] "National Taiwan University" will be abbreviated as "NTU" throughout this chapter. The resulting six focus groups were as follow:

(1) 8 males aged 17 to below 20, with "below university level" education;

(2) 8 females aged 17 to below 20, with "below university" education;

(3) 8 males aged 20 and above, with "junior college or university level" education;

(4) 8 females aged 20 and above, with "junior college or university level" education;

(5) 10 males aged above 20, NTU senior undergraduate and graduate students;

(6) 10 females aged above 20, NTU senior undergraduate and graduate students.

This research design covered all the "categories" of education among the never-married young men and women in 1990s' Taipei. I would argue that as this society at that time was a relatively homogeneous Confucian society, education was the most significant factor affecting opinions and was therefore the appropriate variable, along with gender and age, to define focus groups. Each of the six focus group discussions took two hours, and each was videotaped, transcribed in Chinese and translated into English.[2]

The topics of the focus group discussion covered dating and courtship, marriage arrangement, sex and marriage, premarital sex and virginity. The last topic was elaborated and probed in terms of how each gender thought about it, under what conditions it might be "given up," what the consequences would be for doing so—with and without a marriage following—and what were the imputed causes of the changes in sexual mores expressed in the focus group discussion.[3]

These focus groups have revealed the prevailing perceptions, values, attitudes, meanings and interpretations among young people in 1990's Taipei on topics of romantic love, sexual mores and the value of virginity. In particular, the data reveal "which elements" of the culture or situations depicted were noticed by "which groups" and how they were interpreted.

Virginity: Ubiquitous Assent and Ambiguous Compliance among Men

The Value Affirmed

Among unmarried Taiwanese men in the focus groups, the value of virginity was espoused in all groups (of age and education). Young men perceived that *zhencaoquan* (the value of chastity and virginity) is something that applies to women. However, they saw this value as declining in Taiwan's changing society. One participant went so far as to deny the very applicability of the term *zhencaoguan* precisely because it "moralises" virginity. He preferred to talk about attitudes toward premarital sex.

Even if the value of female chastity and virginity was perceived as declining in 1990s' Taiwan, this value, particularly among men, found expression in the ideal that they would like to marry a virgin. This preference for virginal brides had wide support (at least in terms of public expression) among almost all the men in the groups (regardless of their ages and education). Apart from this quantitative observation, more revealing was the lack of any alternative category of female sexual "accessibility." For instance, no mention was made of women being "on the make." Women were either married or marriageable, with the latter needing ideally to be virginal as well.

Moderator: In mate selection, do you feel a woman's *zhencao* (chastity and virginity) is very important to you?

CL: If I knew in advance a girl had had an affair before and was no longer a virgin, I would have a doubt in my mind. It is very likely that just for this reason I won't chase after her. (M: >20, junior college)[4]

LB: It would be ideal to marry a virgin, if there is one for me! (laugh) (M: NTU)

This last aside (and the laughter it provoked) is revealing. In this context, the reality of declining *zhencaoguan* was acknowledged notwithstanding a preference for its continuation.

Ambiguity in Premarital Sexual Mores

The persistence of the value of virginity among male participants does not necessarily mean that they perceived that young people cannot have premarital sex. The norms and values toward premarital sexual mores were felt as vague and ambiguous in 1990's Taiwan. Engaging in premarital sex would not seem right according to the norms internalised from parents and schoolteachers, normally phrased as something like "Don't misbehave!" By contrast, not having sex can seem strange, given the growing impression that so many people, including their friends, were doing it anyway. This part can lead to feelings of inadequacy at being so "square."

Not surprisingly, participants all said that they could accept *other* people engaging in sexually permissive behaviours, but they *themselves* would not necessarily like to practice them. The justification given, though, related more to practical concerns about responsibility and unwanted consequences such as pregnancy rather than to any blind allegiance to early moral socialisation. The perceived change led to a divergence between attitudes and behaviour. For practical reasons, behaviour was marked by caution while attitudes were expressed in which the person can look "cool," "liberal" and "modern."

Under the surface of ambiguous feelings, a clearer attitude actually did exist among most of the male participants. Change in mores is revealed in the way that premarital sex is seen as appropriate under specific conditions. If the two persons are "in love" and are planning to marry in the future, then they expressed the view that premarital sex and the giving up of virginity may be appropriate. This rationale was however contrasted with another situation in which the loss of virginity could "just happen." Such a "happening" might occur in a romantic context (expressed colloquially as "when we are under the moon and flowers are in front of us"), even if there had been no plan to marry. The rationality of any anticipated plan is lost in the passion of the moment. Discussion here reveals another discrepancy between attitudes and behaviour in that their talk about other people's sexual behaviour allows for the possibility of momentary "accidents." This way, the perceived decline in the value of virginity was expressed in terms of specific excesses of love, rather than of any growth in sexual licentiousness. A few participants did express the view that as long as two persons are "very much in love," premarital sex is all right.

Moderator: How do you feel about young people who have premarital sex?

YC: I always have a conservative attitude toward premarital sex, but I don't think it is a moral issue. It is totally a personal matter. Personally, I have no sexual experience, although there were several times when the atmosphere was very romantic and special and such a thing would have been very easy to happen, but it didn't happen! (Others laughed; he looked regretful.) That was because at those times I was not sure if I really loved her and wanted to spend the rest of my life with her. (M: NTU)

CL: In fact, many people, after they did that, started to think whether they wanted to be together in the future. Because at that specific moment when they did it, it just happened! They just weren't thinking.

Therefore, a further insight can be generated from these two divergences between sexual attitudes and behaviours. Individuals perceived other people's sexual behaviours as often more open than their attitudes, while for the individuals themselves, sexual behaviours were talked about in terms of being more conservative than their attitudes.

Stretching the Value of Virginity and Responsibility for Marrying the Woman

The value of virginity and this premarital permissiveness seem mutually contradictory on the surface, but the cognitive dissonance can be resolved by a temporal extension of the value of virginity. This "stretching" of the temporal reference of "marriage," from a male perspective, is revealed in men's attitude toward premarital sex. In this premarital context (i.e., "in love" and planning to be married), the ideal is still for the woman to be a virgin prior to engaging in such premarital sex with the man.

Moderator: Since you feel it is okay to have premarital sex if two people are really in love and want to be together in the future, do you still feel it would be ideal to marry a virgin?

BC: She could lose her virginity with me but not with other men. (M:

<20, high school)

LC: I would feel very lucky that a woman can give me her "first time," regardless of whether it is occurring before or after marriage. (M: >20, junior college)

Consequently, most male participants still felt that men should take responsibility for a woman's virginity, ideally by marrying her (but not when her virginity has already been given to another). At this point, it is worth dwelling on the underlying logic of legitimation expressed by such views as those quoted above. Despite the noble intention of marrying a woman with whom one is about to be intimate, external factors (from a variety of causes) may intervene to thwart such a plan. Virginity is then taken, but the marriage may not be forthcoming. In such a situation, one might surmise that the man will feel guilty and sorry for the woman—for he imagines (perhaps wrongly) that she will find it harder to marry without her virginity.

This guilt is unlikely to stay unexpressed. One common response would be to rationalise the problem by "blaming the victim": since the woman knew how important virginity was, she ought to have been more restrained and ought to have exercised more responsibility in the first place. The extension of the value leads to conditions which reverse the basis for blame.

Changes in sexual behaviours are such that the men nevertheless saw the growing number of nonvirgins as requiring them to "forgive" women's past "mistakes." Thus, it is possible for women to live in what is termed a "second chastity" in which women get a "second chance" to show sexual integrity and loyalty. However, this loosening does not extend to permitting "serial monogamy," which was simply seen as not being morally feasible.

Moderator: If you found out your girlfriend was not a virgin, how would you feel? What would you do? Would you still marry her?

CL: Well, if I control myself and she controls herself, that's fair. But, if she did not control herself, ... regardless if I controlled myself or not, I would feel very jealous. This may be related to a sense of possession. But, for this kind of thing, it is better that we should just not tell the truth ... Actually, it is not so easy to really tell if she is a virgin anyway. (laugh) On the other hand, it is ideal if she is a virgin, because I still don't think doing this kind of thing is "normal" in the first place! (M: NTU)

HL: Due to advances of medical technology, the hymen can be repaired. So focusing on whether this is her first time is of no use. Past is past. We should concern ourselves more with whether the two are compatible and whether the woman will be faithful in the future. This is what is called the concept of *erdu zhencao* (a second chastity). (M: >20, junior college)

The accomplishment of a "second chastity" is itself highly problematic. As one focus group participant put it: if he found out about a relationship that had led to his partner's loss of virginity, he would either feel jealous of the "other man" or angry at his partner for having been so "loose." There is in this response a basis for "blaming" the woman even though the man decides to continue a relationship with her.

With these changes, some men expressed the fear that some Taiwanese women's sexual mores have become so open and so unrestrained by traditional gender roles that men should be careful about not being "played with" or used by, or losing virginity for, that kind of women.

YC: It seems to me modern girls are very open toward premarital sex. For this reason, I don't dare to date. Because I am afraid that I will be *chikuei* (at a disadvantage) with them! (Everybody laughs loudly.) ... I mean, because I am serious about sex and if the other person is not, I will suffer a loss. (M: NTU)

Responsibility for Risk Management

Although most of the male participants thought that men should be responsible for taking a woman's virginity by marrying her, some NTU male students expressed a sense of responsibility with a completely different underlying logic. They did not think virginity and sex should be linked to the idea of marriage. If two persons are in love and mutually agree, engaging in sex in such a situation would not be immoral or irresponsible, as it is a personal matter. This "amoral" thinking does not necessarily mean there is no sense of responsibility. The "responsibility" here was perceived as being responsible for "making sure there is birth control and safe sex."

How did people with such views feel about the traditional type of responsibility (of virginity loss as a basis for a marriage claim)? The NTU male students were very aware of this traditional "responsibility" and its widespread support in the larger society. If a man decided not to marry the woman who "had her first time" with him, this man would be called "heartless," or would be seen as "deserting a girl after stealing her chastity." They felt that the external pressure from this "responsibility" expected of men would be too large to live with, so to avoid such pressure, they would rather not engage in premarital sex. They would minimise the risk of such encounters and, should it happen, they would seek to minimise "collateral" costs of pregnancy, disease or gossip.

Value Varied among Women

Just like the male focus group participants, female participants also felt that the premarital sexual norms and values were vague and ambiguous in their fast-changing society in the 1990s. There seemed to be no clear rule to follow, although parents and schools had tried to pass on a very distinct and clear rule in terms of no premarital sex. This traditional rule was no longer perceived to be an absolute standard.

Likewise, two divergences between sexual attitudes and behaviours also existed among female participants. From other people's experiences, sex was often seen as having "just happened" in a romantic context; it was beyond rational control and not based on a marital plan. In particular, all of the female participants said that they could accept other people's premarital sexual behaviours, because "The more strange things I see, the less these things look strange!" But, they themselves would not necessarily like to do it. However, in contrast to most men who still prized female virginity (despite the fact that they may have different senses of "responsibility," *zhencaoguan* had different meanings and implications among different age and education groups among unmarried Taiwanese women in my study.

Value Varied with Education among Adult Women

Among participants older than 20, the value of virginity differed according to the educational level of women. Women with university education had the most "rational," amoral and calculating attitudes. They tended to disapprove of premarital sexual behaviours but primarily as a result of the high risks/costs of unwanted pregnancies, including damaging future career prospects as well as devaluing their "marketability" due to their loss of virginity. However, the women said that once a woman has calculated the costs and decided to engage in premarital sex with the man she loves, she should not care about what other people think/feel about her. This independence from "what others think" also enables a woman to break the link between sexual activity and a marriage plan, and thus become more focused in assessing real risks and benefits.

Moderator: How do you feel about premarital sex?

FL: In the past, girls used a moral perspective to view sex. Now they see it as a "cost" perspective. You do it if you think you can afford it. If you care, you don't do it, because the cost is too high ... (W: >20, university)

TY: Among my friends who have had sexual experiences, as far as I know, sex mostly happened in the situation of "*huaqian yuexia*" (before the flowers and under the moon). They, at that moment, did not think about marrying the man in the future. After doing it, they neither regretted, nor did they want to stick with the man they had sex with. In some cases, on the contrary, it was the man who loved the girl so much and felt obligated to "look after" her. (W: >20, university)

Moderator: How about if the man you really love and want to marry really cares about virginity?

FL: Well, if he thinks that my virginity is more important than I am, I would not see him as a smart man whom I would want to marry. I would rather remain single than marry such a man. (W: >20, university)

Women who had finished high school, vocational school or junior college expressed a more conservative attitude. They thought that premarital sex is morally wrong and women should just not do it. The consequence will be lifelong, because a nonvirgin woman will find it more difficult to marry. The fraught nature of the consequences was described in real stories in which premarital sex had led to familial and personal disaster. These stories show that since women with such conservative attitudes had never planned or prepared for premarital sex, they could not have controlled the consequences such as unwanted pregnancies, marriages which lacked strong familial support and lowered self-esteem in a "reverse" relationship (with the woman chasing after the man).

WS: It is better not to have premarital sex. Most men care about whether you are a virgin. I heard there is another kind of man. He was ready to marry his girlfriend and had sex with her. After having sex, he thought less of the girl and decided to break the relationship. He was afraid she would do this kind of thing with other men ... Society puts more moral pressure on women than on men. So, I think we had better not do it, unless you can be sure that this man is trustworthy, reliable and responsible and that you both will definitely marry in the future. (W: >20, junior college)

Yet the view that women should/could avoid disaster by simply not engaging in premarital sex is not as straightforward as it seems. A "no-win" situation for women was revealed in many other stories mentioned by the high school graduate participants. In those stories, sometimes if a woman "refused" premarital sex, her man would terminate the relationship.

Therefore, the female participants aged above 20 in these two groups (university educated and high school educated) dealt with the value of virginity in terms of risk and danger respectively.

Changing Values in the Younger Generation

In the focus group of women aged 17 to 20, with participants who had a high school or vocational school education, a "generational" change can be seen—they blended a romanticism in relationships with what appeared to be a practical sense about marriage as a secure investment. The majority of respondents stated that they would like to "save" their virginity for the handsome (however poor) men with whom they will fall crazily in love. These men need not be rich. They would not marry handsome men, because handsome men would be more likely in their view to have extramarital affairs. The ideal "husband" needs not be especially handsome, but he should be rich and reliable.

CC: In the first year of senior high school, one of my classmates told me she wanted to save her first time for her *laogong* (husband). After one year, she told me she was not a virgin anymore. And in the third year she told me she needed to test for pregnancy. Nowadays, *zhencaoguan* is changing so fast. I, as well as about 10 percent of my classmates, don't think we should save our "first time" for our future *laogongs* ... If I meet a nice man and we like each other, if he asks and I also feel like doing it, I will give it to him. I believe men have sexual desires, so do women ... I will not think about marrying him in the future. (W: <20, high school)

LG: I used to live in a dorm. I saw some girls sometimes sleep over in their boyfriends' places. When I asked, they frankly told me that "I have already lost mine!" I was shocked in the beginning because they were only first-year students and it was hard to know whether they would be able to stay with their boyfriends in the future. However, they had no worries or regret. One of my friends said it was worthwhile, because it was occurring when she loved him the most and she was willing to do this thing just for him ... Now I have this attitude, too. I am prepared to have sex with a man whom I love very much, even though he is just a boyfriend. For the man I find to be my *laogong*, I would not necessarily love him very much. I won't love him more than he loves me. Maybe I just love his money. Before I marry, I hope that I will have a very deep romance. After that, marriage is a lifelong business, and I hope my *laogong* loves me more than I love him. (W: <20, junior college)

Moderator: What kind of a man would be an ideal for *laogong*?

HL: A more stable kind. He won't be chatty with other women. He does not like to show off. [He would be more] considerate and just be nice in general. However, he may not be handsome, because a handsome man would also be desired by many other women. *Laogong* is different from a boyfriend. A handsome man is appropriate for being a boyfriend, because he is good for me to show off. I will lose face if I were going out with an ugly man. Imagine if I do have an ugly boyfriend and I have to introduce him in public, I would have to say that he is my brother! (Everyone laughed loudly.) However, it doesn't matter if my *laogong* is ugly. I would say in fact he is a very nice person and he has *neizaimei* (inner beauty). (W: <20, vocational high school)

CC: I won't think about deep issues when I'm looking for a boyfriend as long as we feel happy. I don't care whether he is less educated, or is younger, than me. But, when looking for a *laogong,* all these factors start to matter. (W: <20, high school)

Had these young women thought through and coped with the possible consequences of devoting their virginity to the man they love but won't marry? A "self-determination" voice was evident in the discussion. This voice tells us that women should not care about how other people (particularly men) think about them because the double standard should be changed or is already changing. As for these high school girls in this focus group talking about themselves, a strong and uniform idea was presented. If they couldn't find the right men to accept their being a nonvirgin, they would rather not marry and develop careers on their own. In addition, these young girls felt entertained by, and laughed at, those men who still hold the traditional sexual attitude of being responsible for taking a woman's virginity.

These young girls in the focus group perceived the sexual mores in Chinese tradition as being too "closed" and suppressed. Their interest in openness and self-determination was, however, tempered by the view that it would not be good to become as open as "Americans." The value of virginity may be declining but not the value of romantic love and marital relationships.

Double Standard

The discussion of both men's and women's valuations of female virginity raises some insights regarding the issue of double standards. All focus group participants showed a full awareness and consciousness of the gender inequality in the double standard of the Chinese cultural legacy. Yet a gender difference in the perceptions of and attitudes toward this double standard was also revealed.

Male participants did want to make the situation more "egalitarian" by "forgiving" women's past "misbehaviour." Equality would imply that both men and women can engage in premarital sex (in an "in love" relationship or a relationship leading to marriage).

Although all female participants perceived that most men in 1990s' Taiwan still cared about female virginity, women's reactions toward this double standard differed according to education and age groups. Most university- and high school-educated adult women held a "compromising" attitude to maintain this double standard by preferring not to engage in premarital sex. Rationales for the "compromising" differed for the two groups of women. The university-educated women used a rational reason of avoiding risks/costs, while high school-educated women used a moral reason of avoiding danger or "bad" morality.

In addition to the idea that women had better "compromise," these adult women also felt that men should "control their impulse more and do less." At the same time, female participants aged below 20 had a radical change in this double standard—basically a "new" double standard: Men should become less sexually permissive while women could become more open. An attitude accompanying this "new" double standard is that women should not care what men think about their being a virgin or a nonvirgin. The logic is that if all women do not care about virginity, men will end up not being able to care about it either. The idea regarding this "new" double standard is consistent with my earlier findings, which were based on a 1988 islandwide survey among adolescents in Taiwan (Chang et al., 1997).

Perceived Causes of Change

The perception of changing sexual mores and the value of virginity were clearly articulated across all of the focus group discussions. Yet the interpretations differed between men and women.

One interpretation is within the Sino-centric framework argued by male participants in the NTU group. They argued that the "change" itself is actually not in sexual mores; instead, it has been related to the level of discretion. They said that in the past, Chinese people had sex, but could not talk about it or make it visible. Now the whole society is more open. Sex can be talked about, and young people behaving intimately has become more visible and acceptable. Sex is no longer a mysterious or shameful concept. The permissiveness is part of the Chinese culture, which does not need to be imported from the West. Therefore, changes in sexual mores in Taiwan are just a result of change in the openness with which sex can be talked about or is found acceptable in the society.

This Sino-centric perception was not held by any of the female focus group participants. It is understandable that, traditionally, sexual permissiveness was only for men, not for women.

A contrasting view from the one just presented was voiced by all of the female as well as many of the male participants. This view sees the openness of the society as the major cause for the changing sexual mores. They described this "openness" in terms of many social phenomena. For example, mass media widely report sex news or discuss sex-related issues, so sex now is much less mysterious. "Sex shops" have also become visible. Young people enjoy buying "fun" things from these shops for friends' birthdays. Contraceptive use is more accessible (such as from condom vending machines). Participants with this view linked such diverse expressions of openness with a positive view about tolerance and a recognition of greater personal autonomy. They perceived that a fundamental cause of this societal openness of sexual mores is the impact of Western ideals such as romantic love, freedom and individualism. This impact is felt mainly through the globalised (particularly American) mass media and cultural industry.

While this openness was perceived to be a worldwide "irreversible" trend, and being open is better than being closed, both male and female participants believed that sexual openness should not go as far as what they saw as American "looseness." Appropriate sexual mores in Taiwan should still be rooted in Chinese culture.

Regardless of their views about the causes of change, the participants were all aware of the exposure, in the media, of sexual mores, particularly the alleged rates of sexual permissiveness applied to Taiwan. Participants tended to compare their own situation to that reported in the media.

TC: In recent years, you can very often see in the newspapers and magazines the statistical figures of young people engaging in premarital sexual behaviours in various surveys. For example, I read some figure like 20 percent of college students have such experiences. Whenever I read this kind of figure, I start to feel different. I felt many of my classmates must have already had such experiences. It seems that I am not living in reality. When the figures go higher and higher, I feel I have to adjust my boundaries. I am wondering: Am I too conservative? Is my concept too out-of-date? I think this kind of media information has a direct impact on us. Whenever we see it, we will be influenced by it. (M: NTU)

Several other comments of this kind were made.

Such perceptions can become self-fulfilling prophecies in which the very trend becomes the basis for its extension as individuals rationalise premarital experimentation.

Implications

A number of insights and policy implications follow from these findings.

Insights about Gender, Generation, Education and Permissiveness

Participants were aware that, behind the phenomenon of changing sexual mores, the values of openness, egalitarianism (particularly gender equality) and personal autonomy are an irreversible worldwide trend (or actually mainly perceived as the American trend). Powerful mass communication and information systems have made the diffusion of such global values possible and quick. Simultaneously, after being exposed to global culture, people are more aware of, and can be critical of, their own culture.

Since the 1990s, a resurgence of indigenous Chinese/Taiwanese cultural elements has occurred. This concurrence of globalisation and localisation has been developing rapidly in Taiwanese society. As a result, as revealed in the focus group discussions, young people in 1990s' Taipei rationally compared, assessed and chose the values most appropriate to their own sociocultural background. People were very conscious that they did not want to become too Western (or too "American").

Beyond changing sexual mores, during my two-month participant observation in 1994 in Taipei, I observed a concurrent trend toward both "globalism" and "localism" reflected in almost all of their political, economic, social and cultural aspects. This blending and elaboration of local and cosmopolitan values can be seen as part of the process of globalisation that has been featured in contemporary sociological theory (Hannerz, 1990; Giddens, 1990, 1991; Waters, 1994; Martinelli, 2005). What is particularly interesting from this study is the different "blends" that occurred between genders.

This study shows that, regardless of age and education level, most male focus group participants in Taipei had fairly conservative perceptions, attitudes and values regarding sexual mores and still prized the value of female virginity. Even though by 1994, Taiwan had been undergoing rapid socioeconomic transformation and cultural change for three decades, the findings in this study imply that the impact of social change, or the "generational" effect, on men's sexual mores was not as significant as on women's.

Two possible reasons can be offered for this greater change among female participants who grew up in Taipei and were living there in the 1990s. One is that men in Chinese culture have always been more sexually permissive, leaving women greater scope (in principle) for further permissiveness. The other reason is that exposure to more opportunities and new ideas for women gained from education and formal employment have brought more changes to women's lives than to men's.

As regards the influence of social change on women's sexual mores, my research reveals two mechanisms. One mechanism is the "generational" impact among women's attitudes. The younger groups (ages 17 to 19) combined a romanticism and practical orientation that marginalised the value of virginity. This marginalisation may be due to the situation of such girls not yet confronting real choices with partners. The girls were thus able to indulge in a more liberal kind of thinking. However, if such discourse is compared with what girls of that age would have talked about even five or 10 years ago, it obviously revealed far more openness and self-determination.

For young adult women (out of the high school system), the value of virginity had a stronger grip on their thinking. This may be due to their greater exposure to situations that threaten virginity, which then require more careful deliberation and compromise. Beyond such situational pressure, there appeared to be a "break" in thinking from women only a few years younger. These adult women in the focus group were showing signs typical of an earlier generation, despite their youth.

The other mechanism works through the impact of education. University-educated female participants were career conscious and rational, calculating the costs/benefits before choosing to engage in sex. As a result, they would be well prepared for whatever choices they made. The views of high school graduates in this study were the most conservative (in a moral sense) and their situations were vulnerable (unprepared) in the process of "accidentally" engaging in premarital sex. This study reveals that the effect of higher education on women's attitudes and values revealed is consistent with findings on the impact of education on women's family and fertility behaviours in the field of family demography (Caldwell, 1982).

Gender roles are skilled accomplishments. Scripts have to be followed. The scripts were changing in 1990s' Taipei, with each of the genders developing variations and improvisations during this transitional period.

For male participants, traditionalism provided a clear line of responsibility: "take virginity, marry the woman." In this study, a small number of more educated "modern" men saw responsibility in terms of minimising risks of pregnancy and disease. They were conscious of the traditional "line" but saw this as something triggered in others rather than themselves. Premarital sex was to be avoided primarily to avoid others forcing responsibilities on them. If the conditions were "right" and the woman doesn't raise the issue of responsibilities, premarital sex might happen. However, the emergence of this possibility, even in thought, had not yet greatly diminished their desire to marry a virgin.

Female participants show more variation. Younger ones—perhaps due to their infrequent exposure to situations that require decisions—tended to combine Western ideas with views of their own personal autonomy. Older women took virginity more seriously: the less educated, as a moral value under threat; the more educated, as a situational value that may be negotiated if the deal offered was worthwhile.

If these responses are combined, a number of viable "dyads" seem possible. Educated and independent women who care less about what "others think" will find in those men who see responsibility in terms of controlling "collateral damage" of pregnancy or disease a common goal of managing their intimacy. Similarly, younger women might be "persuaded" into sexual encounters with these "modern" men if what is being offered seems to transcend the bounds of traditional conservatism while also showing a keen regard for managing risk (and projecting the image of a beautiful couple). These two "matches" might be expected to take on high social "salience," increasing the perception that changes are occurring among the young and the intelligent. Further changes in premarital sexual mores among highly educated young men and women in 2000s' Taipei will be discussed in Chapters 4 and 5.

Policy Implications

The Most Vulnerable Group

As discussed earlier, high school-educated female participants revealed that they were conservative and vulnerable vis-a-vis the changing sexual mores in 1990s' Taiwan. Since they thought premarital sex was morally wrong, they never prepared themselves for it. If they had sex, they would feel guilty and regretful. If they became pregnant (due to the lack of birth control preparation), they would think that the only solution would be to marry the man who made them pregnant. From a policy viewpoint, these most vulnerable women should be the target group for sex education, sex knowledge and information on safe sex and contraceptive use. However, because they have the most conservative attitudes and are seen as "well behaved," they tend to be ignored by the parents, schoolteachers and health education programs. Societal attention and resources usually focus on the more "visible" group of young people, those who speak with a liberal voice and actively engage in heterosexual interactions. The policy implication is that those with liberal attitudes are ready, fully aware of the consequences, and will always prepare for them. Special care should instead be delivered to the "invisible" but highly vulnerable group.

"Responsibility" Issues

The findings from the male discussions in 1994 show that most Taiwanese men perceived their "responsibility" for women to be only for the "first" time—a notion governed by their intention to marry her. In a sense, this means that the woman's virginity, and not the relationship per se, is what has prime value. Meanwhile, if men cannot fully take such responsibility, they will pass this responsibility back to the woman. There will be policy as well as ethical implications about the "responsibility" issues.

In such a rapidly changing environment, society should initiate a deeper and more "current" educational program for young people, one which goes beyond the traditional sex education package. Based on the fact that there is a clear gender difference in sexual mores and the value of female virginity among young people, the meaning of sex and the "responsibility" involved for both genders has to be critically assessed and redefined. Rather than seeing the issue in terms of gender-based responsibility (e.g., what a man "should do" under specific circumstances), it ought to be seen in terms of the quality of the relationship and joint responsibility for its development. It should not only be seen as a matter of personal integrity (as "measured" by chastity for women and responsibility for men).

This learning and redefining process among young people, or actually in the whole society in general, should have a "consensus" feature between the two genders. In other words, men and women should have dialogue and discourse in the hope of achieving consensus about the meanings of a relationship, love, sex and marriage. This redefinition could provide young people with a new decision-making norm, could minimise the risks and danger involved if they decide to engage in premarital sex and could make possible the ideal of gender equality in relationships.

Conclusion

Female virginity is not simply a cultural value from the past which is destined to disappear. Rather, one can see it as a basis for negotiating forms of intimacy and commitment that share some Western characteristics (romance and autonomy) and filter out others that emphasise egoistic individualism as might be seen in promiscuity, serial monogamy or even the justifications to be found for "exiting" from a marriage. Furthermore, the changes in dealing with such a legacy tend to come from Taiwanese women who have experienced and been influenced more by the process of modernisation than from Taiwanese men. Therefore, it is crucial to explore further issues of modern womanhood as well as the dynamics between global/Western and local/Chinese values presented in public discourses. In the next chapter, I will study these themes and issues, represented through *Cosmopolitan*, the most popular women's magazine, in 1990s' Taiwan.

NOTES

1. "Below university level" comprised high school students/graduates and junior college students. "Junior college graduate and university level" comprised university students/graduates and junior college graduates. "National Taiwan University education" in this study comprised in-school senior undergraduate students or graduate students in National Taiwan University (NTU).

2. The recruitment of participants for Groups 1 to 4 was professionally done by the United States Gallup Survey agent in Taipei. According to the selection criteria regarding gender, age and education, the Gallup Company randomly recruited participants. The principal investigator paid NT$1,000 (about Aus$50, equal to the amount which Gallup usually pays) to each participant. The recruitment of men and women participants in NTU was done, for convenience, with the help of my friends who were teaching at the university. I did not pay participants in these two groups. Only snacks and drinks were provided during the discussion sessions. The participants in the six focus groups were all relaxed and appeared to talk freely. They all commented that the discussion was not only to produce "data" for my research, but it was also insightful and useful for themselves, because most of the time they had no opportunity to address and discuss such issues with others.

3. The discussion guidelines concerning premarital sex and the value of virginity were as follows:

   1. How do you feel about the *zhencaoguan* in today's Taiwan? Has it been changing? In what ways?

   1.1 What is your perception of the *zhencaoguan*?

1.2 What does the *zhencaoguan* mean to you?

1.3 Do you want to marry a virgin?

1.4 If you find out that the person you want to marry is not a virgin, how would you feel? What would you do?

1.5 What are the possible consequences for a woman who has lost her virginity?

2. How do you feel about premarital sex? Do you agree with it?

2.1 If "agree," in what circumstances would you agree with premarital sex?

2.2 If "disagree," why?

2.3 How do you feel about those who have premarital sex?

2.4 Do you know people who have engaged in premarital sex? In what kind(s) of situations do they engage in premarital sex? (Is any kind of premarital sex more acceptable than another kind?) What are the consequences to them?

3. How do you feel about the double standard?

3.1 Do you feel that this double standard can be changed? (If yes, how can it be changed?)

3.2 Why have sexual mores been changing in Taiwan? Personally, do you like this change? Is the direction of such a change appropriate?

4. Following each quotation, I identify the participant's

gender, age and education level. For example, "(M: >=20, junior college)" means that this participant is a man who is older than 20 and has a junior college education. "(W: <20, high school)" stands for a woman who is younger than 20 and has a high school education. "(M: NTU)" stands for a man who was educated at National Taiwan University.

Chapter 3

Refashioning Womanhood

This chapter treats the Taiwanese edition of *Cosmopolitan* (1992–'97) as a window into a Taiwanese image of the "modern woman" in the 1990s and as an arena in which Chinese and Western systems and values might clash but, in fact, might also intermesh by virtue of the practice of exploiting Western means for Chinese ends.

The values implicit in women's magazines and advice books have long been studied in the context of a wide range of women's issues, particularly in the West. Previous research has focused mainly on the reproduction of women's oppression by promoting the "cult of femininity" (Ferguson, 1983); the elaboration of a gender ideology of self-help, which emphasised women developing themselves, rather than helping others (Friedan, 1963); an analysis of the role played by this self-help literature in providing women with only "an illusory cure for what ails us, collectively, as a culture" (Simonds, 1994, p. 227); the emergence of a virtual community of women through their shared magazine reading (Shevelow, 1989; Seneca, 1996); and assessments of the polarity of feminism and femininity (Friedan, 1963; Winship, 1987; Stuart, 1990; McRobbie, 1991, 1997; Sheridan, 1995), as well as arguments that such a polarity has now "gone for good" in the West (McRobbie, 1994, p. 8). Most of these findings derive from Western print media, examined primarily from a feminist perspective.

More recently, research using women's magazines in non-Western cultural settings has generally followed one of two approaches. The first uses the same feminist lens to see whether patriarchal values and practices are reproduced in non-Western women's print media (e.g., see Zhou, 1991; Lai, 1994; Ford et al., 1998). The second uses local editions of women's magazines popular in the West (such as *Cosmopolitan*) to study how local and Western values meet and conflict. This research, which grew out of concerns with women's issues, eventually focused on how local editions of "global" magazines, as "cultural hybrids" (Rosenberger, 1995; Leung, 1996), have helped to provide new role models and advice, directed especially at the anxieties and appetites of young women experiencing rapid social change under modernisation and globalisation (e.g., see Rosenberger, 1995; Leung, 1996; Sakamoto, 1999; Kirca, 2001).

This chapter investigates how the Taiwanese edition of *Cosmopolitan* (*Kemengbodan*) may serve to resolve a tension felt by modern women in Taiwan by weaving global and local values together into a tapestry of "modern womanhood" that can dwell within, and yet extend beyond, the local culture. This microexample illustrates not only that contemporary women in Taiwan can be "constructed" as "modern" while remaining "Chinese," but also that such construction achieves a successful and *harmonious* combination, rather than simply expressing a "clash of civilisations," as Samuel Huntington (1996) might call it.

In this study, I examine various issues of the 1990s' Taiwanese edition of *Cosmopolitan* to determine what concerns they addressed, focusing on their propensity to use local and Western sources differently to deal with certain topics, and on how, as portrayed in this magazine, globalism and localism were harmoniously intermeshed in constructing modern womanhood in 1990s' Taiwan.

Cosmopolitan is a popular women's magazine with a worldwide circulation. Its production is both centralised and localised: the various editions can borrow materials from the "central bank"—that is, the New York headquarters—or from "sister" issues in other countries, as well as producing their own articles. Consequently, each issue of *Cosmopolitan,* in Taiwan and in other countries, contains a unique blend of global and local cultural ingredients on topics concerning modern womanhood.[1]

Taiwanese *Cosmopolitan,* which began publication in January 1992, was a leading cosmopolitan women's magazine in the 1990s. Because it deals predominantly with women, we ought not to be surprised that its content is, in effect, continually "refashioning" women—literally, in the sense of offering new styles of clothing and makeup, but also more fundamentally by making available to modern women in Taiwan key concepts of self-definition.

The Taiwanese version of *Cosmopolitan* (or *Cosmo*) sells not only because it symbolises being fashionable, modern and Western, but also because it is a form of popular culture, grounded in local contemporary Taiwanese issues and problems. Its increasing popularity in 1990s' Taiwan was evident in its circulation figures, which rose steadily between 1992 and 1997 from about 230,000 to about 380,000.[2] By contrast, another major local women's magazine in Taiwan—*Women's Magazine* (*Funü zazhi*), the earliest magazine of its type—ceased publication during the same period.

The Taiwanese edition of *Cosmopolitan* is notable in two respects: size and seriousness. Each monthly edition contains at least 200 pages (sometimes as many as 270 pages) and costs about US$10 (a price much higher than in Western countries, including the United States and Australia). Despite its higher cost, in per capita sales, it was one of the more successful editions of *Cosmopolitan* worldwide in the 1990s.[3] And the actual number of readers was likely even larger, as many more people read copies of Taiwanese *Cosmo* bought by their friends, neighbours or classmates, or copies available in public places such as hairdressers, clinics and libraries. These relatively high sales figures, as well as the growing readership, suggest that more and more Taiwanese women in the 1990s had an interest in refashioning womanhood and were accessing the ideas presented and represented in the Taiwanese edition of *Cosmo*.

In what follows, I explore the mechanisms Taiwanese *Cosmo* employed to address concerns about, and provide guidance for, women through the medium of popular culture in the 1990s. I examine the magazine from two angles: as a *window* into a Taiwanese image of the "modern woman" and the concerns that faced her, given the Chinese context of such modernisation in 1990s' Taiwan; and as an *arena* in which Chinese and Western systems and values could have clashed but instead intermeshed, as Western means were exploited for Chinese ends.

In delineating the image of the modern Taiwanese woman in the 1990s, I refer to both physical and spiritual dimensions. The main concerns of modern Taiwanese women in the 1990s are revealed through ethnographic content analysis of a random sample of Taiwanese *Cosmo* from a six-year period (1992–'97). I have identified the major topical concerns as well as which global and local content tackles each. I have also extracted major contrasts underlying the wisdom and strategies found in the global and local content.

In considering *Cosmo* as an arena, I operate at a somewhat more abstract level of analysis and discuss which aspects of globalising Western values for women have or have not meshed successfully with Taiwanese values. The interaction between Taiwan and the West, it should be stressed, appears to be not a clash of civilisations but a filtering as well as a blending, though certain core values from each culture sometimes enter intact. This intermeshing of (filtered) global and local values for 1990s' Taiwanese women is an interesting example of how globalism and localism interacted in a non-Western cultural context.

Methodology

Taiwan's *Cosmo* is published monthly. My research covers the period from its 1992 founding until 1997 (when my data collection for this study was conducted). I selected at random one issue of *Cosmo* per year from the 72 issues available for the six-year period. This yielded a primary data set of 87 articles, features, *Cosmo* "clinics" and columns. For convenience, I call the writing in all these different formats "articles." Each issue normally contains in addition such components as quizzes and tests, horoscopes, advice columns, health and beauty tips, recipes and recommendations on books, movies, travel and so on. These elements were not included in the sample, because most of them are literal translations from other editions that simply transmit information and do not engage in a cultural debate. Instead, only the 87 articles which address issues or can reveal cultural discourses in *Cosmopolitan* are analysed for topical concerns and for cultural sources and strategies for modern Taiwanese women in the 1990s.

The sampling method adopted is *time-based random sampling*, a valid and reliable approach for obtaining a representative sample to discover the main topics and subtopics covered by the magazine, as well as the balance struck among these topics. The alternative approach—sampling by topics or themes—was not feasible, since it requires initially constructing and categorising a complete list of topics or themes, and I could not in advance know what topics would be covered and what the balance would be between New York and local Taiwanese input. Furthermore, a thematic exploration makes more methodological and narrative sense when one is dealing with a homogeneous field, such as a major text or works by a single writer, or with certain themes already associated with that writer. When one is considering instead multiple authors whose texts present competing value positions from different cultures, a predetermined thematic framework is presumptuous and elides much of the variability of content.

Supplementary data, cited briefly here but mainly incorporated in the discussion section, come from a two-hour in-depth interview that I conducted in the Taiwanese *Cosmo* office in Taipei on 24 September 1998. The interviewee was Cai Huiming, a single woman in her late 20s who, at the time, had been associate editor for almost three and half years. In the interview, I focused on whom and what factors have determined the content of the magazine from its inception onward. I also asked her about the target readership groups, the relationship between the editors and the readers and *Cosmo*'s impact on Taiwanese women, as well as the impact of the readers on editorial policy in the 1990s.

Another methodological issue in analysis of the media is whether the values reflected in the contents are mainly those of the editors, the readers or both. *Cosmopolitan*'s dependence on monthly sales means it has to respond to readership preferences—unlike, say, a government publication. Cai Huiming was unequivocal on this point: "In the process of editing Taiwanese *Cosmo,* I have realised that the readers' taste has become the editors' taste." She further explained that the very large increase in local content between 1992 and 1997 was a direct response to the demands of Taiwanese readers for a different take on feminism and on combining marriage and career. Growth in *Cosmo*'s readership had paralleled the growth in the proportion of its articles that came from local sources. These issues are explored in detail at the end of this chapter.

The principal method employed in this research is *ethnographic content analysis*. The first phase of the analysis was to sort the raw material of the 87 articles into *topics,* then into *subtopics*. There were eight main topics covered in 1992–'97: relationships, sex, gender roles, the self, work, marriage, money and life in general. Those that were most frequently covered naturally generated many subtopics—eight in the case of "personal relationships" and seven for "sex." Topics treated less often generated fewer subheadings.

Coding into topics and subtopics proved to be a fairly straightforward, or at least an easily replicable, task. Although in some articles (such as those on "sexual harassment" or "how to be one's self in relationships"), the content incorporated more than one topic, my main criterion in coding was a particular article's *ultimate* concern, its primary discussion and the advice it offered. For example, because articles on sexual harassment were intended to raise women's awareness in dealing with the problem (including their interactions with relatives, friends, colleagues or strangers), I coded them under the topic of "sex" rather than "work." The weight of the discussion in articles on "self in relationships" is on "self," which, therefore, was the coding (rather than "relationships").

After developing the coding scheme and completing the coding myself, I communicated my coding criteria and supplied the coding scheme to a colleague familiar with content analysis but not with the issues of this particular research project. He randomly selected 20 articles to code. Our coding matched in more than 95 percent of cases for topics, and more than 90 percent for subtopics, an acceptable level of intercoder reliability.

The second phase of the analysis involved sorting all of the articles under each topic according to their cultural sources (i.e., global versus local). The third step was to analyse all of the contents under each topic, setting global against local sources, and then to use analytic induction (Turner, 1953) to extract the underlying contrasting focuses revealed in each culture.

COSMO as a Window

A number of topical concerns about becoming a modern woman have arisen in Taiwan as it has modernised and yet has kept alive gender roles rooted in a Chinese familial system (Lu, 1989; Thornton and Lin, 1994; Chang, 1999, 1996; Yang, 1997). Rapid social change in Taiwan has brought more changes to, and had more impact on, women's life courses than men's (Chang, 1996a). Modernisation, as indicated by education and urbanism, has affected family values and attitudes toward divorce more among Taiwanese women than among men (Tsai and Yi, 1997).

In a range of situations in relationships, marriage, family and work, modern life gives rise to tensions and confusions that create an appetite for advice, stories, role models and images on which modern Taiwanese women can draw for application in their own lives (Chang, 1996; Wang, 1997). Therefore, all the main articles and the personal interviews with "successful women" in Taiwanese *Cosmo* provide a window on the construction and propagation of Taiwanese modern womanhood in the 1990s. Through this window, a certain image of the modern Taiwanese woman becomes apparent. The core areas of modern life that seemed to matter to 1990s' Taiwanese women are also revealed. More important for the argument here are the ways Taiwanese *Cosmo* responded to, and provided strategies for resolving its readers' conflicts.

The Image of a Modern Taiwanese Woman

Most obviously, *Cosmopolitan* presents a certain image of the modern woman that varies little across the magazine's content. The data for examining this image are drawn from *Cosmo*'s advertising pages, stories on female celebrities and interviews with successful Taiwanese women. The image of a 1990s' Taiwanese modern woman was one of Western clothes and makeup, an autonomous lifestyle with a professional career, liberal romantic relationships, a healthy diet and workout regimen, travel, a stylishly decorated modern home and, most important, "being in charge." This image was consistent with the worldwide focus of *Cosmopolitan* and with its advertiser base.

However, if we probe more deeply, we find that this image of the modern Taiwanese woman in the 1990s actually contains two different layers. The outer layer is the physical side of this modern woman, while the inner is her spiritual side. The modern woman's physical layer is readily and widely visualised through glossy advertisements for Western fashions, makeup, fitness, beauty and health tips, furniture, room decorating and food and restaurants. Although ads for Taiwanese models and Oriental styles of furniture had increased slightly in the late 1990s' Taiwan *Cosmopolitan*, overall, the *physical* look of this image of the modern woman and her material possessions tended to be primarily "Western."

But the text of 1990s' Taiwanese *Cosmopolitan* also reveals a *spiritual* image of the Taiwanese modern woman, in stories on female celebrities in contemporary Chinese societies (eight in Taiwan and three in Hong Kong) and interviews with successful or famous Taiwanese women. Among the 11 female celebrities profiled in the sample, two were in news media, three were actresses, one was a violinist and five were managers in business or industry. These successful women were depicted as hardworking, conscientious, self-confident and eager to pursue advanced education. Zhao Yu, an adviser with *China Post* in Taiwan, was described as "a traditional woman but a modern manager" (Zhang, 1993). Some had a quite traditional and idealised view of romantic love. For example, Zhang Xiaoxian, a writer in Hong Kong, thought that everlasting love does exist but that it is up to individuals to find it (Huang, 1996). Li Zi, a Hong Kong actress, stated that she would give up everything for love (Cai, 1995a). Their discourse on love and romance led to a series of notions that spiral inward to a spiritual core.

An interview with four successful Taiwanese women about how to become an attractive modern woman suggested to readers what a successful and charming modern Taiwanese woman should be really like in 1990s' Taiwan (Cai et al., 1996). The women were Gao

Yiping and Li Wen, who were performers; Zhang Yaqing, who was a TV news reporter and producer; and Xiao Ai, who was a writer. All of them insisted that physical beauty is not what is most important for a woman's charm or attractiveness, emphasising instead the spiritual aspect, which, in turn, includes several layers. The outer layer pertains to how a modern woman should deal with the world—her attitude; she must work hard and be persistent (Xiao, Gao, Li, Zhang). In this process, she will also find opportunities for self-reflection and self-modification (Zhang), which are the basis for an active and enjoyable life marked by milestones of self-actualisation and progress (Li, Xiao, Zhang).

In the next layer is the kind of personality that drives these attitudes. Here one finds references to the flexibility and friendliness that lubricate social interactions (Gao, Li, Xiao). The "sociable" personality is a "sincere" personality. In turn, this capacity for interaction enables a woman to be natural, secure and confident (Gao, Xiao, Li, Zhang). This strength is not a given, but rather an accomplishment tied to pursuing self-knowledge and wisdom (Gao, Xiao, Li, Zhang). Thus, the modern woman's personality is flexible on the outside and strong on the inside, making it possible for her to have strength without rigidity.

Such a personality leads to a deeper layer of ethical coherence. These interviewees were not hesitant to moralise about the modern Taiwanese woman, whose ethics include the avoidance of being calculating toward people (using them as a means rather than as an end) and a stress on being responsible (Xiao). Such actions create personal assets—good character, manners and reputation (Zhang, Gao). Beneath the ethical layer is the most intimate core of the modern Taiwanese woman, spiritual beauty. All four mentioned the idea of inner beauty and richness in life experiences: every experience teaches something. This learning deepens women's sense of life, allowing them to achieve inner beauty.

In summary, the "hardware," or physical side, of this image of the 1990s' modern Taiwanese woman was portrayed as "Western." At the same time, its "software," or spiritual side, was emphasised as being "Chinese"—working hard; valuing education; being conscientious, ethical, and sincere; improving the self through self-reflection; displaying a personality that is flexible on the outside and strong inside (*wairou neigang*) and bearing inner beauty, a woman's ultimate achievement. Thus, these two sides of the modern woman reflect how globalism and localism were intermeshed in constructing modern womanhood as portrayed in 1990s' Taiwan *Cosmopolitan*: "looking" Western and using modern goods were desirable, but the core values and inner beauty remained Chinese.

Topical Concerns and Cultural Sources

This section looks through the window of *Cosmopolitan* to determine its core content. Table 3-1 summarises the magazine's range of topics and issues concerning modern womanhood in 1990s' Taiwan, as well as the breakdown of cultural sources for each topical concern. Not surprisingly, the topics and concerns follow the major transitions and relevant events and issues in the life of the "modern young woman." The topical concerns in Table 3-1 and in the analysis presented below are roughly ordered by a life-course trajectory. They start with the self and gender roles and identities, expand to an interpersonal level pertinent to relationships, sex and marriage and then end in a wider context dealing with work and money. Articles about relationships and sex have been further subdivided into those that are normative (and "normal") and those that have a transgressive quality about them.

Table 3-1: Major Topics by Source in Six Issues of Taiwanese *Cosmo* (1992–'97)

Topic	Concern	Total (N)	Global (N)	Global (%)
Self	Existence of a woman's self	1	0	0
	Self-autonomy	1	0	0
	Beauty and self-confidence	1	0	0
	Understand self and problems in life	1	0	0
	Woman's self in relationships	1	1	100
	Woman's self in marriage	1	0	0
Subtotal		6	1	17
Gender issues	How different are men and women?	1	1	100
	Criticise conventional gender roles	2	0	0
	Feminist threat to men	2	0	0
	About men	3	2	67
	Female role model	1	0	0
Subtotal		9	3	33
Relationships (normative)	Mate selection and modern dating	7	1	14
	How to create romantic love	4	4	100
	Lack of commitment from men	2	1	50
	Ending relationships	6	5	83
Relationships (transgressive)	Love triangle	9	2	22
	Holiday "loves"	2	0	0
	Women have multiple lovers	2	1	50
	Other	2	2	100
Subtotal		34	16	47
Sex (normative)	Importance of sex	2	2	100
	Sexual skills	8	6	75
	Sexual knowledge	5	1	20
	Sexual mores	1	1	100
Sex (transgressive)	Commercial sex	2	1	50
	Sexual harassment	2	0	0
	Deviant sexuality: cross-dressing	1	1	100
Subtotal		21	12	57
Marriage	Meaning of marriage	3	1	33
Work and money	Success in job interviews	1	1	100
	Salary raise	1	0	0
	Success in being a female manager	1	1	100
	Career planning	1	0	0
	Public relations as a new career	1	1	100
	Mistakes at work	1	0	0
	Investment	2	0	0
Subtotal		8	3	38

Life in general	Make the best out of life	1	1	100
	Empathy brings happiness	1	1	100
	Self-defense, insurance, travel, etc.	4	2	50
Subtotal		6	4	66
TOTAL		87	40	46
Subtotal, 1992[1]		9	7	78
Subtotal, 1997		15	6	40

1. 1992 is the data given in the text and is the logic date here.

All topics deal with women being in control or taking charge of what could be under their control. Under "relationships" falls a mix of topics ranging from the mundane (ending a relationship) to the transgressive (having multiple lovers). But regardless of the range—or perhaps because of it—the tone and the content can communicate an image of a woman taking charge and not being left hanging as a result of not having anticipated the worst or having aimed for the best.

In contrast to the lack of articles on the topic of sex in, for instance, the Hong Kong edition of *Cosmo* in the 1990s, no issue of Taiwanese *Cosmo* would be complete without dealing with matters of sex.[4] The range of topics on sex, too, runs from the mundane (e.g., the importance of sex) to the transgressive (e.g., cross-dressing). Sex and relationships constitute about two-thirds (63 percent) of the 87 articles in my sample. An additional 30 percent of the articles deal with matters more closely related to the life trajectory: self, gender, marriage, work and money. They place a stronger emphasis on strategies for success, though they do cover ideological (feminist) issues such as whether women can maintain "self" and autonomy in relationships and marriage. The sample also covers smaller logistical topics such as travel, and wider questions about life in general—for example, happiness.

Cosmopolitan has a bank in New York from which material for articles can be drawn. The Taiwanese *Cosmo* reveals a unique blend of global (mainly Western) and local influences. Three different sources of content appear within this magazine: imported translations, locally written articles and articles either translated but "elaborated" with local names of people and places or composed locally but from a collage of imported content. I initially differentiated among the three with the labels "global source," "local source" and "mixed sources"; but because the "mixed sources" normally originate with Western material, I have here combined this category with "global source." Overall, the proportion of articles from local sources is slightly higher (53 percent) than that from global sources (46 percent). In addition, the data show that over time, the reliance on global sources had tended to diminish, declining from 78 percent in 1992 to 40 percent in 1997.

One might well wonder whether the sources of the material correlate in any way to the topics. As Table 3-1 shows, the topics of sex and relationships display a significant tendency to have global sources (57 percent and 47 percent, respectively). The sources of the articles on work are evenly distributed, while articles on self, gender and marriage tend to use local sources.[5] In some respects, this disproportionate representation of global or Western sources for material about sex and relationships is not surprising. One of the allures of Western magazines is their openness on such topics, which tend to be taboo in Chinese societies. The following letter from a young woman in Taipei to the *Cosmo* editors reveals the appetite of young Taiwanese women for information and advice on such private matters:

> Dear *Cosmo*,
>
> > I and my female friends all are very grateful to *Cosmo* for providing so much information and reporting on relationships and sex issues, because we all have problems in these areas. Only *Cosmo* honestly faces the need of women and provides us such information and wisdom to deal with relationship difficulties in our lives. Most men do not know that some techniques bringing them sexual

> satisfaction may not suit women ... I am not a sexual libertarian, but I support women having the right to seek and get sexual satisfaction. *Cosmo* can make women like me happier and will make more women happier (September 1996, p. 34).

Topics, Sources and Strategies for Modern Taiwanese Women

The core topics in Taiwanese *Cosmo* show Taiwanese women's concerns over the major aspects of their lives. Articles draw on both global and local sources to provide wisdom and practical strategies for young women through biographical narratives as well as the dreams, meanings and morality pertaining to these major topical concerns. For each topical concern, I analyse and contrast the wisdom and strategies revealed in global and local cultural sources.

The Self and Its Completion

Six of the 87 articles deal with the nature of identity or the "self." Only one of these is Western, with the other five produced locally. A contrast in focus and theme is apparent. The one Western article presents the idea that enjoyment is to be found through autonomy and that, ultimately, trying to please men makes a woman unhappy. The author of *Broccoli and Burgers* declares how much happier she is now that she just eats what she likes and does not try to accede to the wishes of men she is close to merely to "fit in" (Livingston, 1994).

The five local articles deal with identity and self in more complex forms and diverse discourses. Some articles refer to Western feminism but do not adopt that ideology. In one article titled "Huo de yiran zizai" (Women Can Have a Self in Life), the author argues that many women really want a "settled life," defined as "having a stable job and a genuine relationship" (Editor, 1994, p. 10). These women work hard toward this goal and, once they are settled, try to remain so. This settled life may not conform to Western feminist expectations, but the most important thing is that these women feel natural and at peace in their lives. In a biographical sketch, the author of another article, "Nüren de wancheng" (The Completion of Women), reveals how she has discovered that she became "complete" when she had a man. Now that she is without one, she has to admit that there is something "missing" (A Man, 1997).

The topic of self is very much associated with the topic of gender. Quite a few articles acknowledge the impact of social change on gender relations in Taiwan as well as providing progressive and fundamental guidelines for modern women. One author argues that regardless of who chases after whom in modern courtships, the most important principles for a modern woman are "being healthy, natural, and genuine" and "let[ting] yourself be your own master" (Editor, 1994, p. 10). Another article, "Zixin de nüren cai mei" (Confident Women Are the Most Beautiful), expands on this theme of self and autonomy, asserting that a beautiful woman ultimately is one who has self-confidence. Compromising in front of men all the time is no longer a women's "virtue" (Editor, 1993). Yet another argues that *Cosmopolitan* can help women develop a "fashioned self," not only telling them how to improve their appearance with makeup but also informing them of social possibilities so that they can explore and understand their "selves" (Zhang, 1992).

Relationships: Finding Authenticity, Harmony and Growth

The next step after examining how *Cosmopolitan* articles redefine the self and reassess gender roles is to explore the nature of the relationships into which that self enters and the gender politics involved. Thirty-four articles address this topic, more than any other topic in my sample. Most of them concern various aspects of how to successfully move through the major transitions of "normative" relationships (their emergence, consummation and termination). Other articles treat consequences and meanings in certain nonnormative contexts, such as love triangles, multiple lovers and "holiday love."

Western articles dealing with relationships tend to focus on individualism and autonomy. The woman is an autonomous agent who should take her cues from her "feelings," rather than attend to the opinions of others. Whether romance has no basis or is founded on rational calculations, the ultimate rule is to be honest and "true to yourself" (Natalia, 1992). This principle appears repeatedly in Western articles in *Cosmopolitan* on virtually all facets of relationships. Consequently, the only resources a woman can draw on are personal honesty (to her feelings) and skills (how to get a man).

On making the right match, a Western article titled "Give Love a Chance, Give Him a Chance" recommends that "what other people think" should be ignored (Dianne, 1995). All four articles concerned with igniting romance are from global sources. They all treat starting a romance as a technical matter in which readers can gain competence, and thus, their advice is of the how-to variety. One article explains "how to get your man on the first date" (Pietropinto, 1995, p. 138).

There is an irony in the treatment of "romance" in these Western articles. On the one hand, romantic love is depicted as being irrational, as purely a matter of "chemistry." Love is treated as a mysterious injection of feeling into one's life. Yet once this injection happens, once Cupid's arrow has been launched, then the romance begins. On the other hand, such romance is also presented as inescapably embedded in gender politics, and women have to make careful calculations at every step. Women are urged to show themselves to be independent by going home by themselves after the first date. "This is the first step for an equal relationship. If, during the first date, a man wants to have sex with a woman, then this is a sign that he is not trustworthy" (Pietropinto, 1995, p. 138).

The five Western articles on the topic of breaking up also deal far more with gender politics, the ultimate concern being to maintain self-esteem or (re)gain a sense of self. Ending a relationship is justified by the idea that identity has been marred. No relationship can be allowed to distort one's sense of self. Terminating it is a path to survival. The possibility of remaking or renewing the relationship is not mentioned. There is even a suggestion that this termination ought to be brutally frank rather than fudged by a reliance on false niceties—women should be honest and real, and they should avoid the "Let's be friends" line (Kramer, 1994). Truth about one's feelings takes priority over the feelings of others.

Furthermore, a more careful cost-benefit analysis is offered. If the woman's self-esteem and dignity are at issue, then the man should be dumped (Halpern, 1994) or the woman should get even (Barreaca, 1995): she must take action to regain her sense of self, for life moves on and, by implication, people who cause pain should be left behind. Even the involvement of a third party can be viewed as beneficial to a woman. In one case, a woman could not admit the truth about a doomed relationship until literally confronted with evidence that there was another woman; by that time, though, her heart may have been broken, but she was at least facing reality (V. Smith, 1996). Such examples demonstrate *Cosmopolitan*'s skill at selling hope as the magazine instructs women to read life through a positive lens, looking forward and (re)gaining their sense of self.

A similar positive spin is applied even to transgressive situations. The two Western articles on extramarital affairs claim that while they are potentially awkward, affairs can ultimately be therapeutic if people stay true to themselves (in addition, they can be fun and, in the end, have a minimal downside). One discusses becoming involved with your best friend's man, recommending a rational approach. Because men are animalistic, they are never held responsible—it will always be perceived as "the other woman's fault." Moreover, fights between women never end! However, if he is irresistible, "go for it" (Falangxisi,

1994, p. 171). The other Western article describes two married people who used an affair with each other to obtain the fun and excitement that were missing from their own marriages. But when they say good-bye, they still "feel lost and abandoned." When they return home, each observes that it is "still the same me!" (L. Smith, 1995, p. 10).

In contrast with the Western emphasis on the fulfilment of autonomous preferences, the advice provided by most local articles takes a primarily practical attitude toward interpersonal relations. Chinese pragmatism places more emphasis on behaviour and judgement than on feelings. Thus, the local articles suggest that judgements about an "appropriate" mate should be tested by experience and by soliciting the views of others. For example, the theme of "financial incompatibility" is addressed, specifically the tensions that may arise when a woman earns more than her boyfriend. In this situation, he may want to borrow money; how should she respond? The author advises caution. In such cases, the woman should find out more, noting in particular how he deals with money with his other family members or friends (Ye, 1995). Rather than ignoring what others think, as suggested in the Western article, this local article recommends seeking out others' points of view.

Furthermore, a relationship's harmony is more important than its intensity. The notion of "the perfect" is challenged. The author of "Ta bu cha, ta shi wo de qingmi airen" (Mr Perfect Is Not Your Only Choice) argues that women who think they can develop a perfect relationship are doomed to self-torture, because no one is perfect (Cai, 1995b). Instead, women have to be flexible and know how to compromise.

An unmistakable emphasis on harmony even appears in the local articles on how to end a relationship. Starting and terminating a relationship are explicitly Western concerns that lack strong local cultural grounding. Only one article (out of six) on breaking up comes from a local source, and it emphasises empathy for how the other party might feel. It even recommends that a good rationale to justify a termination is to say that some family member does not find the man acceptable (Wu, 1994). Such arguments reveal a strong familial sense and the importance of avoiding conflict and hurt. Also, romantic relationships are in a sense embedded in other relationships, most notably familial ones. *Cosmopolitan* sends its female readers the message that when a woman has to dump a man, she must be empathetic and protect his ego by trying to find a "family" excuse.

The local articles make clear that the Chinese advice tends toward caution and responsibility. In response to the rapid social change in Taiwan, one article reports on the diversity of types of relationships young women in 1990s' Taiwan could choose to have in Taipei (Snowden, 1996). The choices included "single and proud", a dual-income couple without children, and unwed mother. The author certainly acknowledges the variations, making no moral judgements except to suggest that "people take responsibility for themselves." This underlying value of responsibility is articulated as a basis for behaviour in times of uncertainty about the forms that relationships may take.

There is an ultimate emphasis on moral integrity, particularly in approaching transgressive events. Unlike the Western articles, which perceive transgressions as fun and even beneficial for individuals, the local articles approach the prospect with greater seriousness. For example, Chinese articles dealing with affairs concentrate on the "other woman." The advice starts with "character building": being rational, facing reality and thinking through the consequences. It is important to be honest and genuine. "Being able to be passionate is a good thing, but self-discipline and control are *necessary*" (Wan, 1995c, p. 147). A moral tone always accompanies this counsel.

One extramarital affair that was much publicised involved a PhD student, Lee Annie, who loved her thesis supervisor, a rich and famous married man, and stated publicly that she was happy to simply be a "concubine." The media portrayed her as the "most horrible woman."

On top of that, as a competent modern woman and a PhD student, she "should not just aim to be this man's concubine! She should not want to just take advantage of a rich man!" (Li, 1995, p. 40).

In addition to advice, warnings are also given to women having affairs with married men. In "Being a Competent Other Woman," the author sets out ten criteria for competence; but she also admits that in reality, no woman can meet all of these criteria. Moreover, she concludes, women who get involved without meeting these criteria risk tears and endless regrets (Wu, 1997). The theme that affairs are dangerous is present in every local article. The life of the other woman is described as tough and lonely, "just like a tree in the desert," and she is warned that "playing with fire will burn you" (Zhong, 1993, pp. 22, 24). None of the seven Chinese articles on the subject denies the possibility of affairs, yet their feasibility is far more circumscribed. The authors suggest that the whole area is fraught with danger, unstable and bad for women; their tone is moralistic, and under no circumstances do they urge a woman to "go for it," as the two Western articles suggest.

There are two articles on the topic of women who stray, one local and the other Western. The contrast between the two is revealing. The Western article actually recommends having multiple lovers so that a woman can make more informed choices. There is no need to get into a marriage at an early age, so it is not worth "going steady" too soon with a man (Snowden, 1996). In contrast, the Chinese article explores what a woman who had had multiple lovers actually lived through. She acted as though she did not care in front of other people, but she still cared about it very much in her heart. There was always a sense of shame. Eventually she was caught in public. She felt humiliated by the whole experience, and swore that she would never do it again (Gao Shi, 1994). The messages of the two articles seem contradictory, but they are actually focused on two different levels. The Western one speaks to self-centred calculation, while the Chinese one emphasises moral integrity.

Finally, women are given the goal of spiritual growth, as the two local articles on "holiday loves" demonstrate. Unlike most Western editions, which offer techniques for finding a partner for the holidays, these articles focus more on spiritual themes. One pertains to the strengthening of the self—using holiday experiences for self-validation and spiritual growth.

In a personal discussion, the author reveals how the Christmas season can make a woman feel lonely. She feels she should go overseas and find romance. On one occasion this happened, but when the woman returned to work, she realised that "the beautiful romance was not real...not because I was really lonely, but it was because I used romance to demonstrate that I must be good. When I knew I was good, I was able to love myself and didn't need to go to 'blind dates'!" (Wan, 1995b, p. 131).

A second theme is self-growth: "It is possible to use loneliness during the holidays to grow up, because in loneliness you can clearly hear your own inner voice. Otherwise, 'have a crazy Christmas Eve' is okay too!" (Wan, 1995a, p. 14). In other words, Taiwanese *Cosmopolitan* adapts this sexy-looking "Western topic" to highlight a Chinese value, encouraging women to seize the Christmas holiday as an opportunity to grow on a spiritual level.

In all 34 articles on relationships analysed above, regardless of whether the subtopics are about normative or nonnormative arrangements, the 16 Western articles treat relationships as paths to individual ecstasy. Love is mysterious but precious, and their primary concern is creating the conditions to ignite love and consume it as an elixir of life. All else—other people, opinions, consequences and commitments—is secondary.

In the process of seeking ecstasy, the authors suggest techniques and skills to enable individuals to carefully calculate their self-interest and to make the best of their circumstances. But coexisting with this Western tone of focusing on individuals who seek to have fun is an even louder voice from the 18 Chinese articles. They are denser and more serious than the Western articles, and they take into account many more specific pragmatic considerations and many more "players," notably family members. Furthermore, they show greater emphasis on issues and fundamental Chinese concerns: family and interpersonal relations, moral integrity and spiritual growth.

Sex: Being Streetwise and Wise

The more relationships are characterised by the modern form of intimacy, the more such relationships raise the central issue of their consummation: sex. Here, *Cosmopolitan* delivers its blend of sexual coaching within the confines of Chinese sensibilities and decorum. Sex sells! This topic is the second largest in my data set (21 out of 87 articles). Eight of the articles focus on sexual skills; these are mainly Western in origin (six of the eight). Six articles are on knowledge and "wisdom" regarding sex; these are mainly written by local authors (five of the six). The remaining seven articles deal with various non-normative sexual issues such as sexual harassment, male prostitutes and cross-dressing as an expression of sexual rebellion.

The ten Western articles on normative sex deal primarily with skills rather than issues. Such skills include how to perform oral sex (Meade, 1992), how to build up self-confidence in the bedroom (Bakes, 1994) and how to use sex as a good tonic. One article lists 25 reasons for wanting sex "tonight" (R. Smith, 1993). Women are encouraged to take the initiative so that men do not have to "do all the work" in bed (Hill, 1994), but they also are encouraged to enjoy themselves and receive pleasure, rather than solely focusing on giving men pleasure (Jacoby, 1993). Also, "Yushuizhihuan shi de gangga yiwai" (The Ten Most Awkward Things that Happen in Bed) are described and preventive strategies are offered (Hill, 1994). Finally, an article gives ten reasons why men don't want to make love and how to overcome them. The how-to strategies embedded in gender politics include trying to be understanding and to support one's man, not looking down on him, letting him communicate what is bothering him and letting him regain confidence and feel "in control" in the relationship (Davidson, 1995).

Overall, in these six Western articles, the focus on pleasure and the emphasis on skills, techniques and strategies are mutually reinforcing. Pleasure does not "just happen": competence makes a difference. Conversely, the more pleasure that is achieved, the more confident people become, so the more they can do and enjoy.

In contrast, the six local articles on this topic have a much more serious tone; they focus on the quality and the meaning of relationships, rather than on skills and strategies. For example, one local article contains interviews with four Taiwanese men regarding their experiences of oral sex (Ye, 1996). All four men think that oral sex is even more intimate than intercourse. In order to be able to enjoy oral sex, a couple needs a longer and deeper relationship, as the two parties need to have more trust in each other. The emphasis is not on what to do to get it right, but what is right about a relationship that gives oral sex its quality.

Also, four out of the six local articles focus on knowledge and wisdom regarding sex. One article on women's orgasms argues that the process of aging is linked to the growth of confidence, self-awareness and openheartedness—attributes that are the basis of achieving good orgasms (Ye, 1997). Another article develops the theme of aging by addressing the myth about sex and the elderly. The elderly can and should enjoy intimacy rather than focusing on performance or acting like sex machines (Jiang, 1994). Two other articles address the issue of whether the body's smells can be arousing (Qiao, 1995, 1997). It is significant that the local articles are much more engaged with aging and the body, rather than with the tactical issues of how to keep young, act young and get what one wants. There is an openness to letting good things emerge from a lifelong natural process, rather than relying on short-term strategies in negotiating gender politics.

A final issue dealt with is sexual harassment, which has drawn attention in Taiwan's society only since the early 1990s. Li Ang, a local feminist, wrote both articles on this topic. In both, she advocates increased autonomy for women. She argues that the way to eliminate sexual harassment is for women to dare to express themselves and respond to others based on what their bodies feel. For a woman, listening to what her body says is more important than listening to her mind, because the mind is the locus of conventional gender roles: it, thus, cannot solve the problem of sexual harassment (A. Li, 1996).

Li Ang also comments on a now famous phrase: "No sexual harassment, but sexual orgasms!" Over time, people have forgotten that this saying originated as an antiharassment slogan. People today tend to focus on the last part of this slogan, which, as Li Ang points out, challenged two things. One is the "good woman" morality; that is, the inseparability for women of love and sex. The other is male sexual competence: the more active and stronger women become, the more pressure men feel and the less likely they are to achieve or maintain an erection (A. Li, 1994). Li Ang views the latter as a particularly useful insight in dealing with sexual harassment.

Work and Money: Strategies with Integrity

Six articles are on work, three Western and three locally sourced. Two articles on money are both Western-sourced. The three Western articles on work focus on the strategies for success—in the first job interview ("Gongwubuke de miantan EQ," 1997), in being a female manager (Kleinman, 1993) and in pursuing a new career path in public relations (Newman, 1992)—linking prospects for advancement to the operation of gender. These are not stories of simple discrimination, but instead, offer strategies for women to achieve their goals by mobilising what is within their control in the work domain. Similarly, two articles on money also teach concrete skills for investing.

The three Chinese articles on work deal with salary raises (Cai, 1996), career planning (Newman, 1992) and mistakes made at work (Wu, 1993). Again, they have a very different tone than the Western articles, emphasising moral and ethical integrity. A feature common to the three is that in stating their argument, the authors don't address women readers specifically, even though they are writing for a women's magazine. On this front, the authors see moral and ethical integrity as gender-neutral. In addition, such integrity is "status-neutral." For example, a local author argues that for both employees and employers, making a mistake at work is a golden opportunity to learn and to improve, not something to fear. The employees "should face the mistake you made honestly and peacefully"; the employers "should fight *with* your subordinates and not blame your subordinates for making a mistake or threaten to fire them!" (Wu, 1993, p. 26).

The View through This Window

The discussions above begin with the self and end with the world. In between there are "gendered" relationships, either personal or work related. In comparing the local and the foreign articles, we can see the difference between a process-oriented and a structural view of womanhood. The Taiwanese articles tend to focus on process, presenting experience as a teacher. Some contain nuances of shame and morality that mark areas as "dangerous," not only as regards gender but also as regards being a decent person. By contrast, the approach of the Western imports, even as they offer ways to change the status quo, is more static. The self is already fully formed, and there is less to be learned from experience. Choice, rather than experience, is the source of success, and the tone is more technical and strategic.

In many of the Western articles, the self is identified as a site of enjoyment. Thus, identity is based on consumption. In the local articles, identity is the site of coherence, implicitly producing social outcomes rather than seeking all-consuming stimulation or attention. For instance, *Cosmopolitan* is not simply to be read as a manual for makeovers or for learning how to make do in the "battle of the sexes"; rather, its purpose is to inform and deepen the value of the reader as a woman. This value has its own life trajectory, as women seek coherence and stability with a robust form of integrity. Women have to be true to their natural selves, cultivating self-confidence and feeling certain that when they have what they want, they should keep it.

Implicit in the Chinese articles—with the exception of one that explicitly makes the point—is the idea that women need men to round out their lives, a position quite contrary to that revealed in the Western articles. But this view that man completes woman does not imply the woman must therefore be subservient or dependent. Indeed, there may be insights here of use to a Western readership.

COSMO as an Arena

As long as social change exists, the potential for tension between traditional and nontraditional values will always be present. *Cosmopolitan*, which relies on the medium of print, must actively select the material it publishes. The *Cosmo* editors thus function as cultural modulators, managing an arena where different discourses or values come into conflict. Rather than seeing the *Cosmopolitan* editors as cultural gatekeepers, I suggest that they filter, mix and match content in ways that satisfy their readership while also remaining within Chinese cultural parameters. The editors thus both select certain Chinese and Western values, identified here, and fail in their efforts to filter out certain other Chinese and Western values, despite their preselection of market-appropriate topics regarding modern womanhood. Those values that manage to break through the filter can thus be seen as core aspects of the respective cultures.

Furthermore, while the local sources tend to emphasise local or Chinese values, some local articles may strategically employ certain global values either to support or to criticise the local system. In addition, though the overall feel of the magazine may give readers an impression of multiple values, one may nevertheless find an overall tone that emphasises some values as fundamental. Therefore, another way to validate empirically that Taiwanese *Cosmo* is an arena of cultural discourses is to map the topical concerns and the ultimate value being emphasised in articles from the global and local sources.

This analysis can reveal several features: (1) how *Cosmo* editors function as cultural modulators in (re)constructing a Chinese form of modern womanhood, (2) how long-standing Confucian insights are implicated and reemphasised in this "discursive" modern womanhood, (3) in what areas of modern womanhood is Chinese wisdom becoming less relevant or is being criticised by Western values, and (4) how global or Western values, views and knowledge are drawn on as a means to support the Chinese values in the local Taiwanese system.

Filtering

It is important to ask whether magazines such as Taiwanese *Cosmopolitan* accentuate and provoke cultural clashes and inflame local sensibilities, or instead, mediate conflict and assuage ruffled sensibilities. Taiwanese *Cosmopolitan* is situated between two major cultural blocks. There are many opportunities for cultural conflicts to arise, such as the clash between Chinese familial values and Western individualism. Should a woman give up her career for her family? One culture recommends "yes," the other "no." Should money earned be given to parents out of filial piety or be saved for the sake of personal autonomy?

The challenge for the magazine is clear. It has to maintain as large a readership as possible in order to maximise advertising revenues. To that end, it cannot become too radical or too closely identified with Western values that may disturb a local readership. At the same time, it cannot simply reiterate local values until it loses its hint of the "cosmopolitan." On this front, *Cosmopolitan* mediates between two cultures, reprocessing content from both.

The American edition contains many more articles on sex, sexual techniques, exotic sexual encounters, sexual experimentation and homosexuality. These topics simply do not appear in the Taiwanese edition.[6] Conversely, local values about filial piety do not appeal to young women readers who are enjoying the fruits of personal autonomy in Taipei's nightlife. They cannot be expected to warm to homilies on such topics! Therefore, certain specific sources or values from both cultures are already blocked from Taiwanese *Cosmo* to avoid overt conflict with readers. In other words, the editors apply filters to each side before global and local values even enter into this arena.

After the filtering occurs, no major cultural clashes in constructing and refashioning Taiwanese modern womanhood are found in the Taiwanese edition of *Cosmopolitan*. Instead, the preselected global values are geared to Chinese values and the local Taiwanese social system.

Values that Slip Through

The filter is a permeable one, for certain fundamental Western and Chinese values occasionally still slip through. This seepage is visible in the way some articles end. After describing some behaviour considered to be "deviant" (e.g., having sex with a best friend's boyfriend or participating in an extramarital affair), the writers recommend courses of action that constrain the behaviour or mitigate its bad consequences; but rather than ending the piece there, they add a sentence that removes the deviant tone and rationalises the original act. For instance, they may say that if the love is "true" and mutual, then it is okay to go for it. In other words, while topics translated directly from Western sources are made acceptable by filtering, in some circumstances, core values such as individualism nonetheless slip through.

Similarly, although none of the articles in the sample is specifically about education, education is emphasised in most of the locally written articles. Normally, the least likely place for educational values to surface would be in coverage of the private lives of actors or actresses. However, in 1990s' Taiwanese *Cosmo,* a story on a popular award-winning actress, Lu Xiaofeng, indicates that she was busy studying at UCLA. "She came back in the summer term break and has become a much deeper person" (Lu, 1992, p. 112).

Intermeshing Globalism and Localism

The 1990s' Taiwanese *Cosmo* data show two kinds of intermeshing. First, global or Western sources were used to support local Chinese values. For example, the title of a translated story on Clint Eastwood was "tough-looking in films but gentle in life," thereby depicting this celebrity as a good family man (Segell, 1993). Dennis Quaid was characterised as "sexy in film but straightforward and a competent and kind father in real life" (Mills, 1994, p. 136). In most articles on extramarital affairs, the ultimate tone was basically cautionary—for example, how miserable it could be to be a mistress (Zhong, 1993)—and they end with the husband eventually going home (Falangxisi, 1993). Or the final outcome for a woman who has multiple lovers is getting caught (Gao, 1994).

The second kind of intermeshing appears in several articles written by local Taiwanese. Certain global or Western values such as feminism were drawn in to challenge aspects of the local gender system: sexual harassment, difficulties for women under conventional gender roles and so on.

Overall, my analysis of major topical concerns and their cultural sources presented in the section "*Cosmo* as a Window" suggests that in the 1990s' Taiwan *Cosmo,* the local or Chinese sources tended to *moralise* topical concerns. In contrast, the *Cosmo* editors tended to *instrumentalise* the global or Western sources, mostly to support—and in a few cases to challenge—the local values and social system. In other words, the *global or Western* sources tended to be used as a *means* to enter new contexts (e.g., relationships, sex and jobs) and to deal with issues of "efficacy," while the *local or Chinese* sources tended to highlight the *ends*. For modern Taiwanese women, the desired ends are achieving inner coherence, being ethical and balancing various roles—especially those pertaining to work and family.

This division in Taiwanese *Cosmo* between ends and means in the fashioning of a successful modern cosmopolitan woman in 1990s' Taiwan can explain why globalism and localism tend not to clash with each other. In other words, these are not just "competing discourses" that "reproduce and magnify" that anxiety of modern young women about love, marriage, work and freedom, as Nancy Rosenberger found in her study of Japanese women's magazines (Rosenberger, 1995, p.156). Rather, as represented, the two values were operating on different levels in the 1990s' Taiwan *Cosmo*; the Chinese "moral" level was dominant, guiding Taiwanese women toward their ultimate destination. An indication of the ascendancy of Chinese values is that Taiwanese *Cosmo* had increased the proportion of Chinese articles (compared to Western articles) during the 1990s, as sales and the cover price had also increased (as noted previously).

I would extend this interpretation, suggesting that the 1990s' Taiwan *Cosmopolitan* had achieved a coherent intermeshing of values by organizing specific oppositions of means and ends, each of which was then open to resolution as one read the various articles in a specific issue of the magazine. Indeed, by analytical induction, I have extracted three such intermeshed oppositions that situate and control the apparent tensions between Western individualism and Chinese familism: *skills* versus *integrity*, *choice* versus *responsibility* and *moments* versus *processes*. In each case, the dangers of the first (Western) term are resolved by the counteraction implicit in the second (local) term.

As mentioned above, in the 1990s' Taiwan *Cosmo*, within each of the topical concerns, the Western articles tend to be about skills while the corresponding local articles are about integrity. Implicit in this contrast is the challenge that to be "too skilful" is perhaps to risk being seen as opportunistic, manipulative and shallow. The blend of articles creates the impression that this risk is diminished if the enhancement of social (or even sexual) skills is kept in check by a reflective awareness of personhood and inner spiritual coherence.

Similarly, the deployment of skills necessarily implies the making of choices. While there are attractions to making autonomous choices based on calculating self-interest, the contrasting articles in the 1990s' Taiwan *Cosmo* suggest that self-interest alone does not deliver happiness. Inner depth and living one's role with integrity are the sure paths to happiness for women. Thus, the local articles in *Cosmopolitan* counter the allure of autonomy by referring to issues of harmony and responsibility.

Finally, the Western articles tend to emphasise moments of insight, pleasure or drama, while the local ones stress process. This contrast contains an implied resolution: moments gain depth if women attend to the process of bringing them about—if, through reflection, they are stitched into episodes of an unfolding biography.

Readers Become Editors: Inferring Modes of Readership

According to a survey conducted by 7-Eleven stores in 1998, among the chain's 1,800 branches in Taiwan, international women's magazines sold much better than local women's magazines. Moreover, among all international women's magazines, the sale figures of *Cosmo* were the highest. Such high sales of the Taiwanese *Cosmo* mean that the editors had succeeded in filtering and constructing the right mix of global and local content in the magazine, satisfying local readers' appetites and avoiding the issues perceived to be irrelevant to the 1990s' Taiwanese women. My interview with Cai Huiming, an associate editor, shed light on the process:

> The earlier years of the Taiwanese *Cosmo* had more translated Western articles, but now we have more local articles: from 100 percent, then 50–50, to currently 30 percent imports versus 70 percent local ... Because readers don't like topics or contents to be too radical ... What kind of topic is seen as too radical by local women? Mmmm ... Western feminism is seen as too radical and Western feminists are seen as too angry—they are not relevant to local women here. Local women perceive that those Western feminists themselves don't have good personal life experiences, so the feminists want to mobilize other women to support their views. But most other women, like our local Taiwanese women, don't feel the same way, and they perceive their own life experiences as not being bad at all! (Cai Huiming, interview with author, 24 September 1998).

The "feminism" appearing in earlier issues (which were translated directly from the Western sources) was perceived as "Western feminism" by the editors and local readers. In talking with Cai, I did not get the sense that she viewed *Cosmopolitan*'s brand of "Western feminism" as but one of several possible versions; it, and thus all feminism, was regarded as irrelevant.

The editors not only filtered out some Western articles but also borrowed content from others to construct a promising and positive image that makes sense to local readers. Cai explained,

> We don't want radical feminists. Because, after all, romance, relationships, marriage and family are good things in life—they sometimes may have problems but can always be improved and become better and better. We at *Cosmo* want to give our readers a *positive* image that things can be improved, and we at *Cosmo* aim to provide advice and the means to improve them. And the advice and means we provide have to be acceptable to local women. This is why the issues of recent years have many more articles written by local authors than earlier years. Now most articles are written by local authors and even the fashion models in the advertisement pages are Chinese!

This positive image constructed by the editors was seen by readers as distinct from "Western feminism" and had an inspiring effect on the editors themselves. Cai Huiming felt that she had become a successful cosmopolitan woman since she took over the magazine's editorship:

> My personal view and lifestyle have been gradually changed since I came to work for *Cosmo* more than three years ago. I feel more positive toward life in general, and I feel I can be in control. In the process of editing Taiwanese *Cosmo*, I have realised that "Readers' taste becomes editors' taste!" I have become much more upbeat. I started to wear makeup. I dress well, not to please men, but for myself, feeling good and confident … and I feel I can succeed. I still want to get married, have children, and have a very balanced life in which I can play both my family role and my career role well. All

my old friends are amazed by how I look and my positive attitude toward life now!

It thus can be argued that Taiwanese *Cosmopolitan* was a niche publication in 1990s' Taiwan: it targeted a specific audience consistent with its advertising brief.

Who were *Cosmo*'s readers in 1990s' Taiwan? Were they a homogeneous group? Did they consume similar material in this magazine? These questions lead to the issue of modes of readership. The associate editor's personal impression was that the magazine's readers were likely to be unmarried women with a high school to postgraduate education, between the ages of 18 and 35. In 1998, the Taiwanese *Cosmo* office conducted a survey: a short questionnaire was attached to an issue with a request to readers to complete the items and mail it back. Because the sample was not representative of the *Cosmo* readership, it cannot be used to generalise about those readers. Moreover, identifying what the different modes of readership might be is difficult or impossible, because the population of potential readers extends far beyond subscribers and occasional purchasers. Yet we can draw on clues in the data and findings presented above to speculate about certain aspects of the 1990s' Taiwanese *Cosmo*'s readers, about possible modes of readership and about the kinds of functions *Cosmopolitan* might be performing within each mode.

We can surmise that there were three socio-demographic clusters of Taiwanese women in the 1990s, to each of which *Cosmo* may have had a unique appeal. These included local Taiwanese women in both the lower and the upper social strata who were likely to read *Cosmopolitan* as "spectators." While family values might have differed among women with different education levels, and between women living in the major cities and the regional areas in Taiwan (Tsai and Yi, 1997),[7] women in these two social locations tended to take interest in "modern" issues, for different reasons.

Women in the lower social strata (e.g., factory workers) viewed the West as a source of glamour and excitement. For them, *Cosmopolitan* provided an accessible window onto a world that might remain forever out of their reach. Those in the upper social strata had an abiding interest in trends of fashion and stories about the famous, particularly local celebrities.

Another group of women were the Westernised and highly educated who might have studied in Western countries and were well established in their careers. They might view *Cosmopolitan* (the Taiwanese edition or the United States version) as overly concerned with issues of appearance, relationship management and success on the job market. Such women would have already solved many of these problems for themselves. But another part of *Cosmopolitan*—the commentaries on being a Chinese modern woman—provided a basis for, or even a provocation to, self-reflection. Such women could have pondered their own personal journeys away from Chinese culture and considered some of the pathways of reconciliation that *Cosmopolitan* offered.

From the content of this magazine in the 1990s' Taiwan, we can surmise that the primary target group was likely to be women on the move, who were therefore puzzled by the many choices and conundrums in their lives. These women were relatively young and perhaps had not yet completed their education. They were fascinated by Western glamour and perplexed by the issues that arose in a more autonomous style of dating. They wanted to have a professional job, be free of conventional control and have a high, disposable income. They had not yet considered the costs of forming a family, however.

It was these women whom the 1990s' Taiwanese *Cosmo* was refashioning by providing them external guidance and internal direction. The emphasis on efficacy made more sense to individuals who were no longer tightly held in the bonds of tradition and had yet to establish themselves within more cosmopolitan settings. For such a group, too, the quest for balance and integrity would have seemed all the more pressing and problematic because there were so many choices and risks before them. Thus, these women used *Cosmo* more practically than the other readership groups mentioned above. Their mode of involvement was more as participants learning about, wanting to be and "making it" as modern women rather than as spectators.

Therefore, the initial appeal of *Cosmopolitan* in 1990s' Taiwan was its cover photos and headlines that offered entrée into various worlds. As women read the magazine, their initial interest in getting access deepened to matters of efficacy, on the one hand, and a concern for balance, on the other. In turn, these functions raised issues of internal coherence and moral character. Thus, the magazine can be seen as having drawn into its semantic web those women considered to be on the move and likely to be interested in refashioned self-definitions that covered a wide range of issues. The targeted women were thus empowered to enjoy greater mobility without being a threat to the local culture in 1990s' Taiwan.

Conclusion

In 1990s' Taiwan, Taiwanese *Cosmopolitan* was not just a popular cultural artefact in a global consumerist world. It was a revealing social phenomenon of considerable complexity. Viewed from the perspective of social change, *Cosmopolitan* can be seen as a vehicle for the Chinese cultural modulators to have filtered, reprocessed and reconciled values from Chinese tradition and Western globalisation. Treating Taiwan *Cosmopolitan* as a window reveals a layered image of 1990s' Taiwan modern womanhood mediating Chinese and Western values. The surface aspects of women (makeup and fashion) were Western, but in moving from pictures to text, one noted an influx of Chinese views that defined deeper, internal aspects of womanhood.

Taiwan *Cosmopolitan* operated as an arena for intersecting cultural contexts from diverse sources. But its very capacity to achieve such a mix of influences raises the question of whether some initial filtering of the material had taken place. The absence in the local edition of certain articles found in Western editions suggests that the local editors did, in fact, filter what appears in the magazine. Yet the filtering was not perfect: values from both cultures had slipped through. The seepage was not as serious as it might have appeared, for the Western values were attached to strategies and function as a means to an end, while the local values were reestablished as moral ends. In this way, the global and the local can have coexisted harmoniously on two different levels within the same pages.

The 1990s' Taiwanese *Cosmo* thus had enabled potentially conflicting values to be brought into some productive alignment. Beyond this, however, the magazine may have wider significance, as it demonstrates that modernisation need not mean Westernisation, even if it relies on veneers of Western images. This possibility—that Taiwanese *Cosmo* can aim to transform local Chinese values in a way that gives them global significance—deserves deep study. Here, in a postcolonial scenario, we see the peripheral tail wagging the central dog (Darby, 1997). The ultimate test of success will be when issues of *Cosmopolitan* in Rome, Istanbul, Sydney or New York contain some articles translated from the Taiwanese edition into their languages.

NOTES

1. In 1996, the "sister countries" were Argentina, Australia, Brazil, the Czech Republic, France, Germany, Great Britain, Greece, Holland, Hong Kong, India, Italy, Japan, Portugal, Russia, South Africa, Spain and Turkey; there was also a general "Latin American" edition. The global and Western ingredients in the Taiwanese edition were drawn mainly from the English-language editions (i.e., the United States, Great Britain and Australia).

2. Sales figures courtesy of the marketing department of Taiwanese *Cosmo.*

3. In 1996, the circulation of *Cosmo* in Australia (population 18 million) was about 100,000; in the United States (population 250 million), about 2,560,000. As noted, in 1997 in Taiwan (population 18 million), circulation was about 380,000.

4. Because Hong Kong readers were found to be uninterested in articles on sex, perceiving the topic as "Western" or "foreign," the local editors were persuaded by the parent company to publish very few such articles (Leung, 1996).

5. Since topics other than those falling under "relationships" and "sex" are represented by few examples, it is inappropriate to draw conclusions about the global/local breakdown of their sources.

6. Such articles about sexuality did not exist in the 1990s' Hong Kong edition of *Cosmopolitan* either (see Leung, 1996).

7. For example, in a 1991 Social Change Survey of a random sample of 2,488 respondents in Taiwan conducted by the Institute of Sociology in Academia Sinica, the proportion of

women agreeing with the statement "Financial security is an advantage in marriage" decreased as years of schooling increased: 70.6 percent of those educated at the elementary school level; 54.1 percent, junior high school; 38.6 percent, high school; 27.3 percent, junior college; and 13.8 percent, university and above (see Tsai and Yi, 1997, p. 140, Table 1). Such attitudes also varied by residential area: 55.2 percent of rural regional women; 48.3 percent of women in major cities; and 41.6 percent of women in Taipei agreed with the statement (see Tsai and Yi, 1997, p. 152, Table 3). Women's attitudes toward another statement, "People without children lead an empty life," varied significantly by different educational levels: agreeing were 82.5 percent of those educated at the elementary school level; 65.8 percent, junior high school; 51.5 percent, high school; 30.8 percent, junior college; and 26.4 percent, university and above (see Tsai and Yi, 1997, p. 149, Table 2). Agreement with this statement also varied by residential area: 66.5 percent for rural regional women; 62.6 percent for women in major cities; and 56.9 percent for women in Taipei (see Tsai and Yi, 1997, p. 154, Table 3).

Part 3:

1950s to Present

Taiwan, Hong Kong and Mainland China

Chapter 4

Pathways to Changing Sexual Mores

The previous three chapters have generated insights regarding changing premarital sexual mores accompanied with the rapid process of modernisation and exposure to Western influence in Taiwan. To explore whether there is something common, or "Chinese," regarding modernisation and changing sexual mores, my findings from Taiwan have to be compared with those in other contemporary Chinese settings, such as mainland China and Hong Kong. This chapter reviews trends and pathways to the liberalisation of sexual mores in each of the settings of China, Hong Kong and Taiwan.

Overall, it is commonplace to assert that Chinese societies (China, Hong Kong and Taiwan) are "modernising" and their older mores are being liberalised. This is illustrated by the claim that sexual mores are becoming more permissive. There has indeed been a trend away from arranged marriages toward love matches in the courtship process, with increasing premarital sexual intimacy. Even some "nonnormative" sexual practices (such as pornography, prostitution and homosexuality) have become more visible and prevalent in these rapidly changing societies. This modernisation argument, however, is insensitive to specific processes internal to these societies and to variations between them. Specific questions can be posed. Regarding changing premarital sexual mores in Chinese cultural contexts, why did Hong

Kong high school students exhibit more liberal sexual behaviour, but have more conservative attitudes, than their counterparts in Taiwan from the mid-1980s to the early 1990s (Chang et al., 1997)? Why did university students in Shanghai evidence more permissive sexual attitudes and behaviours than university students in Taiwan and Hong Kong, even though the latter are seen as more "modern" than the former in the mid-1990s (Fan et al., 1995)?

There has been a converging trend of premarital sexual mores among major cities in China, Hong Kong and Taipei since the mid-1990s (Chang, 2005a). And then, after "converging," would there be a common direction among these major cities, a "real," rather than just quiet, sexual revolution following those in the secular West? Meanwhile, regarding the increasing visibility and prevalence of pornography, prostitution and homosexuality in these Chinese settings, have these "nonnormative" sexual practices been the products of modernisation?

Before examining the changing sexual mores in contemporary Chinese settings, I first briefly frame sex in the Confucian tradition: the famous Confucianism saying "*Shi se xing ye*" (Eating food and having sex are in the nature of human beings) provides an interpretative key to Chinese sexuality—a natural urge. The exercise of sex was not normally associated with feelings of sin or moral guilt as long as sex was with the right party in the right place (van Gulik, 1974; Hsu, 1983). Historically, the "right" party for Chinese men could include wives, concubines (*qie*) and prostitutes, whereas the right party for Chinese women was husbands only. The right place for sex was the bedroom. Beyond the bedroom, neither sexual behaviour nor sex talk was appropriate. The violation of the right party and/or place was associated with shame in the individual who violated these norms as well as in his/her family.

In this chapter, I address issues regarding "normative" versus "nonnormative" sexual practices in Chinese traditions, as well as review and identify pathways for changing sexual mores in both normative and nonnormative areas in contemporary China, Hong Kong and Taiwan. There had been varied pathways of liberalising "normative" premarital sexual practices due to different political economy and colonial experiences from the 1950s to the mid-1990s, whereas there was a common pathway of changing the "nonnormative" into the "normative" sexual practices under modernisation. At the end of this chapter, I briefly explore, after the mid-1990s, which direction of a converging trend in premarital sexual mores in these contemporary Chinese societies appears to be going, with an implication for the modernisation argument.

Varied Pathways: Liberalising Premarital Sexual Mores (the 1950s to the Mid-1990s)

This section examines the trend toward sexual liberalisation in contemporary Chinese societies which is not part of the Chinese traditions, particularly premarital sex for women, which was "nonnormative" in historical China. Premarital sex has become "normative" in the West since the 1960s' sexual revolution, which has influenced and "normalised" the nonnormative premarital sex practices in Chinese societies in recent decades.

Taiwan and Hong Kong began the modernising process in the 1960s; China started it in the late 1970s. The speed of the process and what has been accomplished in these societies have been described as "Asian miracles." The first dimension regarding modernisation is structural transformation, namely, industrialisation, urbanisation and the expansion of education and migration. The second dimension is cultural change through exposure to new ideas, particularly those of the West, such as romantic love, freedom, individualism (in the name of autonomy and choices), egalitarianism, gender equality and consumerism. Since the 1990s, growing access to the Internet and globalised media and popular culture have sped up the diffusion of these ideas, ideals and images of global icons in these contemporary Chinese settings.

In the past several decades across all these Chinese societies, there has been a change from arranged marriages toward love matches with increasing premarital sexual intimacy. As we saw in Chapter 1, this trend was evident in a 1986 islandwide survey of about 5,000 married women aged 20 to 49 in Taiwan. The incidence of premarital sexual intercourse had substantially increased from 9.5 percent for the birth cohort of 1936–1940 to 38 percent for the birth cohort of 1956–1969, but most of them had had their first sex with their future husbands after engagement or in a relationship that led to marriage.

There was no comparable cross-sectional survey data, i.e., a sample covering a wide range of 20-year birth cohorts, in Hong Kong to reflect such change. Less satisfactory data sets were a serial of household surveys of a random sample of out-of-school youths aged 19 to 27. In these Youth Sexuality Studies, among men, 36.7 percent (out of 581) in 1991 and 39.8 percent (out of 517) in 1996, and among women, 32.7 percent (out of 578) in 1991 and 39.4 percent (out of 447) in 1996, had experienced sex (Hong Kong Family Planning Association, http://www.famplan.org.hk). These figures can be expected to be higher than the extent of premarital sex because the sample in these surveys included married people who may not have had premarital sexual experiences.

Since the Reform Era started in China in 1978, a similar trend has shown itself in both major cities (since the 1980s) and in some of villages (since the 1990s) (Zhou, 1989; Whyte, 1990; Xu and Whyte, 1990; Geng 1991; Liu et al., 1992; Zha and Geng, 1992; Fan et al., 1995; Li, 1996, 1991). In rural China, a "dating" culture emerged in the 1980s and the early 1990s, but dating frequently occurred *after* a young couple had become engaged or had made a commitment to marry. This Chinese style of dating was accompanied by an increase in premarital sexual intimacy (with the future spouse). Since the late 1990s, a significant proportion of couples have had premarital sex after engagement (about one-third in the northern village studied by Yan) (Yan, 2003). Arranged marriages have become a minority phenomenon for young people in rural areas.

As for urban China, in the 1980s and the first half of the 1990s, some university students engaged in premarital sex. Various surveys in major cities reveal that between 10 percent and 20 percent of university students had had sexual experiences (a higher proportion of males than females having had sex) (Zhou, 1989; Geng, 1991; Zha and Geng, 1992). The largest national survey on contemporary sexual attitudes and behaviours in China—done in 1991 (with 20,000 respondents) by the Shanghai Sex Research Centre—found much higher figures due to its nonrandom sampling bias (Liu et al., 1992).

Other data also reveal a picture of premarital sexual activity: reports from various parts of urban China indicate that between 30 and 50 percent of abortions done at urban hospitals were performed on unmarried women (Lyle, 1983; Honig and Hershatter, 1988; Riley, 1989). Another research survey comprised of nine studies (seven in urban, one in rural and one in both urban and rural areas) studied data from compulsory premarital physical exams conducted for about-to-marry women between 1978 to 2002, and found that most women had had premarital sex (estimates ranged from 54 percent to 82 percent) (Qian et al., 2004).

Beyond these trends in changing premarital sexual mores, I wish to further discuss the variations of processes and pathways of these changes across these societies prior to the mid-1990s.

Regarding the microlevel determinants of sexual practices, it can be expected that age, rural/urban background, educational level, gender, generation, living arrangements before marriage and belief in Christianity would impact young people's premarital sexual mores in each of these Chinese societies. But these microlevel factors cannot explain the different pathways to changing premarital sexual mores across the three Chinese societies, because the notion of "pathway" is on an aggregated societal level which is beyond the socio-demographic factors of an individual.

Regarding the meso-level determinants, most of the institutional factors were actually similar across these three contemporary Chinese societies prior to the mid-1990s, such as (monogamous) marriage law, a divorce law based on fault, lack of adequate sex education, abortion being officially legal for married people only (but accessible underground for unmarried women) and lack of social welfare for single mothers. These cannot explain the different pathways of sexual liberalisation evident in urban China, Taiwan and Hong Kong. The only major institution-level factor which differed among these societies was that Hong Kong was the only society to allow official birth control access for unmarried people.

Regarding the macrolevel determinants, I argue that political economy and colonial experience were the two major societal-level factors which varied across these contemporary Chinese societies and that these were particularly useful to explain the different processes and pathways to changing premarital sexual mores in urban China, Hong Kong and Taiwan, given the fact that most of the microlevel and meso-level determinants to individuals' sexual practices were largely similar across the three societies prior to the mid-1990s.

Of particular significance here was the variety of contexts in which premarital sexual practices had come into being: Chinese socialism had aimed to replace "feudal" Confucianism as the only ideology for nation building as well as for people managing their everyday lives from the 1950s to the late 1970s. It was part of Hong Kong's specific blend of the Chinese familism, British colonial administration,

Christianisation and international trade; and they were embedded within the Taiwanese drive for modernisation and cultural consistency with the Confucian heritage. These societies had, as a result, quite distinct macrolevel determinants that had conditioned premarital sexual practices in the everyday lives of Chinese before the mid-1990s.

Communist China: Negation of "Tradition"

There are many interpretations of the nature of Communism implanted in China, particularly in the first three decades. For the purposes of a study of sexuality during this period, the key issue to be explained is what kind of "repression," if any, there was of sexuality.

The goal of building a new China, from the 1950s to the mid-1970s, meant that Communist political ideology and action were the priority, as well as the only standard of defining morality in the everyday lives of both men and women. Sexual thought, talk, interest or behaviour in public were seen as either feudal or capitalist immorality. In this period, although research found that a range of materials published were on sex-related issues such as adolescent hygiene, contraception, love, extramarital relations and the breakdown of marriage (Evans, 1997, p. 2), it has been argued that the general atmosphere was that sex was a taboo subject and displays of romantic feelings or gestures in public were frowned upon (Zha and Geng, 1992). During the Cultural Revolution (1966–1976), both men and women wore gender-neutral "Mao-style" clothes to defeminise the female appearance and reinforce political-puritanic sexual mores.

On a gender-ideology level, Mao's slogan that "women hold up half the sky" mobilised women into nation building. The new socialistic woman was called "Iron Girl," for she was as strong as a man (Honig and Hershatter, 1988). The policing system mobilised all-level nonfamilial structures, from communes, schools, work units and committees, from the neighbourhood to the state level. Serious sanctions against immoral sexual practice meant that transgressors could be sent to labour camps in remote regions or be sentenced to jail. Chinese people and Westerners perceived the period of the 1950s to the 1970s as being the most sexually repressive period in Chinese history, even if the Communist state was trying to "liberalise" China by destroying the "repressive" feudal system defined by Confucian cultural ideals.

But I argue that this political/puritanical sexual morality, as applied to both men and women in Communist China, may simply be a sexual "suppressor" (like the suppressor in the neo-Confucian period in terms of emphasising female chastity). The only difference in this political/puritanical era was that the "right party" outlets were reduced to the wife only as a result of monogamous marriage and the abolishment of prostitution. The "right place" to express affection was limited to the bedroom.

Furthermore, the political/puritanical sexual morality under this political/puritanical nation-building process did not mean that young people had no romantic involvement before marriage. Even in the early phase of socialistic China, there had been a ten-year period of sexual "puritanism" in public during the Cultural Revolution (e.g., men and women wearing the desexualised Maoist uniform; no "falling in love" based on sexual chemistry but on political criteria). People violating the sexual norm were seen as shameful and guilty of political incorrectness, and they were sent into forced labour camps for thought correction. Even so, research found that young women still managed to wear decorations on their Mao style-uniforms (Ip, 2003), and some young people sent to the countryside during the Cultural Revolution did have (premarital) sexual experiences in various circumstances (Honig, 2003).

The survey that Whyte (1990) conducted of 586 ever-married women aged 20 to 70 in the two main urban districts of Chengdu in 1987 shows that premarital sex, with the future spouse, increased during the Communist period. Whyte used both minimum and maximum measures[1] to estimate Chengdu women's premarital sexual experience with their future husbands. The two measures show a significant increase in premarital sex between the pre-Communist and the Communist periods. The figures for the pre-Communist period are: 4 percent (a minimum measure) and 12 percent (a maximum measure) for women who married between 1933 and 1948, i.e., the last 10 years of the Republican period in China. The figures for the Communist period are: 15 percent (minimum) and 21 percent (maximum) for women who married between 1949 and 1957; 15 percent and 24 percent for women who married between 1958 and 1965; 19 percent and 25 percent for women who married between 1966 and 1976 (i.e., the Cultural Revolution period).[2]

In the aftermath of the Cultural Revolution, the Reform and Open Era started in the late 1970s. Capitalistic socialism, based on the market economy, has modified the Communist socioeconomic system. Major cities and regions have been undergoing a rapid modernising process. Economically, decollectivisation and decentralisation have meant that farm and business operations are now privatised to an extent. The speed of industrialisation, urbanisation and growth in international trade and investments from foreign countries has been record-breaking. The Shenzhen region in Guangdong has gained a reputation as the "Fifth Little Dragon" of Asia. Politically, the eager demand for democracy and human rights from Chinese intellectuals was evident in the Tiananmen Massacre on 4 June 1989.

On the cultural front, the "open-door" policy during the Reform Era has exposed China, particularly the major cities and the east coast regions, to modern cultural influences from Japan, Korea, Taiwan, Hong Kong and the secular West due to business contacts and popular culture that are diffused through the mass media in a globalised world.

Since the late 1980s, modern ideas, ideals, images and lifestyles have been pouring into China due to the amount, speed and irreversibility of its reforms and opening to a market economy. One impact of the economic growth on the post-Mao family system is that Chinese have been reacting to the newly gained wealth in this socialistic capitalism by practicing the conventional marriage rituals (Davis and Harrell, 1993). The exchanging of presents from both families and the staging of extravagant weddings contrast significantly with Maoist weddings where both parties wore Mao's uniform and bowed to his picture. This post-Mao wedding behaviour shows that a core aspect of Chinese familism has persisted and Chinese people have been fulfilling an old "wish" which had been suppressed for almost three decades during the Communist period.

However, using the new means of wealth to achieve an "old end," namely a "traditional" wedding as defined by Confucian familism, does not mean that the reformed economy has returned social morality to the prerevolutionary days. The loosening of premarital sexual mores since the 1990s has taken place in a context of a double negation of traditions. The reason for using the term "double negation" of traditions here is that the Communist revolution was supposed to negate the Confucian values (seen as "feudal" tradition by Communist ideology) from 1949 to 1978,[3] while "Reform-open"/modernisation negated the Maoist values in the post-Mao period from 1978 to the mid-1990s. Consequently, moral values had eroded (Chu and Ju, 1993), and all new or different values, particularly those from rich countries or societies, have "poured into" this environment that has been through double-negating of traditions.

Romantic ideal and sexual intimacy are part of the relationship, an expression of love from the secular West (mainly from the representations in the imported popular culture) which has been perceived as being "modern" by many urban young people. As a result, premarital sexual mores had been loosening—premarital sex was acceptable after engagement or in a relationship leading to marriage prior to the mid-1990s.

Many Chinese, in both media and everyday life, have perceived that a new value which Chinese have is "looking at the money," [4] because opportunities to earn big money are now both a "means" (to survive in a system of decreased access to welfare benefits) and an "end" (some people in society have become so rich!). This was not the case during the three decades of the Mao period. Chu and Ju conducted a survey in 1987 regarding value changes in the Reform Era for about 2,000 residents in Shanghai, Qingpu County and villages nearby. The authors found rapidly rising material aspirations among Chinese, and money has become something very important in Chinese social life (Chu and Ju, 1993). They interpreted in their book *The Great Wall in Ruins*:

> The preoccupation with material gains in contemporary China is partly the result of an abrupt policy change from Mao's revolution to Deng's economic reform. After a prolonged period of austerity and deprivation, Chinese people are shocked to find an outside world dazzling with modern amenities beyond their wildest imagination. Poverty is no longer a symbol of revolutionary strength, as it used to be under Mao's policies. Getting rich is now not only acceptable, but even given an official sanction under the mantle of economic reform. People do not want to accept poverty as a way of life. They want material comfort, and they want it now. Both traditional virtues and revolutionary ideals are thus pushed aside (Chu and Yu, 1993, p. 317).

To some young women, the "look-at-money" mind-set placed against a background of liberalising sexual mores led them into the sex industry, to sexual encounters with Westerners who have liberal sexual behaviours, or to be "kept" (so-called *baoernai*) by Chinese businessmen from Taiwan and Hong Kong who were engaging in "pseudo-concubine behaviours" (with the legacy of traditional sexual norm justifying the concubine as a "right-party").

Taiwan: Orthodoxy with Modernity

Before the Han Chinese migrated and settled in Taiwan in the seventeenth century, Taiwan had mainly indigenous people who had had some Portuguese contacts when they passed through Taiwan in 1517. While parts of Taiwan had been under Dutch control from 1624 to 1662, Jilong had been occupied by Spain from 1626 to 1642. Spanish influences were mainly in the northern region in Taiwan. After Zheng Cheng-gong expelled the Dutch during the Ming Dynasty in the seventeenth century, Chinese from Fujien and Guangdong started to migrate to Taiwan, bringing their traditional Chinese lifestyles from the mainland and developing their new home into an agricultural society. Cultural, educational and social developments in Taiwan were framed under a policy of "domestication" during the Qing Dynasty. A Confucian society was created and administered by the intelligentsia (The Story of Taiwan, March 2004; Rubinstein, 1999).

Taiwan had been a Japanese colony for half a century (1895–1945). The infrastructure for advanced agriculture and proindustrialising in Taiwan was started during the Japanese colonial period in order to produce agricultural products for Japan. On the sociocultural front, the Japanese colonisers did not intervene in the local family and kinship system, and they let the Taiwanese maintain Chinese family structures and values (Barclay, 1954).

In 1949, the Nationalist Party (*Kuomingdang*, or "KMT") lost the civil war to the Communists, fled from mainland China and took over political power in Taiwan. In order to continue the political fight with the Communist Party in mainland China and to earn international recognition of, and claim to, being the only "real China," the

Nationalist government constructed an "orthodox" Chinese identity, implemented Mandarin as the official language and committed itself to implanting the core aspects of traditional Confucianism (such as familism and respecting authority) into the ideological system and cultural institutions of Taiwan (Chun, 1994). In particular, a major countermovement called the "Cultural Renaissance Movement" was proposed to counterbalance the most forceful "Cultural Revolution" that took place in mainland China from the 1960s to the mid-1970s. All levels of school curriculum, national entrance exams and civil service exams have had Confucian classics as a compulsory subject. The heritage of Confucianism has been strategically and politically implanted in Taiwan, and this has reinforced and strengthened the Chinese values brought to Taiwan by the migrants from southeast China.

During the 1960s and 1970s, Taiwan experienced a rapid process of industrialisation, urbanisation and educational expansion as well as exposure to Western values. Women gained opportunities for formal schooling and work outside home. They were even able to live away from home before marriage (Chang, 1996). The value of virginity was emphasised, and young people "had a say" in mate selection (but in most cases with parental approval). In the 1980s and 1990s, Taiwan was hailed as one of the newly developed countries for its economic miracles and significant progress in democratic politics.

Since I fully explored the topic of changing premarital sexual mores in Taiwan by utilising both quantitative and qualitative approaches in Chapter 1 and Chapter 2, I only need to highlight two major points from those two chapters. The first point is that although in the process of rapid modernisation there has been a dramatic increase in premarital sexual intimacy in Taiwan, based on my 1986 survey data (analysed in Chapter 1), this so-called quiet revolution was not a real revolution at all, because premarital sex usually occurred only in relationships where marriage was already planned (the couple were engaged) or being seriously considered. This implies that romantic love, dating and premarital sex were seen as changes from the 1950s to the mid-1990s in Taiwan, but that premarital sex in a marital context remained within the Chinese tradition.

The second point is that based on the focus group data I collected in 1994 and analysed in Chapter 2, the insights into the perceptions, interpretations and idioms of sexual mores among young people in Taipei suggest that a realignment was underway between the genders regarding their roles in, and expectations about, intimate relations. The outline of this realignment did not appear to be a direct importation of the contemporary Western ideas about sexuality. Hybrids of global and local values were discernable in addition to specific local variations due to gender, age, generation and education. Chinese ideas about virginity arose when virginity was lost. Men were confronted with the challenge of making good their responsibility to marry the woman, given the premarital, rather than promiscuous or exploratory, nature of the sexual encounter.

In anticipation of any risk of virginity loss or in the "aftermath" of it happening unexpectedly, women were challenged to assess the loss of "marriage value" from no longer being a virgin and to assess the risks of nonmarriage. New economic independence for women means that marriage is no longer the sole path to a secure or a coherent life. Women can therefore downplay the value of virginity. A new balance can be expected through women's expectations of the fidelity of their future husbands and the downplaying of women's past "indiscretions" by men.

Hong Kong: Doubling Traditions

Hong Kong was a British colony for 99 years (1898 to 1997) as a result of the Qing Dynasty's defeat in the Opium War. The British government developed Hong Kong into an international trading port and generated a rapid momentum for industrialisation and urbanisation in the 1960s (Buckley, 1997). Women gained access to work opportunities outside of the home and formal education (Salaff, 1981; Pearson and Leung, 1995).

By the mid-1970s, Hong Kong had earned a reputation among local and foreign investors, as "a heaven for economic gains," due to its attractions, namely, the nonintervention policy of the government, the well-developed infrastructure and telecommunication system, low taxation and the colony's well-trained labour force (Chan, 1986). In the 1980s and 1990s, Hong Kong (like Taiwan) became one of Asia's "Four Little Dragons" in recognition of its economic miracle. Hong Kong's economic success benefited both the colonised and the coloniser.

On the social front, the British government did not intervene in the local Chinese family structure, which is evident in the fact that the polygamous system of concubinage and maids was not abolished until 1971 (Pegg, 1986). On the cultural front, Confucian culture was not able to be passed on through the colony's formal institutions of education or local Chinese elites. Chinese in Hong Kong were exposed to Chinese culture mainly through the family (Lau and Kuan, 1991). The situation of Chinese culture in Hong Kong is insightfully revealed in a book entitled *The Ethos of the Hong Kong Chinese*.

> The tenacity of tradition in the Chinese society of Hong Kong has been drastically weakened by the absence of the agrarian-landlord and gentry-scholar-official classes in the colony. The nonexistence of these classes means that there have been no powerful custodians to uphold and enforce Confucian morality and virtues, nor is there any cultural hegemony to influence the substance of education. The disappearance of Confucianism from the content of Hong Kong's civil service examinations even deprives the residual Confucian presence

> of instrumental values and relegates it to cultural backwaters. Confucian influence lingers on, but this is contingent more on the natural influence of social customs and family socialization than on any institutional underpinnings (Lau and Kuan, 1991, p. 34).

Since Hong Kong was a British colony for almost a century, Western cultural influence in the colony could be expected to be quite significant. As has been noted, Confucian cultural influences on Hong Kong Chinese mainly existed in, and through, the family. Most of the "public" arenas are typically filled with "inputs" from the coloniser, and so they show the influence of British culture, systems and institutions. Hong Kong people, as Chan (1986) has argued, "[Hong Kong people] were both Chinese *and* British, Hong Kong people were *neither* category" (Chan, 1986, p. 210). In the colonial system, everything categorised as "Chinese" was regarded as inferior to things "British" and "Western" (Tsang, 1990).

The missionary culture, in particular, was quite influential in Hong Kong society. Most elite schools were run by Christians. The compulsory school curriculum taught and practiced Christianity, not the Confucian classics. Moreover, people in Hong Kong were exposed to a "presecularised" Christianity and did not go through the "sexual revolution" that Christians in the secular West experienced. It is not surprising, then, that Hong Kong young people's sexual mores were found to be influenced by Christian values (Tsang, 1986) in which nonprocreating sexual pleasure or the violation of sexual mores would be tied to sin and guilt.

Meanwhile, the value of familism[5] (Lau, 1981, 1987) and the "right party/place" requirement (and the attendant sanction, "shame") regarding sexual practice have no doubt influenced Hong Kong Chinese through their families. This unique mix of Christian cultural influences from the wider society and Chinese cultural influences from the family meant that Chinese people in Hong Kong were exposed to the most conservative elements, as well as to the fullest sanctions (including sin, guilt and shame!) regarding sexuality, from both cultures.

One impact of this "double sanctions" system is evident in comparisons of statistical figures of sexual practices between different Chinese societies. In a 1991 survey of a sample of 10,410 first-year university students in Hong Kong and Shanghai, Hong Kong students exhibited more conservative sexual attitudes and behaviours than the college students in Shanghai (Fan et al., 1995). Hong Kong college students lived with double sanctions (sin, guilt and shame) from both Christian and Chinese influences, while college students in Shanghai faced few, if any, sanctions (at most, some shame due to the Chinese legacy from their families) in post-Mao China.

Further evidence can be drawn from my own comparative study of the sexual attitudes and behaviours of high school students in Hong Kong and Taiwan in the late 1980s.[6] I found that the sexual behaviours of Hong Kong students were more permissive, but their sexual attitudes were more conservative, than their counterparts in Taiwan. Regarding sexual behaviours, in Taiwan, 2.3 percent of 3,021 female students and 10.7 percent of 1,537 male students had engaged in sexual relations, while 13.5 percent of 721 female students in Hong Kong had had sex, and 17.4 percent of 750 males had engaged in premarital sex. Regarding sexual attitudes, Taiwanese high school students' attitudes varied by the level of the seriousness in the relationship. In a relationship where "a woman is fond of a man," 21.2 percent of males and 2.9 percent of females agreed that sex was permissible. In a relationship where "a woman is in love with a man," 33 percent of males and 7.2 percent of females agreed that sex was permissible. As for an engaged relationship, 53.6 percent of males and 14.6 percent of females agreed that sex was permissible. In contrast, for Hong Kong male students, 11.4 percent approved of sexual intercourse in dating while only 2.6 percent of female students approved (Chang et al., 1997).

The 1986 Hong Kong data suggest that the impact of these values was probably more visible at the behavioural than the attitudinal level among high school students, as their behaviours were more permissive than their attitudes. One of the possible explanations is that modelling or mimicking behaviour might have been easier than altering deeply entrenched attitudes.

Another explanation, which is not incompatible with a cultural influence theory, is that there may be facilitative and inhibitory mechanisms at work within a given social context. For instance, in the 1980s, the higher availability of birth control aids and abortion facilities in Hong Kong—both of which can be seen as products of Western culture—might have been a facilitative factor for more permissive sexual behaviours.

On the other hand, the fact that Taiwan students evidenced more permissive attitudes than behaviours, while the reverse was the case in Hong Kong, suggests that Western influences had been able to creep in to influence attitudinal shifts without affecting behaviours due to more limited access to birth control and abortion in Taiwan. Here, the factor of birth control access shows how a meso-level institutional factor had been able to determine people's sexual behaviours.

In summary, three different processes and pathways of changing premarital sexual mores show themselves in these contemporary Chinese societies in the years prior to the mid-1990s. The conservative attitudes of Hong Kong Chinese stemmed from the mutual reinforcement of Confucian and Christian norms as a result of almost a century of British colonisation. As a result, the pathway of Hong Kong youths' liberalising premarital sex was through "doubling traditions" but with easy access to birth control. Conversely, mainland China experienced a "double-negating of traditions" in which Confucian tradition was attacked as being feudalistic from the 1950s to the 1970s and Maoism and puritanical elements of Communism has been undermined since the start of the Reform Era in 1978. This double-negating has resulted in new values "flooding in" (Lu, 1995) and old premarital sexual mores loosening.

Finally, in Taiwan, the upholding of orthodox Confucianism combined with explicit modernisation had led to the careful reworking of Western values in terms of Chinese traditions. As a result, the loosening of premarital sexual mores among young Chinese had been accomplished via a pathway of *doubling traditions* for Hong Kong, *double-negating of traditions* for mainland China and *orthodoxy with modernity* for Taiwan.

These different pathways can answer the questions I posed in the beginning of this chapter. Prior to the mid-1990s, it was due to double-negating of traditions that university students in Shanghai were found to have more liberalised sexual attitudes and behaviours than their counterparts in Hong Kong and Taiwan (Fan et al., 1995), even the former started "modernising" after the latter. Doubling traditions (and sanctions) and easier access to birth control aids made Hong Kong high school students exhibit more conservative sexual attitudes, but more permissive sexual behaviours, than was the case in Taiwan (Chang et al., 1997).

A Converging Trend since the Mid-1990s —A "Real" Sexual Revolution Underway?

More young people have had premarital sexual experiences in the three contemporary Chinese societies since the second half of the 1990s than those prior to the mid-1990s, regardless of whether the couple's relationship was leading to marriage. Survey data, based on fragmented samples, are limited. A 2001 study of youth sexuality in Hong Kong revealed that 8.7 percent of 1,186 males and 5.2 percent of 1,678 females in a sample of in-school students (ages 13 to 18), and 44.9 percent of 633 males and 35.2 percent of 579 females in a sample of out-of-school youths (ages 19 to 27), had had sexual experiences. But the out-of-school sample included both single and married/cohabitating youths, so these figures included premarital and some marital sex experiences (Hong Kong Family Studies Association, http://www.famplan.org.hk).

In Taiwan, studies of premarital sexual experiences have tended to focus on in-school students. A 1997 study of Taipei junior college students, ages 19 and 20, found that 35.2 percent of males and 26.7 percent of females had had sexual experiences (Yen et al., 1998, p. 8).

In China, a few studies have been conducted through small and fragmented samples. A study of high school students in Shenzhen found that 10.30 percent of males and 4.4 percent of females had had sexual experiences (Xie et al., 2003). A study of university students in Yunnan found that 39.4 percent of males and 20.8 percent of females had had sexual experiences (Yu and Zhao, 2004). A study of unmarried women, ages 15 to 49, in Jiangsu Province found that, among those who had had romantic relationships, 28.57 percent had experienced sex (Yue et al., 2004). Li Yinhe, a researcher in studies of sex in China, commented in an interview, "In 1989 I did a survey that showed only 15 percent of Beijingers had had premarital sex. Now the figure must be three or four times that" (*Asia Week*, 6 July, 2001).

Although these figures from limited survey data cannot present a coherent or general picture regarding premarital sexual practices in the three Chinese societies since the mid-1990s, my own qualitative research on social trends has shown that there has been a converging trend among the highly educated young people growing up in major cities of China, Hong Kong and Taiwan. This segment of young people has been exposed to avant-garde values. There is a significant contrast in findings between the in-depth interviews I conducted with university students in 1994 and those I conducted in 2005. In 1994, when I conducted interviews in Shanghai, Hong Kong and Taipei, university students had primarily linked the appropriateness of sex to contexts of engagement or relationships leading to marriage. They thought that the virginity value for women was crucial—most female interviewees believed that a nonvirgin woman would have trouble finding a husband, and most male interviewees wanted to marry a virgin.

In 2005, my interviewees, growing up in Shanghai, Beijing, Hong Kong and Taipei, all approved of premarital sex when two people are in love and in a committed relationship, and they said that sex *is* an important part of the relationship—it is a given. Most interviewees estimated that significant proportions of people they knew had had premarital sexual experiences, with estimates ranging from 50 percent to 80 percent.

As for smaller towns and semirural areas in China, some young people reported having sex in a relationship in which the couple had not yet reached the stage of talking about getting engaged. A qualitative study conducted in a semirural region bordering Shanghai by Wang and Davidson (2005) found that in some cases the parents or one of the other of the youngsters somewhat "consented" (at least did not discourage) the first sex intimacy, because parents wanted the relationship to be stabilised for their children, and they must have thought that sex could have produced that result (Wang and Davidson, 2006).

The converging premarital sexual mores revealed in my qualitative research between urban China, Hong Kong and Taiwan since the mid-1990s may be associated with similar levels of economic development, easier access to birth control aids for unmarried people, and increased exposure to Western sexual mores and romantic ideals from the Internet and globalised media. Is it possible that beyond convergence there is a common direction evident that shows a "real" sexual revolution (not just a "quiet" one), similar to that in the secular West? I would argue that there has been no "real" sexual revolution in these Chinese societies, for premarital sex still occurs primarily in committed, or long-term relationships, and young Chinese continue to define themselves primarily by their familial roles and living through familism in their everyday lives. An indicator of this orientation toward "familial harmony" is that among the 29 young people growing up in urban China, Hong Kong and Taiwan whom I interviewed in 2005, a crucial criterion in selecting a mate is "having to get along with my parents and treat my parents very well" (Chang, 2005a).

Such a familial orientation will no doubt increase in evidencing the three "converging" Chinese societies, especially given that the Chinese Communist Party has been promoting a top-down cultural policy to return to the Confucian philosophy and values generally. An official celebration (through the medium of state-controlled television broadcast) of Confucius's 2,556th birthday, on 28 September of 2005, was the biggest such occasion since Socialist China was founded in 1949. More than 2,500 individuals, including many fairly high-ranking Communist Party cadres, made a pilgrimage to Confucius's birthplace at Qufu in Shandong Province to celebrate the occasion (*Asia Times*, 16 November, 2005).

The latest government line is that Confucianism can serve as a moral foundation to fill in the "void" due to the negation of "tradition" and/or to counter the "flooding in" Western values as well as to restore the social harmony and stability disrupted by the worsening social inequality that has come with the rapid social change driven by the market economy in the Reform and Open Era. This cultural policy has reinforced and strengthened the awareness of Chinese culture in post-1997 Hong Kong.

As I briefly mentioned in the preface, in 2007, I had conducted in-depth interviews with 12 cultural elites in Beijing and Hong Kong.[7] The notion of "harmony" has been spontaneously mentioned by all my interviewees as a good traditional value/element that should be preserved in today's world and for an ideal modern China or Hong Kong regardless of how the "tradition" was defined by these elites. In particular, the cultural elites I interviewed in Beijing deeply lamented the lack of harmony in the wider Chinese society today due to the worsening gap between the rich and the poor and how disturbing some employers have been by so inhumanly exploiting their workers.

It seems to me (as a researcher) the notion/value of harmony is so deeply rooted in my interviewees' hearts in both Beijing and Hong Kong that seems beyond the recent Chinese government's cultural policy or slogan for developing a civilised harmonious Chinese society. Even among those interviewees who were critical of the Chinese government and believed that the ideal values for a modern China should be freedom, democracy and pluralism, termed as *pushi jiazhi* (universal values) by these elites, they all (still) mentioned the traditional value of harmony. I would like to call it as "the habit of a Chinese heart"! Most interviewees perceived this value as "If we don't have harmonious relations with our family members and important people in our life, we won't have inner peace within ourselves. It will be awful to live a life with inner tension." They wholeheartedly agreed with the old Confucian saying "Harmony in family will make everything prosper in our lives." They also felt that Chinese people are good at working out practical ways to reduce tension with others and ultimately within themselves.

Having harmonious relations with others (emphasised in Confucianism) is a primary factor to reach a state of having inner peace or a peaceful mind within oneself. Even an interviewee who is editing the Beijing edition of an imported women's magazine and promoting its slogan of the New York headquarters for young women, i.e., the three f's (fun, fearless and feminine), emphasised the notion/value of Chinese "harmony," particularly the harmony within ourselves. To her (a 30-plus married woman having a young child), such inner harmony is closely related to another Chinese notion/value *zhongyong* (the middle way). She said, "Anything too extreme or radical won't bring peace to the society or to ourselves. This is why I don't agree with Western feminism, because men and women are so different and the two gender roles are complementary to each other. Demanding two sexes being the same is too extreme and not helpful!"

The concepts of "not being too extreme" and "complementary" gender roles are shared among most of my male and female interviewees in Beijing and Hong Kong. The editor also argued that the Beijing edition is a localised magazine, promoting both Western and Chinese values. The former is referred to: "being honest to yourself, making your own choices and taking your consequence, so don't blame others when things go wrong." The Chinese list is much longer. "I think that some traditional Chinese virtues are very good such as being gentle, kind, polite, using money carefully (and saving), reserved (in interpersonal relations), sacrificing, tolerant, and the emphasis on family."

All these Chinese virtues are to do with a woman in relation to others and/or her family. While the two sets of values she recommended might look contradictory on the surface, the Chinese virtues can seem more fundamental. A tolerant, reserved and gentle woman emphasising on, and sacrificing for, her family would not likely blame others when things go wrong due to her own "choice."

Finally, all my interviewees in Beijing and Hong Kong perceived filial piety as a core of the (good) Chinese tradition that should be preserved. As complained by a female interviewee who is a feminist academic in Hong Kong, aged 30-plus, and an advocate for heritage preservation, "The public housing policy in Hong Kong since 1960s has aimed to solve the over-crowded dwelling problem, but has unfortunately prevented us from living with and actualising our filial role to look after our elderly parents. Each adult can apply for a small public housing on his/her own. Now, aging population has provoked the government to revisit this un-thoughtful policy." Even so, another male interviewee in Hong Kong (an editor for a major newspaper) mentioned that his elderly parents are living with his older brother. His brother and the wife look after his aging parents while his parents help looking after his children. The female director of moral/ethics education of an elite school in Beijing commented, "We teach students to be grateful to what parents have given to us (*ganen*). In return, it is our responsibility to be filial and look after (*shanyang*) our parents when they are old. Besides, there are laws to penalise unfilial people who neglect their elderly parents."

Therefore, Taiwan is no longer the only Chinese society preserving the core Confucian values.

A Common Pathway: Twists and Turns in the "Normative" Becoming the "Nonnormative"

Having explained the "liberalising" of premarital sexual mores (i.e., more permissive sexual attitudes and behaviours before marriage in recent decades due to modernisation and exposure to Western ideas), I will now address aspects of sexuality in Chinese history (e.g., erotica, prostitution and homosexuality) which were once defined as "normative" but in modern Chinese contexts have become "nonnormative" due to the modernisation process (mainly Western influences).

Erotica

Within the Confucian tradition (as briefly introduced at the beginning of this chapter), erotic materials (paintings and fiction) and pornography have existed for a thousand years, and historically, prostitution had been "normative" or acceptable for Chinese men. In socialist China, Maoism/socialism was based on Marx's political ideology, which *was* a particular kind of Westernisation. Right after Socialist China was founded in 1949, a strict ban on erotic materials and prostitution was implemented and there was no major difficulty in implementing this policy. In the two decades of the Reform Era, printing and video forms of pornography have flourished, and pornography is now the primary source of sex education for youth in both urban and rural China (Wang and Davidson, 2005).

In Hong Kong and Taiwan, printed erotic materials are graded by age groups. Owning or consuming erotic materials is not an offence punishable by law, but distributing them, particularly to people under 18, is a legal offence. In Hong Kong, a 1996 study of 964 youths aged 18 to 27 revealed that 70.2 percent of males and 43.4 percent of females had purchased or rented some type of sexual media, via magazines, videos, movies, comic books, the Internet or telephone (Janghorbani, 2003). In Taiwan, according to a 1996 study of high school and junior college students, 90 percent of males and 60 percent of females had consumed erotic materials (Lin and Lin, 1996).

In China, studies show that a side effect of pornography is that it has taken the place of parents and schools in providing sex knowledge and skills to youth in Hong Kong and Taiwan (Lee and Yan, 1996; Ng and Ma, 2001).

Prostitution

The reoccurrence of prostitution in China has been particularly challenging for government officials, and consequently, laws have been toughened. In some cases, owners of underground brothels arrested in antiprostitution drives have even received the death penalty (Ruan and Lau, 1999, p. 368). Based on Farrer's and Yuen et al.'s fieldwork and qualitative data obtained in the 1990s and the early 2000s, we see that prostitution began reappearing in the 1980s and has been booming since the 1990s in major Chinese cities.

One major source of "supply" has been young women migrating from rural areas in poor inland provinces (Farrer, 2002; Yuen et al., 2004). The sources of "demand" are businessmen from other countries, Hong Kong and Taiwan and local men who can afford the price. A 1999–2000 Chinese health survey conducted by the University of Chicago found in a random sample of 1,890 men aged from 20 to 64 that 3.3 percent of married or cohabitating men and 2.6 percent of unmarried men had visited prostitutes in the last year (Merli and Hertog, 2004).

In Hong Kong, prostitution has been a crime ever since 1935, under British colonial rule. Although prostitution remains illegal today in post-1997 Hong Kong, the sex industry exists underground in various forms, including hostess bars, fish ball stalls and escort and gigolo services. Three surveys of out-of-school male youths aged 19 to 27 in Hong Kong revealed that 36.2 percent of respondents in 1986, 28.4 percent in 1991 and 30.7 percent in 1996 approved of single men having sex with prostitutes (Ng and Ma, 2001, p. 224). In the same 1996 survey, 10.2 percent of Hong Kong males got their first sexual experience from prostitutes and 13.9 percent had had sexual experiences with at least one prostitute (Ng and Ma, 2001, p. 234).

In Taiwan, prostitution was legalised under Japanese colonial rule, with state-run licensed brothels. Taiwan was reunited to China in 1946 and since then, the Republic of China government in Taiwan has officially banned prostitution and has stopped issuing new licenses. Already-licensed brothels were allowed to continue until the original owners died (Taiwan Judicial Yuan Web site: http://coswas.org.tw/). However, the sex industry has always existed underground.

The capitalist market economy in all three contemporary Chinese societies has enabled some young women on one level to use this "means" (a new means for the sex industry in post-reform socialist China) to achieve old ends (such as sending money back home to poor areas to fulfil filial duties), or on another level to use the old "means" (prostitution) to achieve new ends (such as buying famous brand consumer goods).

Homosexuality

Male homosexuality in historical China was not ideal (due to the encounter not being with the "right party") but tolerable (as long as men married and had children to continue the family line), or even an acceptable or noble activity for the emperor or upper class (Lau and Ng, 1989; Hinsch, 1990). Lesbianism was less visible than male homosexuality, but its existence can be seen in the Chinese term *mojing* (rubbing mirrors). *Mojing* refers to lesbian sexual behaviour that was tolerated (Hinsch, 1990; Ruan and Bullough, 1992). In socialist China, homosexual activity has been redefined and included in "hooliganism," and all hooligans are subject to arrest and sentencing (in some cases up to five years in jail) (Ruan and Lau, 1999, p. 362). Public figures tend to condemn homosexuality, particularly blaming Western influences. It is referred to as "spiritual pollution" or "Western social diseases" (Ruan and Lau, 1999, p. 363). The irony is that the contemporary Chinese government tends to blame the homosexual activity itself as if it has only emerged in recent times due to capitalistic and secular Western influence, rather than frame the issue in a historical context.

First, homosexuality should be grounded and traced to its "tolerable" tradition in historical China. Second, there should be reflection on and a revaluation of the process by which social, cultural and political changes in the first half of the twentieth century had converted homosexuality from "normative" into "nonnormative." In the beginning of the Republic of China, leading intellectuals in the May Fourth movement advocated the view that modernisation meant Westernisation, with an emphasis on science. Scientific discourse in the early twentieth century viewed homosexuality as a disease. In Communist China, modernisation was influenced by Russian and Maoist Marxism and its morality, which viewed homosexuality as moral degeneration (Evan, 1997). Therefore, homosexual activists in modern-day mainland China have had to fight for the "normalization" of these contemporary "nonnormative" sexual practices defined by the "normative"/ socialist Chinese moral standards of the Chinese Communist Party. This fight has been primarily based on the globalised secular Western values of human rights and entitlements, rather than being grounded in the relevance of its existence in the past. Similarly, Western scholars also tend to use the Western notion of "sexual citizenship" with an argument of "democratisation of desire" to approach the issues regarding homosexuality in contemporary China (Jeffreys, 2006).

The inadequacy of primarily using Western notions to approach Chinese homosexuality issues can be indicated by the following revealing examples of the lived experience of one gay man (in Beijing) and one lesbian (in Shanghai) whom I interviewed in 2007. They both were in their mid-20s. The man was a PhD student in an elite university and planned to apply for a postdoctoral fellowship in Euro-America, and the woman was working and graduated from a vocational school. None of their parents knew about their sexual orientations; they didn't want their parents to "lose face" because of them "being different." They claimed that their friends "in their circles" normally do not let parents know. They both said (seemingly without much regret) that they and their homosexual friends would be willing to "leave their circles one day for the 'big picture,' getting married and having children." It sounded as if being a homosexual can be treated as a phase (before marriage). The homosexual lifestyle can be limited within their "circles," and does not necessarily need to continue into a "real adult" life stage with "many more important things to do or responsibilities to carry."

They both mentioned some pragmatic strategies utilised by some people in their circles, such as some would get married and have children for their parents and then get divorced. Or, some gay men would marry lesbians but each has their own lover. These pragmatic arrangements would likely impact the well-being of their (innocent) children and/or their (ignorant) spouses. However, to these homosexual interviewees themselves and those people they mentioned in their "circles," their narratives reveal a stronger sense attachment to traditional family values than a sense of rights as a sexual citizen. It appears that being filial to parents and a familial duty to continue the family line (for the gay man) remained as much more significant aspects of who they are than their sexual orientations.

In Hong Kong, homosexual activity was criminalised via Westernisation for most of the British colonial era; it was only decriminalised in 1991, toward the end of British rule. Conviction for any act of "gross indecency" was punishable by a two-year jail term, and anal intercourse could bring life imprisonment (Ng and Ma, 2001, p. 228). In Taiwan, homosexual activity has not been specifically criminalised, but that which is seen to be against individual will or hindering good social customs (*fangai fenghua*) in public is punished (Taiwan Judicial Yuan Web site: http://coswas.org.tw/). Before martial law was lifted in Taiwan in 1987, discourses regarding homosexuality were not prevalent. Since then, the sociopolitical issues regarding the human rights of homosexual citizens have emerged.

As in China, Western scholars tend to primarily use a lens of sexual citizenship to approach homosexual issues in Taiwan, interpreting the "silence" on this topic as a result of the dominance of the Nationalist Party, and arguing such silence as the marginalisation of homosexual people (Damm, 2005).

In contrast, I would interpret it differently. The silence regarding homosexuality before the end of martial law had little to do with political repression. Homosexuality was not an issue like the Taiwanese political independence movement which indeed had been "tabooed" under martial law. Sexual issues and behaviours (whether heterosexual or homosexual) tended not to be topics for the public arena, because the "right place" for such matters was the bedroom.

Furthermore, heterosexuality in the Confucian tradition is far more significant than homosexuality given the emphasis on the continuity of the family, so public discourse and policy making were focused on heterosexual issues. In this sense, before human rights issues were imported into Chinese societies, homosexuality was not an ideal on the individual level, but as long as the family line was continued, an individual's homosexual preference was just not a big deal.

In recent years, Taiwanese people's awareness of, and support for, homosexual rights have been increasing, evidenced by more participants at the annual *tongzhi* parade in Taipei (estimated as 500 in 2003 and 30,000 in 2010). The theme of 2010's parade was "voting for *tongzhi* (homosexual) policies," because activists complained that none of the major political parties has proposed concrete policies in this area (*Lianhebao*, 30 October, 2010).

In spite of the increased publicity of what *tongzhi* activists have promoted, many *tongzhi* people's lived experiences seem quite similar to their counterparts in China, as revealed in this Taiwanese lesbian couple's story. This couple was in their early 30s. They hadn't informed their mothers of their lesbian relationship until several years later after they returned from studying overseas and lived together in Taipei. One woman has not informed her father, because she thought that he has a "rigid" personality. The other woman's father had passed away, and she imagined that her father would not be that flexible either if he were alive now, because "he was a military officer." In other words, they imagined their fathers would not be tolerant of their unconventional sexual orientation due to their personalities.

Their mothers had accepted their sexual preference for different reasons. One mother thought having a good partner to look after her daughter matters the most. The other mother didn't make a big deal either, telling her daughter, "It is for now, and one day you may change your mind anyway!"

The young couple thought, "Perhaps because we don't have the issue of continuing the family line, so to our mothers, this relationship (despite a bit unusual) is acceptable (or at least tolerable). Besides, nowadays, many highly educated women may not get married anyway. We know gay men generally would have a much more difficult time to get their parents' approval because of the issue of continuing the family life. But nowadays, many parents wouldn't care so much about the family line issue, and if more and more parents wouldn't care about this issue, gay men's lives would become easier and easier."

In summary, "normative" sexual practices in historical China have become "nonnormative" through modernisation and Westernisation in modern times. Moreover, these "nonnormative" sexual practices in these contemporary Chinese societies have become normalised and liberalised due to Western secular trends and the global values of human rights and justice, e.g., "professionalising" sex workers for prostitution, "free speech" for pornography and decriminalising homosexual acts. These trends made it look like the contemporary Chinese societies are following the irresistible Western/secular trends, but underneath, the common pathway to "liberalisation" of these "nonnormative" practices in the Chinese societies differ from those in the West, because the "nonnormatives" were part of the Chinese traditions in the first place, and beneath the surface, they have always been there!

Conclusion

The pathways to the "normalisation" and loosening of premarital sexual mores were different in urban China, Hong Kong and Taiwan from the 1950s to the mid-1990s. Since the mid-1990s, the premarital sexual practices of young Chinese may look like they are converging with Western trends, but the underlying meanings are not the same. Yet, due to modernisation, there has been a common pathway in defining, "nonnormalising" and then "liberalising" pornography, prostitution and homosexual practices in the three contemporary Chinese societies.

This chapter, therefore, has argued and illustrated that the modernisation argument is indeed inadequate when it focuses only on trends, particularly those trends which are "converging" to the West, and fails to ground the trends in the traditions and histories of specific societies. This inadequacy or even fallacy is due to making "truncated" comparisons between societies, particularly societies rooted in different cultural traditions. In our fascination with our "neighbours" in this global village, we run the risk of imagining that we are all becoming alike, without asking where our neighbours came from, or indeed, where they might be going!

I will ground the trends of changing sexual mores in Chinese and Western traditions in the last chapter of this book. But first, I will explore what being "modern" means for young people in these contemporary Chinese societies in the next chapter.

NOTES

1. Whyte's study uses two measures for estimating premarital sexual experience. The "minimum" measure is based on a comparison between the age at which the woman first married and the age she said (in a separate part of the questionnaire) she had her first sexual experience. The "maximum" measure makes use of more information: women who either cohabited or were estimated to have had a premarital pregnancy, as well as whose first sexual experience was younger than their age at first marriage (Whyte, 1990, p. 193).

2. These figures are extracted from Table 3 in Whyte, 1990, p. 192.

3. Scholars have tended to emphasise rural-urban differences—noting, in particular, that traditions regarding marriage and family die hard in rural China (Baker, 1984; Croll, 1981; Hooper, 1985; Lang, 1968; Parish and Whyte, 1978; Wolf, 1984; Zhou, 1989).

4. This view was revealed in numerous commentaries in the popular press in China in the mid-1990s. See, for example: "Ten Changes in Chinese Social Attitudes." *Shanghai Fazhibao* (19 November, 1993); "The Wealthy New Generation in Shanghai—Perceived by Hong Kong Female Writers." *Gongtaixinshibao* (31 March, 1994).

5. The primacy of familial interests in Hong Kong was strongly argued in Lau's work (1987): "That the Hong Kong Chinese would put their familial interests above any other kind of social interests is obvious to anyone who cares to observe Hong Kong. Moral leaders and the mass media have crusaded to castigate the Chinese people's lack of public spirit. Moreover, in Hong Kong, it is not only the middle-aged and elderly who

consider the familial group to be of overwhelming significance, but this point of view also is the norm for young adults in Hong Kong" (Lau, 1987).

6. The data for this study were taken from two nationwide surveys of high school students undertaken in these two regions. The data were collected by students (aged 14 to 18), anonymously filling out self-administered questionnaires. The questionnaire was designed to allow for issues of privacy and embarrassment on the part of the respondents. The Taiwan survey was conducted in 1988 by the Department of Public Health of National Taiwan University (sample size 4,897); the Hong Kong survey was conducted from November 1986 to February 1987 by the Family Planning Association of Hong Kong (sample size 1,710). The high school students in the two samples had grown up in a period of similarly rapid socioeconomic transformations and exposure to Western influences during the 1970s and 1980s.

7. With the assistance of my three key informants in Beijing and two in Hong Kong, I used "purpose" sampling to identify eligible cultural elites in the three sectors as defined above and used "snowball" sampling to obtain willing participants. My key local informants were in different fields. It was a methodological plus, because it had diversified my paths and "pools" for identifying potential elites as well as for obtaining a variety of referrals and securing cultural elites via snowballing in different social circles. Each in-depth interview normally took two hours. In Beijing, the snowballing process stopped once the state of "theoretical saturation" (Strauss and Corbin, 1997) was reached during my 12th interview.

Chapter 5

Are Highly Educated Urban Youths Becoming Less Chinese?

As discussed in Chapter 4, over the past decades, economic development, political liberalisation and sociocultural changes, the whole package of so-called modernisation, have all been occurring in mainland China, Hong Kong and Taiwan. All of these modernising changes have impacted the courtship process, mate selection, marriage arrangement and premarital intimacy. The loosening of sexual mores is one indicator that these societies are becoming more open, modern and Western. This trend in these Chinese societies fits well with the modernisation argument—in Western societies, sexual mores became more permissive under modernisation; in non-Western societies, sexual mores also appear to have become more permissive under modernisation and Westernisation given that exposure to Western ideas has been part of the package of modernisation in these societies.

Building on my previous research and fieldwork as presented in Chapters 1 to 4, this chapter further argues that the loosening of sexual mores is a surface manifestation that may not signify the kinds of social changes and modernity that occurred in the West. In 2005, I conducted a study, utilising a grounded theory approach (Strauss and Corbin, 1997), to explore deeper cultural processes and ongoing trends among highly educated youths who were coming of age in the major cities of the three contemporary Chinese societies in a time of rapid modernisation and globalisation. For instance, do the changes in behaviour (e.g., premarital sex) reflect an underlying attitudinal trend toward secular Western mores (e.g., permissiveness)? More fundamentally, are these highly educated young people "loosening up" in general relative to core traditional values in the three Chinese societies? What are the "traditional" values perceived by these youths from the most modernised Chinese settings? Are these traditional values fading away or are they still lived by these young Chinese? Are these highly educated young people who have grown up in the urban contexts of Shanghai, Hong Kong and Taipei all becoming alike? What does being "modern" mean for these young Chinese?

Methodology

This research uses a grounded theory approach with in-depth interviews to explore how highly educated young Chinese in the major cities perceive, feel, articulate and live through the social and cultural changes in conditions of rapid socioeconomic transformation and exposure to Western and global ideas. Their words reveal what core traditional values/"Chineseness," as well as "Western" values, actually mean in their daily lives.

"Ground theory" is an approach—to generate theory from data, and the theory generated will therefore be *grounded* in data (Punch, 2005). A strength of the grounded theory approach is that it uses "analytic induction" to glean insights from data that emerge from elicited sentiments of interviewees, which can diminish the possibility of researchers essentialising culture(s) or people in specific societies. Consequently, in this research, I (as an academic researcher) have deliberately not defined up front the notions of what it means to be "Chinese" or "Western" and what "traditional core values" are.

In this study, I conducted 29 in-depth interviews with young men and women who were growing up in the major cities of these three societies, as well as having romantic relationships there. I used snowball sampling to identify and obtain eligible young Chinese for this study—using specific eligibility criteria. The first criterion of eligibility was the level of current familiarity with their own societies. I defined this criterion as currently living in one of these Chinese societies or coming to Melbourne in recent years but having returned for visits and having had close contact with relatives and friends as well as being knowledgeable about their views regarding major sociocultural issues in their societies.

The second criterion was their exposure to the avant-garde of mores in their country of origin. One aspect had to do with settings. Where the young Chinese grew up had to be major cities, because major cities (such as Shanghai, Beijing, Hong Kong and Taipei) are leading the socioeconomic development and cultural changes in each of the Chinese societies. The other aspect had to do with education. Highly educated young Chinese in the major cities were more likely to have been exposed (more than any other youthful sector of these societies) to modern, Western and global influences.

This research explored the values of highly educated urban youths who would be leading future developments in these societies. Being "biased" toward those who were most exposed to Western and global influences actually tested more sharply the ongoing impact or persistence of traditional Chinese values. If this group showed any Chinese leanings and (still) embraced certain values they considered "Chinese," the rest of the Chinese population—the less educated or rural Chinese—could be expected to be even more traditional in orientation.

The snowballing process started with one interview from each of the three Chinese societies; one led to another. Emerging patterns were discerned between the interviews within each society and across the three societies and were elaborated further with each additional interview. The snowballing process stopped once the state of "theoretical saturation" (Strauss and Corbin, 1997) was reached—no further information was likely to be obtained or deeper insights developed about the issues being explored by conducting additional interviews.

Among the 29 interviewees, eight were from major cities in China (including Shanghai, Beijing, Guangzhou and Siquan), nine from Hong Kong and 12 from Taipei. The majority of the interviewees, 22 out of 29, were living in Melbourne; most had been here less than one-and-a-half years. Seven interviewees were living in Chinese societies (five in Taipei and two in Hong Kong). For the interviewees in Melbourne, a two-hour in-depth interview was conducted in Chinese with those from China and Taiwan and in English with those from Hong Kong (the researcher did not speak the Cantonese dialect). For interviewees outside of Melbourne, the interview questions were posted in Chinese with answers obtained via e-mail. The researcher also followed up and clarified questions which were unclear to interviewees or answers which were unclear to the researcher until all answers were adequate.

All interviewees had a university education (four were postgraduate students); most of them were full-time students (only two were working professionals). There were 14 males and 15 females. Most of them were aged 20 to 24 (only five interviewees were aged between 25 and 35).

Loosening Premarital Sexual Mores

Virginity Value and Double Standards Have Weakened and Changed Their Meanings and Objects

My exploration suggests that the application of "loosening of sexual mores" was primarily articulated in terms of the reduced value of virginity and its double standard. All of the male interviewees across the three societies said that they *themselves* did not care if their girlfriends were virgins. Some said, "If she were, it could be a bonus!" They mentioned, however, that "some men [not themselves!] may still wish to marry a virgin, as in the phrase 'a man wishes that he is the first man his woman has dated while women wish that they are the last woman he dates!'"

In contrast to all male interviewees who saw themselves as not caring about whether a potential marriage partner was a virgin, most female interviewees (particularly the ones that grew up in China or Taiwan) perceived that many men (if not most men) still hold the virginity value inside their hearts (but without admitting so). When probed, "how to respond to this apparent double standard in men," they would reply, "I don't want this kind of man to be my boyfriend anyway! I will find a man who doesn't care about whether I am a virgin."

There are cross-gender perceptions. Most male interviewees perceived that nowadays it is not so much men but *women* themselves who still care about the virginity value: "Many women only want to give their first [sexual experience] to the men they really love or want to marry." Some women did mention, "I treasure my virginity, and I only wish to give it to someone I really love." To these women, however, virginity is valuable in itself, which is meaningful to the woman herself—"saving" it for someone special rather than fulfilling an expectation or a requirement from (any) man. Therefore, the virginity value has not only declined but also changed its meaning and its object.

Premarital Sex Lodged in Love and Responsibility

All of the interviewees across the three societies (wherever they were living) linked the appropriateness of premarital sex to the existence of love and a steady and long-term relationship. Both male and female interviewees viewed sex as "natural" when two people are in love and are committed to one another; sex is "part of the whole package." All the women made a statement like, "Sex is an expression of love!" but conceded that such a view may not apply to all men. Even all male interviewees had a view or a stereotype that sex could just be a physical need for men, but they also spontaneously added, "Sex without love is meaningless to me!"

All interviewees emphasised a sense of "responsibility" comes with engaging in premarital sex. There are different aspects of the sense of "responsibility" being referred to by interviewees.

One aspect of being "responsible" is referred to as "safe sex," particularly in the sense of not getting pregnant. If a premarital pregnancy were to occur, interviewees in Hong Kong and China thought that abortion is a solution, while Taiwanese interviewees thought that if the relationship was steady and mature enough, marrying would be a better solution and abortion should be the last resort.

Regarding birth control, among the three societies, Hong Kong was the first to let unmarried people have easy access to birth control aids (e.g., pills sold in pharmacies without prescription and condoms sold in vending machines or convenience stores); young people in Taiwan and China have only had such access since the mid-1990s. Accordingly, some male interviewees described the awkwardness or embarrassment they had experienced when purchasing condoms in Taiwan or China if the salesperson was of the "older generation." It felt like, "They looked at me through a 'colourful' lens (*youse yanguang*) in a somewhat disapproving way!"

Another aspect of responsibility emerged in the case of "taking responsibility for the woman I have had sex with," stated as such by more male interviewees in China and Taiwan than in Hong Kong. When probed, "How would you take responsibility?" the answers tended to be like, "it would be more difficult for me to break up with her" or "I feel like I have to look after her more." To these Taiwanese and Chinese men, premarital sex has not only translated into intimacy and closeness but also into a sense of a "man to woman" long-term responsibility. Despite that these same men claimed that they don't care about whether their girlfriends or wives are virgins (i.e., not demanding a virgin girlfriend or wife), they could not help feeling "responsible" after they have had sex with a girlfriend, particularly if their girlfriend was a virgin.

A Liberalising Trend since the 1990s

All interviewees have observed a liberalising trend since the 1990s in each of the major city settings. One 24-year-old male interviewee from Beijing said, "In the past, we referred to some people being 'open.' Nowadays, we are only describing some people being conservative." He meant that in the past, people who were sexually open were in the minority, where today, people who are sexually conservative have become the minority. Another 22-year-old male interviewee from Guangzhou described the change in people's language: "Nowadays, when we ask how many *real* girlfriends you have had, it means the one(s) you have had sex with. The one(s) without sex don't count as 'real' girlfriend(s)!"

All female interviewees thought that sex before marriage is important, for if the parties found themselves sexually incompatible after marriage, it would be too late! All divorce is really bad and particularly bad when there are children. Premarital cohabitation was also perceived as valuable, "Otherwise, how would two people know if they could get along on a routine daily basis?" Most interviewees thought that their parents would not approve of their premarital sexual behaviour or co-habitation (if their parents knew at all), but they wished to go ahead anyway. However, all mentioned that such an arrangement would be much easier or more feasible for people who had already left home than for those still living with their parents.

All interviewees attributed this liberalising trend in loosening premarital sexual mores to Western influence, meaning the "huge amount of information every day distributed through the Internet and global media." However, they don't wish liberalised premarital sexual mores resulting in them becoming "too loose like the West," because "sex without love or commitment would be meaningless!" They all disapproved of casual sex, one-night stands and extramarital affairs.

Persistence of Traditional Values Focused on Family

Mate Selection Partially for Parents

If their parents did not like the partners they had chosen, interviewees said that they would persuade their parents to gradually get to know and to accept their partners. While sounding like autonomous, most interviewees also mentioned that one crucial mate selection criterion for themselves was that "this girl (or boy) has to get along with my parents and treat my parents very well." In particular, most male interviewees in China and Taiwan mentioned this criterion without giving it a second thought. A 22-year-old male from Guangzhou described his "priority" as, "It is like half-half, 50 percent we love each other and 50 percent she treats my parents well!" This half-half "priority" actually involves two equally "must" conditions. Most female interviewees from China also mentioned "treating my parents well" as a crucial condition in mate selection.

One reason for insisting on this condition for both male and female interviewees in China is obviously related to the outcome of the one-child policy which this cohort of young Chinese grew up with. The interviews revealed this strong sentiment: "I am the only child, and

I want to look after my parents when they are old, so the woman (or the man) has to support me to look after my parents." In addition, to female interviewees, regardless of which society they grew up in, "treating my parents well" requires material capacity (not just being a nice person!), and such capacity was clearly stated as a crucial criterion, "It would be good that the man is well off or at least has to be financially stable so that he can give me and [our] children a secure family, and support me to look after my parents."

In summary, the appropriateness of premarital sex has been lodged in a loving relationship and implemented through a certain amount of discretion (or even deceit) on the part of the highly educated urban young Chinese I interviewed, but the salience of parental concerns remains and the concerns for their parents have always been in the hearts of these young people.

Filial Piety

These mate selection criteria were consistent with the orientation of all the interviewees. These young people still held and treasured the family values, and their ultimate concerns were in and for the family, particularly their parents. Family values were perceived as the "core traditional values" by these Chinese, the most modernised sector of the young generation in their societies. The core traditional value that was mentioned constantly was filial piety (*xiaoshun*), particularly responsibility for looking after elderly parents. All the men and women interviewed believed this to be their responsibility, although some said that their parents do not really expect them to look after them. Male interviewees asserted statements of the kind, "Of course, it is my responsibility, because I am a son!" Young women expressed the filial duty in a similar way, "I know my parents still want me to go home to see them very often even after I marry out." Young women growing up in China particularly emphasised, "I am the only child and I have to, and want to, look after my parents when they are old."

As to the practical question of *how* to look after elderly parents, all interviewees said, "I want to give my parents money so that they can have a better life or not have to worry about money anymore. But, looking after elderly parents is not just giving money to parents. I know my parents want me to be around and spend time with them." They also mentioned a preference for not living under the same roof but living with their parents nearby (e.g., in the same apartment building but on different floors or next door).

When asked, "Where or in which country would you like to live permanently?" they all answered, "I want to live wherever my parents are!" A 23-year-old female interviewee from Guangzhou and a law student in Melbourne expressed her determination in this way. "Even if I end up staying in Australia for whatever reasons, I want my parents to join me and live with me here. But, of course, my parents may not like to live here for too long, because they can't speak English and all their friends are in China. They will be bored. If so, I think eventually I will return to China in order to be with my parents."

Interviewees mentioned other aspects of filial piety as well, such as not doing things which would make parents worried or ashamed; doing things to make their parents proud; trying to learn to be independent and responsible "so that I can look after myself well and my parents don't need to look after me;" or trying to fulfil parents' expectations. Most interviewees who were there studying in Melbourne felt a self-imposed pressure (and stress as a result) to perform well in their studies, expressing sentiment like this. "My parents are using their life savings to finance my studying here. I owe my parents a lot and want to reciprocate one day. Now at least I have to study hard and do well. But, sometimes I end up being too nervous and not doing so well on exams. I hate to disappoint my parents like that!"

When probed about how they learned what filial versus unfilial behaviours are, they all referred to the behaviour of their parents relative to their grandparents. They also mentioned that they had heard their parents commenting on the behaviour of others, commenting on what counts for unfilial practices, such as sending elderly parents to a nursing home when the parents did not want to go. However, when I asked, "In those instances, why was the parents' wish not factored in? And how could it have been?" a common response was, "The children were too busy to look after parents, because both the son and daughter-in-law had to go to work." When I probed further, "How did the son feel?" a more subtle sentiment was revealed in answers such as, "Of course, the son felt bad, but, in fact, it was normally the daughter-in-law who insisted on such an arrangement!"

Is there some truth in laying the "blame" on unfilial daughters-in-law (rather than on unfilial sons)? In a different topic when all interviewees expressed their strong wish and determination to look after their *own* parents, I asked, "How about looking after your parents-in-law?" All male interviewees replied, "Of course! I will support my wife to do so." Female interviewees didn't have such a unanimous response, however. The responses ranged from "I will do my best!" to "Depends on how my parents-in-law treat us." In other words, interviewees had unconditional filial love toward their own parents, but female interviewees tended to have a "conditional" attitude toward their in-laws.

This is not surprising. The filial attitudes and behaviour of sons toward their in-laws tend to be on the level of *support*, including generously contributing (their) money and (their wives') time to looking after their in-laws. If most of the routine care or housework tends to be done by women, it is no surprise that women put their parents as a top priority on the list of "filial" responsibilities, particularly those women who work outside the home. This flows as a consequence of China's one-child policy: a married couple is responsible for two sets of elderly parents. Given the wish of all my female interviewees to have a job and be married with children and the fact that their paid employment allows them to be more assertive at home, their "depends" response to my question was actually quite genuine and realistic. This finding and interpretation is consistent with the finding of another recent study. Greenhalgh and Winckler (2005) found that parents with single child daughters are the biggest beneficiaries of the one-child policy (p. 282), because young women are now much more able to contribute to looking after their own parents after marriage, at least in some emerging situations where the daughter has a good income.

Finally, when asked, "What are the core values you would like to pass on to your children one day?" the first item the majority of interviewees mentioned was filial piety, even though most of them didn't expect their children to look after them when they themselves become old (because "society is changing so fast"). One 21-year-old man from Shanghai said, "I think filial piety value is the most important value. If people can't even be filial to their parents, how can they treat other people well? How can they really treat their jobs seriously or be loyal to their employers?" Therefore, this cultural ideal of *xiaoxun* is indeed a *core* value and remains alive in the hearts of these young Chinese, despite the fact that in reality, the preference of some of their parents may have to be compromised one day in certain circumstances.

"Self" Defined by Familial Roles

Another orientation toward families can be seen in responses to questions regarding self-definition. All of the interviewees had difficulty answering this question: "How do you define yourself in terms of who you are?" Initial responses were statements like: "I have never thought about this" or "I don't know." A main reason given was, "So far, I have been trying to do what my parents expect me to do." Only two female interviewees answered, "I think I am a nice person; I like to help others." But most interviewees tended to easily answer another question, "How do you define yourself in terms of being a man or a woman?" All the males said, "To be a man means being responsible and to be able to take responsibility for his family." "To be a man also means to live through all stages of being a son, a husband, and a father."

All the females made statements like: "To be a woman means being a wife and mother. She can be good at cooking and child-rearing. I am not a woman yet in that sense." Two women with divorced parents also emphasised the importance of financial independence for womanhood. "To be a woman means having an ability to earn money so that she can leave her husband and still run a life independently if her marriage doesn't work." A 22-year-old Hong Kong woman even said, "My mother has had to work so hard as a waitress to raise me and my sister by herself after her divorce; she even sent me here to study. My dad abandoned us when I was 15, and recently, my parents were talking about getting back together. Both my sister and I told my mother not to take my dad back, because we will look after my mom when she is old. She doesn't need any man, because she has us! We will have jobs, and will give money to my mother."

When I asked, "What kind of life do you want to have when you reach 40?" males mostly answered in this form: "By age 40, I want to have a stable job with a good income for my family. I will be able to look after my elderly parents well and establish a good family for my wife and children." All the females wished to have a good job and be married with children, and have a balanced life between work and family. It seems that the loosening of premarital sexual mores has not given rise to a generation of young Chinese with an individualistic sense of "self"; the primary definition of manhood and womanhood still remained framed by familial roles.

Other Core Values

Other values which consistently emerged in the interviews related to working hard for the family (e.g., a man should be responsible—a good provider to provide a better life for his family; a woman should manage her home well and not let her career hinder family); emphasising education; worshipping ancestors in major festivals; fostering harmony between people, being dutiful and loyal to one's family, friends and work; and not harming others.

Living Confucian Values without the Name

Despite these values' origin in Confucianism, highly educated young people who grew up in China or Hong Kong in my study did not necessarily understand or call these core values "Confucian." Taiwanese interviewees, however, did call these Confucian values (even those who identified with the prospect of political independence and a revival of Taiwanese culture).

Taiwanese tend to have a strong sense of Confucianism and equate "traditional values" and "Chinese culture" with Confucianism, as revealed in my in-depth interviews. This is due to the compulsory curriculum in Taiwan which teaches the comprehensive Confucian classics from elementary school to university. Conversely, the exposure to Confucian classics in China and Hong Kong has always been much more limited. Only selected chapters are included in the subject of "Chinese language and literature." In China, the whole education system was disrupted and Confucian values were challenged during the 10-year-long Cultural Revolution (Chu and Ju, 1993).

Although China had gone through a socialist revolution, the Cultural Revolution and, since 1978, the socialist capitalism of the Reform Era, my interview data show that some core aspects of Chinese culture have persisted, even if these highly educated urban youths in my study do not know that these were from Confucianism or they have lost the labels to name them. The interviews revealed that these core Confucian values have survived significant social-political-economic changes through family and being "lived" by people in their everyday lives. Even if premarital sexual mores have been changing, as discussed in Chapter 4, young people in my sample have not been in a "value vacuum."

Furthermore, while interviewees from China's major cities have developed a consumerist desire to buy globally recognised brands, their sense of nationalism (evident in the phrase "loving my country") was stronger than the interviewees from Hong Kong and Taiwan. They desired Western brands and wanted to have fun, but they were still loyal to China and were intent on making a future in China (saying, for example, "China has so many opportunities for young people!") for their families, rather than just for themselves as individuals. A 20-year-old university student from Shanghai said, "I want to study hard, be capable, return to China, find a good job and earn a good income. I want to treat my parents well and buy good brands for them! My parents' generation just couldn't buy those things."

Interviewees who grew up in China tended to treat "Confucianism" and "traditional Chinese culture" less as values than as artefacts. They viewed "Confucianism" primarily in terms of the classics by Confucius and Mencius, and they felt that their exposure to those classics had been limited in the school curriculum. They also equated the term "traditional Chinese culture" more with folk art and activities in major festivals, heritage preservation (e.g., temples), sophisticated Chinese characters *(fantizi)*, calligraphy, traditional arts and literature and the classics of Chinese philosophy and history. They spoke positively about the promotion of traditional cultural activities during the Reform Era. Quite a few interviewees said that China should go back to using the traditional (sophisticated) Chinese characters: "All other

Chinese societies still use *fantizi*. It is a great Chinese art! We should not continue to lose our traditional culture!" This general awareness and sentiment in favour of restoring or reviving the "artefacts" of traditional culture is associated with the government's new cultural policy of promoting traditional Chinese culture in general as well as its admission of the Chinese Communist Party's errors in undermining it for more than two decades.[1]

In Hong Kong, the young people interviewed appreciated the fact that their familiarity with both cultures and languages enabled Hong Kong Chinese to have a broader perspective than their counterparts in Taiwan or China, but they all felt that the British colonial experience had not eradicated traditional Chinese familism and human relations. As discussed in Chapter 4, Hong Kong high school students were more liberal in their sexual behaviour but had more conservative attitudes than their counterparts in Taiwan. The more liberal behaviour was due to easier access to both control aids in Hong Kong than in Taiwan before the 1990s. The conservative attitudes of Hong Kong Chinese, as we have seen, stemmed from "doubling traditions," that is, the mutual reinforcement of local Chinese values and the impact of Christian norms from British colonisation. However, such differences in sexual attitudes and behaviours between Hong Kong and Taiwan did not exist among these interviewees who had had romantic relations in the late 1990s and 2000s in Hong Kong and Taipei. Interviewees in both those settings referred to the liberalisation of premarital sex as being due more to the exposure to Western ideas through the Internet and global media and easy access to birth control aids.

Extensive exposure to Western ideas worried the Hong Kong interviewees: "Western influence has made the young generation so materialistic, particularly consuming famous brands, and so individualistic that they only care about themselves." However, when probed about what "they only care about themselves" means, the reply was, "They only care about themselves and their families. They don't care about Hong Kong society and the wider world, unlike young people in Taiwan, who feel strongly about Taiwanese independence." Thus, being "individualistic" remained within the boundary of one's family, rather than only the individual him/herself.

Compared to the Taiwan and mainland China interviewees, Hong Kong interviewees were less patriotic and cared little about the wider society. They tended not to know if core values were being promoted in Hong Kong society. They had difficulty thinking of anything inspiring in Hong Kong aside from cheap and fantastic shopping (as all the female interviewees mentioned). They were most progressive in caring the least about the virginity value, but all female interviewees thought that men should pay all the expenses on dates and buy them presents (while Taiwan and mainland China female interviewees thought that sometimes women should contribute or that the two parties could rotate to pay for dates).[2] This sort of Hong Kong spirit, or actually a lack of "spirit," is not inconsistent with other, more general, research findings about Hong Kong.

Both in the pre-1997 handover and after, Hong Kong people have been a migrant society with "displaced" Chinese primarily from the southeast coast of China. The almost 100 years under British colonial rule and the "reunion" with China in 1997 have certainly not helped Hong Kong people build a sense of belonging or establish "roots" in the wider society. This displaced or rootless feeling enables Hong Kong Chinese to "move on" wherever they migrate as well as adapt to other "host" societies. Perhaps because they don't attach themselves to, or identify with, the "host" society, Hong Kong people do (or have to) preserve their Chinese familism, maybe even in a stronger sense than Chinese in Taiwan or mainland China, because the family is all they have and belong to.

In contrast to the "doubling traditions" in Hong Kong, as presented in Chapter 4, there has been an upholding of orthodox Confucianism in Taiwan since the 1950s. As indicated in Chapter 3, the "modern"/ Western values (e.g., the glamorous image of sexually autonomous young career women portrayed in imported women's magazines or the TV program *Sex and the City*) have been reworked via this "orthodox tradition" to fit into Chinese familism. Consequently, their sexual attitudes can be more liberal (with Chinese and Western values co-existing) than their "orthodox" behaviours. A 23-year-old Taiwanese female interviewee commented, "Many Taiwanese women in my generation, including me and my close friends, can be very open, but only in our minds! We won't do it because we have been taught by parents and teachers not to do it."

It should also be noted that Taiwan has undergone a successful transition to democracy. The pro-Independence Party has won presidential elections since 2000. A Taiwanese identity has developed in recent years with a new state-directed school curriculum which highlights Taiwanese history and culture. Nevertheless, the four-decades-long cultural policy of Orthodox Confucianism has established a solid foundation, and traditional Chinese values have taken root in Taiwan (despite the fact that those "roots" were strategically "implanted" by the Nationalist Party which came to power in 1949) (Chun, 1994). The Taiwanese interviewees felt strongly about the merits of having more Chinese traditional values than their counterparts in Hong Kong and China, regardless of whether their political standing was pro-independence or pro-unification with mainland China.

Young people interviewed growing up in each of the Chinese societies had clear impressions of "the other." Taiwanese were perceived by people in all three settings as the most "traditional"/"Chinese"; Hong Kong people as the most "Westernised" and Chinese in the mainland as falling somewhere in between (except for Taiwan and mainland Chinese female interviewees wondering why Westernised Hong Kong women would want men to pay all expenses on dates).

All interviewees, however, complained about the most worrisome social phenomenon of most people "only pursuing money," and they wished to see no decline in their traditional values under the influence of Western values, particularly individualism (perceived as being selfish), materialism, and/or consumerism (perceived in terms of no spiritual-level ends or pursuits). As one 24-year-old male interviewee from Beijing said, "Some Western things are good, like modern technology, but we can't lose our Chinese base, the traditional values and the purpose of being Chinese. After all, we are not Westerners."

Conclusion

A consistent theme in the interviews was a commitment to family. Familism, the core traditional value, has not just survived but has also been authentically *lived* by all of the urban and highly educated young Chinese I interviewed, regardless of which cities they grew up in or whether they recognised that this value was (called) Confucianism.

Therefore, changing sexual mores have not been accompanied by highly educated urban Chinese youths in my study disengaging from Chinese values or becoming less Chinese. Consumerism and an appetite for Hollywood movies and TV programs like *Sex and the City* have not made Shanghai, Hong Kong or Taipei into a "sex city." Highly educated young people in these metropolitan cities use Western skills to pursue their Chinese dreams, which were articulated in terms of ultimately establishing a happy family for themselves while providing good care for their elderly parents and the best education for their children.

NOTES

1. I acknowledge this point made by Professor Hao Ping, president of Beijing Foreign Affairs University, in a conversation with me in October of 2005. Professor Hao stated that the Chinese Communist Party (CCP) has officially reflected and admitted (*zongjei*) that undermining traditional culture was a mistake.

    1) In 1979, an "assessment of the Cultural Revolution" was done by Deng Xiaoping at the Sixth Central National Assembly (*zhong-quan-hui*). In that meeting, the CCP reflected and "summarised" (*zongjei*) that it was a mistake to have overthrown the so-called feudalistic Confucian tradition during the Cultural Revolution. Chinese socialism should include the Chinese tradition. This is a different cultural policy compared with the years 1950 to 1978.

    2) Since the Reform Era started in 1978, the CCP's top priority has been to reform the economy according to Deng Xiaoping's four modernisations. In a way, cultural reform has lagged behind despite official government policies which have emphasised both material and spiritual (re) construction and development. The former has to be accompanied by the latter, and the latter is built upon Chinese tradition.

    3) But, gradually, traditional Chinese culture is being included in the school curriculum, particularly since the 1990s.

    4) Recent government campaigns on promoting cultural development include these:

        - 2003 *fangrong zhexuei shehui kexuei* (making

philosophy and social science thrive)

- 2004 *hexei shehui* (harmonious society)
- Since 2003, the government officially has sponsored a few major projects to revive the Chinese traditions, particularly Confucianism:
- restore Kuoxueiyuan (national classics studies)
- compile and edit the treasures of Confucianism (*ruzang*); in the past, similar work has been done for the treasures of Buddhism and Daoism (*forzang, daozang*)
- compile Qing history
- Tang studies (*shengtang yenjiu*)

But China doesn't have "family studies" in an academic sense, except for demographic studies related to population control since the 1970s.

2. Among male interviewees, Hong Kong men also mentioned that men are expected to pay while dating, but they themselves wouldn't mind women sharing some of the costs sometimes. Mainland Chinese men thought that men should always pay on dates, even if they have to borrow money (to show that they have the capacity to pay). Taiwanese men tended to think that men should pay for the initial date, but once the relationship is formed and stabilised, both parties could share the costs on a rotating basis.

Part 4:

Western

Chapter 6

What Women "Make of Men"

After comparing pathways of changing sexual mores and what being "modern" means in contemporary Taiwan, Hong Kong and Taiwan in Chapters 4 and 5, a further question is whether all this diversity and commonality regarding changes between these societies points to something which can be called "Chinese sexuality." The only methodologically prudent way to proceed is by more comparison, and this comparison has to be extended to non-Chinese cultural settings. I have chosen the secular Western cultural settings as "the other" for purposes of comparison, given that the major cultural impacts on the three Chinese societies today come from the West and the two settings are built upon two fundamentally different cultural bases. As discussed in previous chapters, on the surface, social trends have converged in the Chinese and Western cultural settings, but beneath the common trends, culture-specific elements remain, as I will show.

A vast amount of social science literature regarding sexuality was produced in the West in the last century. Rather than attempting to summarise this literature, for the purpose of this book, I will instead focus on original research using the same kind of data and discourse analysis as I did with Chinese materials of the Taiwan edition of *Cosmopolitan* as presented in Chapter 3. This chapter, therefore, will focus on the issues, difficulties and ultimate solutions regarding relationships as presented in popular discourses (represented by the American edition of *Cosmopolitan*) to provide a background understanding of gender politics, relationships and individualism in the secular Western cultural settings. This chapter and Chapter 3 are, therefore, a prelude to the comparative studies of self, gender, relationship and sexuality in the Chinese and Western cultural settings presented in the next two chapters.

Many studies have analysed the effects of popular women's magazines and advice books on women's lives in the West. For instance, women's magazines have had been found to provide women with survival skills and outlets for daydreams (Winship, 1987), to promote the "cult of femininity" and to reproduce women's oppression (Ferguson, 1983). Few of these works have questioned how women perceive men and what men mean or could mean to women. To open up this fundamental domain of cross-gender perceptions in studying gender and relationships in secular Western settings, "Agony Columns" are an excellent but underutilised source of data in scholarly research.

This chapter will examine the perceptions and depictions of men in the Agony Column of a leading women's magazine, *Cosmopolitan ("Cosmo")*. The Agony Column in *Cosmo* was chosen for this study because of its mundane "everyday" nature: it is a direct medium for expressing, sharing and consuming difficult experiences in gender relations among *real* people in their everyday lives.[1] Unlike other print sources used, the Agony Column provides a highly structured set of data, since each Agony letter involves a problem, an Agony Aunt and a "solution."

I have two rationales for this study—one has to do with the self-disclosing nature of Agony letters; the other with the pivotal role played by the Agony Aunt in defining and specifying norms of cross-gender encounters. The first rationale suggests that when women are in "agony," their perceptions of men may be "distorted" toward the negative, but the "distortion" itself may actually reveal more about women's *fundamental* values, ideology, stereotypes and projections of deep-seated anxieties about men than what women perceive in happier moments. In addition, the publicly portrayed anxieties in advice columns give insights into the range and richness of worries that women have about men.

The second rationale was that the adviser (or the "Agony Aunt") plays a pivotal and legitimating cultural role in identifying, validating or challenging who is to blame, what is blameworthy, and what reasons "count" in problematic gender relations. The Agony Column combines popular concerns with more "expert" or "experienced" voices. Such "expertise" provides another basis for the legitimacy of any advice, while giving highly specific insights about the construction of modern womanhood, in particular, and gender relations, generally, in the secular West. It is from this passing parade of intimate "agonies" that this chapter draws its material.

A central focus of this chapter is on what women in agony "make of men." But since the Agony Column is full of problems about relationships that women report, the same agony "data" can also reveal how they perceive what men "make of women." Of course, this second focus is from the women's perspective as well, but this is an important perspective to explore (i.e., cross-gender perceptions). Therefore, this chapter examines some of these largely unnoticed perceptions in an attempt to promote a new engagement between the genders. It is a first tentative step in the exploration of cross-gender perceptions, and is limited to women's perceptions in the United States. However, this "United States" limitation is not as "limited" as it seems. The American version of *Cosmopolitan* is the headquarters "bank" for the *Cosmopolitan* editions in 44 countries, so the impact of such Agony Columns reach beyond the United States.

Methodology

Data and Units of Analysis

A sample of Agony Columns was selected for this study from all of the issues of American *Cosmopolitan* magazine published between October 1982 (when the Agony Column started) and December 1996 (when my data collection for this study was conducted). All three issues published in 1982 and three randomly selected issues per year thereafter were analysed. This yielded a total of 45 issues, from 1982 to 1996.

Due to the nature of advice columns, each "entry" in the Agony Column involved a pair of items: the woman "in agony" raising a problem and the Agony Aunt offering a solution. To keep the focus on gender-based relationships, I eliminated problems which were not related to romantic relationships. Such problems included being stuck with a demanding boss or mother-in-law, helping a lesbian daughter or a gay friend and dealing with sister rivalry, competitive colleagues or insecure housemates. Each "problem and solution" pair constituted a single unit of analysis. This study analysed a total of 130 units. Each unit is called an "agony resolution" in the following analysis.

The Nature of Data and Its Implications

Two aspects related to the issue of selectivity regarding the nature of the Agony Column data should be addressed here. The first aspect has to do with the editorial process involved in selecting which agony letters were to be published. The editors could be expected to look for "interesting" (i.e., with "odd" episodes) and/or "relevant" (i.e., "this is my problem too!") letters.[2] There was likely to be a bias toward oversampling the extremes as well as the ordinary. Consequently, this bias could actually make the data from the Agony Column capture a very wide range of variation or possibilities regarding problems and potential solutions in heterosexual romantic relationships.

For the purpose of generating theoretical insights about gender relations by using a grounded theory approach, this kind of bias became an improvement of coverage from the point of view of the analytical inductions to be developed. The logic of the "sampling" or the "representativeness" regarding the data analysed in this study (in terms of being a grounded theory study) was therefore "theoretical" rather than enumerative (Barton and Lazarsfeld, 1955; Glaser and Strauss, 1967; Strauss and Corbin, 1990; Turner, 1953).

The second aspect of selectivity has to do with the issue of readership. *Cosmo* readers are adult women, married and single (Winship, 1987). Compared to the readership of *Cosmopolitan*, the demographics of other women's magazines tend to be more specific (e.g., some are targeted to teenage girls while others are published for highly educated young professionals), and their specific readerships may be expected to receive and respond to different kinds of relationship problems in those magazines targeted to specific group(s) of women. Therefore, the theoretical insights about gender relations in the Western cultural settings generated from the Agony Column of the American edition of *Cosmopolitan* in this study could be further verified against, and deepened by, more data (i.e., the advice column material in other Western women's magazines) in future studies.

Coding and Data Analysis

Coding

Developing a reliable coding scheme for this kind of data involved a few steps. The first step was that I randomly chose 10 units of "problems and solutions." I asked a colleague of mine in sociology to be the other coder. Although the content of the problems and solutions might seem different across all the units, a number of *generic* components or elements were actually visible to both of us. These were then used as "codes." These codes include a summary of the problem regarding the relationship, who was the fundamental instigator (self or the man) in the eyes of the woman in agony, whether the woman perceived herself in control of her man (yes or no), whom to blame ultimately (self, the man or the norms) in the eyes of the Agony Aunt and a summary of the solution given and the focus of the solution (self, the relationship or the norms). Some units of "problems and solutions," at first glance, might seem to have more than one clear-cut cause and/or solution, but when reading deeply, a *fundamental* cause and an "ultimate" solution could be identified for the purpose of coding. The other coder and I read through the 10 units and basically came out with a quite similar coding scheme.

The second step was that I randomly chose another 10 units for myself and the other coder to read more deeply in order to check the validity of the coding scheme developed from the first set of 10 units. The coding scheme remained valid with these 10 extra cases. Then, we both used this coding scheme to code the second set of 10 units and to assess intercoder reliability. The other coder and I were consistent in our coding. Then, I coded the remaining 120 units.

Identifying Dimensions

I randomly chose 10 coded units for myself and the other coder to analyse and to discern major dimensions of variation in these units of problems and solutions. Again, we both discerned the same major dimensions of variation.

One dimension was regarding the variation in the *form* of the relationship that had caused the woman the agony disclosed, i.e., the agony woman is or is not in control of her man. The other dimension was regarding the *focus* of advice in terms of who or what was best placed to offer a solution, i.e., a focus on the agony woman, the relationship or the norms. This should not be surprising for a column dedicated to personal relationship problems. There is a certain analytic closure to this dimension. When relationships go wrong, there is a tendency to blame someone, or the relationship that brings people into contact or the rationale that keeps people in the relationship. With these two dimensions isolated, I then read through the remaining 120 coded units of problems and solutions and checked these two dimensions against each unit. These two dimensions of variation remained valid across all the units.

Generating Theoretical Typology

With these two major dimensions of variation extracted from the data (i.e., "the form of the agony relationship" and "the focus of advice"), it was possible to develop a theoretical typology from the cross-classification of the two dimensions. This is a theoretical typology that defines an "encounter" between the woman in agony and the Agony Aunt. Each cell, in defining an "agony-resolution" encounter, can be grounded and "elaborated" by referring to the raw data of the Agony Column. There are recurrent themes across all the cases revealed in each cell in terms of the linkage of a certain form of the agony-producing relationship to a specific focus of advice on how it was to be resolved. Within each cell, a specific type of "agony resolution" can then be extracted from the data.

Dimensions of Variation in Agony and Resolutions

Across all 130 units, two prominent dimensions of the variation were visible: one was the *form* of the relationship that had caused the woman the agony she disclosed; the other was the *focus* of advice in terms of who or what was best placed to offer a solution.

The Form of the Agony Relationship: The Woman Is or Is Not in Control of Her Man

As only the agony letters that deal with problematic heterosexual relations were analysed in this study, one dimension of variation that emerged within the agony letters stems from whether the woman in agony saw herself in control of her man or not. To be in control meant that she had a relationship, but it was not satisfying enough in some way; e.g., she liked the security she had from her man but wanted more excitement. In the sample of 130 cases, 20 cases were of this type. The other category was far more common: the woman in agony felt that she was not in control of her man. No middle category was revealed in my data. Indeed, the only way a "middle category" could function in this context is temporally: being in control only some of the time. In the letters, however, only episodes and individual mishaps are reported, rather than longer temporal spans of a relationship within which a middle category might emerge. It should not be surprising that the distribution is so skewed. We can expect that Agony women who write for advice are much more likely to see themselves as not being in control of their men than vice versa. The majority of Agony cases included scenarios such as the man was "cheating" on her, she could not get personal autonomy from a possessive husband or she could not elicit commitment from her boyfriend. Of the 130 cases, 110 fell into this category.

The Focus of Advice: Focus on Woman, Relationship or Norms

Independently of how the woman in agony defined her problem, the Agony Aunt had three different types of changes to recommend: one solution centred on the Agony *woman*, regardless of the man; another solution involved making a decision about *the relationship*; and the third solution focused on the general gender *norms and values* that impact the relationship.

Regarding the first focus—the solution is lodged in the woman in agony herself—63 out of 130 advice columns had such an orientation. In 61 of the cases, the woman was advised in one of three distinct ways: to make a range of changes by herself and for herself, i.e., "self-help" (such as improve her fitness, join clubs, go out with others); to be assertive in dealing with her man; or to just enjoy what she has and ignore the rest.

Regarding the second focus—the solution involves making a decision about the problematic relationship—25 out of 130 advice columns revealed this orientation. Again, the woman was advised to decide and take firm action about the relationship in one of three ways: leave her man, accept him, or "hang in there" to see whether her feelings toward him would change.

Regarding the third focus—the solution as tied to gender norms and/or values—42 out of 130 advice columns revealed this orientation. In these cases, the Agony Aunt may remind the woman of some normative expectation and advise her to modify her behaviour accordingly. Or, based on conventional gender roles, the woman might be advised to be more "realistic" in terms of what can be expected from a man. Or, the Agony Aunt may relocate the problem in the processes of human maturation, the nature and principle of love, marriage, relationships in general or a philosophy of life.

A Typology of "Agony Resolution"

The combination of the categories of the two underlying dimensions can determine the types of agony resolution. Six cells result from this cross-classification (i.e., two forms of "agony relationships" multiplied by three "focuses of advice"). In other words, six theoretical as well as empirically grounded types of "agony resolution" can be generated from the Agony Column material in this study (see Table 6-1). Each of the six types of agony resolution is discussed below.

Table 6-1: A Typology of Agony Resolutions

Advisor sees solution as:	Woman in an agony relationship sees herself as being: NOT in control of her man (N=110)	Woman in an agony relationship sees herself as being: In control of her man (N=20)
Centred on the woman (N=63)	1. Reliant (N=57)	4. Carefree (N=6)
Centred on the relationship (N=25)	2. Robust (N=22)	5. Hedging (N=3)
Resting with values and norms (N=42)	3. Realist (N=31)	6. Authentic (N=11)

Type 1: Reliant

Typically, the woman in agony felt that she was not in control of the man (or men). This was why she was in agony: something had gone wrong in the relationship with the man/men and she did not know what to do. The Agony Aunt normally challenged this assessment as misplaced and focused instead on what the woman could do with what she did control—notably herself. In this situation, the agony resolution was described as recommending self-reliance. Fifty-seven out of 130 cases were this type.

Self-reliance emerged when the woman in agony was advised to focus on those aspects of her life that can be controlled: her appearance could be improved; her friendship network could be extended; her self-criticism could be countered with positive interpretations; the impositions of her man could be more resolutely questioned and rebuffed; her own problems could be more clearly defined and her expectations could be more explicitly formulated and communicated to her man.

Two examples give a feel for this type.

Agony: "I hate my marriage. I seem to live in a velvet-lined prison, a centrally heated cell ... Sometimes I feel so unhappy, bored, frustrated, neglected, forgotten and useless I want to sleep forever ... I have lost the art of being me ... How can I live with the guilt of knowing I don't want any of it?"

Agony Aunt: "You are fighting with a genuine, full-blown depression ... so you had better see your doctor ... If you still feel rotten, why don't you do something radical and brave? Persuade your husband that you need a vacation alone ... How long has it been, I wonder, that you've had anybody to confront or care for just yourself? ... Do something unorthodox and courageous ... You will just possibly be able to see from a cool distance who you were, who you are, and who you want to be ... Start listening to your inner voice. It is a free voice, a happy voice and the only voice that can tell you what to do." (Question 2, January 1984, p. 58)

We can see here that the woman in agony did not feel in control. But the Agony Aunt focused on what this woman in agony could do for herself and by herself.

In another example,

Agony: "I am 23 and made love for the first time last summer ... but I'm finding that the men I meet are used to having sex much sooner than I am. I'm torn between my desire and guilt. I want some type of strong mutual feeling and commitment before I go to bed with a man, but I'm not sure I'll meet too many men who'll be willing to wait that long ..."

Agony Aunt: "Any woman with standards about sex is not going to meet 'too many' men who will wait. Isn't that precisely the point? To meet not 'too many' men, but the few whose standards are as high as your own and who attach the same importance to making love that you do?" (Question 4, November 1988, p. 68)

Here the woman in agony could not control the behaviour and expectations of the men she dated. Yet, control was possible through selection, rather than through the woman's pleas or explanations to "unsuitable" men who should have been "filtered out" in the first place.

The above examples reveal a certain amount of variation within this type of agony resolution in terms of the modes of involvement in the "pathway" to resolution. Self-reliance could be inwardly directed, in which case it was really a mode of "self-help." Alternatively, it can be outwardly focussed, in which case it embodied self-assertion.

Type 2: Robust

In 22 cases in the Agony Column, the woman in agony viewed herself as not being in control of her man, and the Agony Aunt advised the agony woman to focus on how to deal with the relationship. The agony resolution emerged from a recommendation to be robust. Robustness refers to the need to "grit one's teeth" and bear the consequences of putting up with or ending the relationship.

Two examples give a feel for this type.

Agony: "I feel like I'm in competition with my boyfriend's porn magazines ... I've found out that he would buy dirty magazines and masturbate while reading them! I simply cannot accept this ... How can he possibly think my body is any match? ... He swears he loves me as I am, but don't all men say that? ... No matter what he says, I feel very unattractive ... How can I forgive my boyfriend for something I see as unforgivable, as well as increase my self-esteem without cosmetic surgery?"

Agony Aunt: "If you want to solve your problem, stop harassing your boyfriend and get to work on your own insecurities." (Question 1, March 1990, p. 50)

Again, the woman in agony implied she is not in control. However, in this case, the Agony Aunt placed the resolution with the man in this relationship—to whom the woman should adapt.

In another example,

Agony: "I had been married almost four years when my husband, whom I adored, shattered me by leaving ... My life is in ruins ... All I do is cry, and my self-respect is nonexistent. When he came to see our son recently, I begged him to stay the night. He did, but made it clear once again that he no longer loves me. We had sex, which we both enjoyed, but then, of course, he left again. I'm lost, confused, angry, a mess. Will this hurt ever stop?"

Agony Aunt: "If you want the pain to stop, you'll have to get tough with yourself—and with him ... Why not start getting over him *now* by staying away from him? The only place I suggest you do get together is in a court of law, to make certain he fulfils his obligation to support his child financially." (Question 2, January 1992, p. 32)

The woman felt that she could not control her man but the Agony Aunt spoke directly to the importance of the woman taking control of what this man was doing to her: he, not her, was the cause of the problem; but she, not him, was the one to implement a solution.

As the above examples reveal, one can be robust in two distinct ways. The "problematic man" can be removed from the emotional horizons of the woman in agony by her being "robust enough" to simply leave the problematic relationship—the exit solution. Alternatively, the robustness was revealed in her putting up with what was problematic on the assumption that not much could change the man.

Type 3: Realist

In 31 cases, the woman perceived herself to be not in control of her man and the Agony Aunt saw the solution as involving the very norms of the kind of relationship the woman in agony was confronting. Norms are the conventional expectations that apply to social interactions. Often, the intensity of a relationship may create the impression that particular norms or mores "do not apply to me." Thus, a woman having an affair with a married man may think his not giving up his wife has to do with the wife's "manipulations and threats" or the man being "too weak." But the adviser normally replied in this context that it was simply unrealistic to expect a married man, particularly one with children, to give it all up—whether his wife was being manipulative or not. There are many other examples.

The agony of the women may be caused by their having fallen in love with a work colleague; or wondering why a "friend" did not wish to deepen his/her relationship; or whether a lover should have gone back to his wife for the sake of his daughter or whether a husband should have spent so much time with an ex-girlfriend at a school reunion. In these examples, the Agony Aunt focused on the question of what was normal to expect in the situation and, as a result, to compromise. That is, the Agony Aunt elaborated what is known as the jurisdiction of norms, i.e., how specific expectations about relationships are to apply. In this regard, the agony resolution involved the construction of a realist—one who does not dream that she transcends the expectations that apply normally to *anyone* in such a situation.

Agony: "My boyfriend is divorced and has two children ... I know it's ridiculous to be jealous of children, but they seem to mean more to him than I ever will ... He says that theirs is a civilised divorce and it is much better for the children for everyone to be friendly ... The effect of all this is to make me very bitchy about his wife ... Am I being unreasonable?"

Agony Aunt: "Whenever you fall in love with a man who has children, there is a part of him you cannot share ... If you want him, you will have him as a husband; let them keep him as a father." (Question 6, April 1983, p. 60)

In this context, the Agony Aunt simply reiterated a "fact of nature" that cannot be ignored. The woman in agony resolved the matter to the extent that she "faced facts."

Agony: "Is there anything I can do about premature ejaculation? ... I have tried to make him feel at ease and reassure him that it doesn't matter, but deep down inside I feel it does ... I really love him, and we have a very good relationship except for this problem."

Agony Aunt: "One thing you can do is stop saying it doesn't matter. Because it does matter, doesn't it? And when a couple has a problem, it's better if they both acknowledge it. Otherwise, how can they hope to do anything about it? There are a number of things that you can do about premature ejaculation. Books ... your doctor ... It will probably be so easy you'll both wonder why you waited for so long." (Question 4, March 1989, p. 64)

In this context, the woman in agony already confessed to a certain realism (about what matters!). The Agony Aunt reinforced the view with a norm in terms of "what a couple should be" as well as trying to work it out as a couple.

As with the other pathways, this one also had two forms. One form of realism was to acknowledge what norms apply to a situation. This is a process of the woman in agony realising she was not *that* special, that her man was not *that* "free" and that the world was not *that* fluid. As a result, she could acknowledge the constraint and compromise. But it also becomes possible for a problematic couple to be more active in terms of working things out together given a certain norm.

Type 4: Carefree

Although the incidents were far less frequent, six women in agony wrote in about a problem that had emerged even though they felt in control of their man. In these cases, it might be that the woman enjoyed sex with her boyfriend but did not really love him as much as he loved her; or her marriage had lost sparkle and she had had an affair, etc.—How was the good to be enjoyed while the bad was there too?

Agony: "For the past two years, I have been living with my boyfriend, with whom I was deeply in love at the beginning ... Since his suicide attempt, he has come to rely on me even more than before. A few months ago, I discovered suddenly that I no longer love him, although I am very fond of him. My dilemma is that if I leave him he will probably try to kill himself again. I'm too fond of him to let him down so badly, but I don't feel it's fair to him to build himself up on my lies and deceit."

Agony Aunt: "You are aware, I suppose, that you are in the process of being victimised? Your strength, which is your sense of honour and responsibility toward others, is being turned into a weakness, and you are being blackmailed for it. Blackmail is a crime in which two people are guilty ... As long as you are there, no matter how reluctantly ... why should he rely on himself? ... I can tell you that if you stay, you will not help him and you may destroy yourself. The longer you stay, the weaker you both become." (Question 2, October 1982, p. 32)

In another example,

Agony: "My marriage has not been a failure in every respect ... but sex has been a disaster ... I began to find other men attractive, since I felt so physically and mentally turned off by my husband, and we grew apart ... I have now fallen in love with another man ... I haven't told him about my lover—there seems to be no point at the moment, with our children just starting a new school term. The first priority must be them ... Practical advice is what I am seeking."

Agony Aunt: "Nobody in love has ever been known to listen to practical advice. Go on enjoying your love, then, for just as long as it lasts, but if it lasts forever, never stop enjoying it. Should your extramarital affair start to falter or bring you confusion, it might be a good idea to try professional counselling before you give up altogether on your marriage ... In due course, you might even want to share that tender secret with your husband." (Question 1, September 1986, p. 60)

Again, there was a loosening of constraints and the recommendation to enjoy what was there.

The examples revealed two ways in which "carefree" could be implemented. The woman could learn to "block out" the problematic nature of her partner's behaviour. Here carefree was "careless" in the sense of learning not to care about irksome aspects of another person. Conversely, a carefree spirit could become more explicitly hedonistic: enjoy what there is and for what it is.

Type 5: Hedging

In three cases, the woman was in control of the man, but the Agony Aunt saw the resolution of the problem as focused on the relationship. The woman might not have wished to make a commitment or felt that her love was not as strong, but was afraid of hurting her man or living by herself. In these contexts, the Agony Aunt normally saw resolution in a "hedging" (of bets). The woman was advised to focus on what actually occurred in the relationship, particularly on her feelings, and then make a decision.

Agony: "Although my boyfriend is very caring, I am not attracted to him sexually ... I especially love the way he supports me in everything I try to do ... I do have warm feelings for him but no real passion. Am I expecting too much? I've never been in such a caring and supportive relationship."

Agony Aunt: "The passion *and* emotional support that add up to love and sexual attraction are certainly not too much to ask from life. But you've known this man for only six weeks, and love can take much longer than that to develop. Right now, it seems that you simply like your boyfriend, and there's nothing wrong with that. Your feelings will probably become clearer as times goes on. ... If, at some point, you realise there's no chance you'll ever feel more strongly about him, then it would be best—for both of you—to break up. Although support is wonderful, support from the wrong person is worse than none at all." (Question 3, January 1992, p. 32)

The advice here is significant. Insofar as the woman in agony had some control, she should "wait and see." If waiting revealed nothing new, then she was not in control and therefore should leave, i.e., become robust rather than hedging.

In another example,

Agony: "I've been going out with my present boyfriend for over four months now. He is deeply in love with me, and we get along very well. I have grown to love him, and everything was going fine until I realised that what I thought was just a friendly interest in his best friend was much more than that and I was falling in love with him. I tried to stop it since he already has a girlfriend and my feelings of guilt are affecting my present relationship ... Can you help?"

Agony Aunt: "Stop seeing what you want to see, and try to see what is really there, which may or may not be what you wish were there. Your infatuation with your boyfriend's best friend could simply indicate your lack of real affection for your boyfriend, and in that case, give serious thought to ending one relationship before you think of starting a new one." (Question 4, December 1982, p. 60)

Here, the woman felt in control of her emotions regarding her boyfriend (though not his best friend), and the Agony Aunt suggested that the resolution should be focused on the relationships—to see what was really there in the relationship with the new man as well as what was missing in the relationship with her boyfriend.

As with the other examples, there are two ways in which "hedging" can be implemented. On the one hand, it can be "passive"—"wait and see," on the other hand, it can be more active—"communicate and provoke responses."

Type 6: Authentic

Finally, in 11 cases, the woman might have felt in control of her man, but the Agony Aunt sensed that the woman was not adequately oriented to the norms or principles that applied to her situation. Perhaps she thought she could avoid certain responsibilities, or she hadn't thought through the implications of some values.

For example,

Agony: "For the last two years, I have been going out with a boy who is 10 years younger than I. I am 29. The problem is that he has asked me to marry him. I am worried because of all the responsibilities he will have on his shoulders at such an early age ... I would like to stay with him, but his age makes me unsure."

Agony Aunt: "I would suspect that it is not your boyfriend who will be burdened with responsibilities, but you ... Like it or not, you may find yourself cast in the mother's role ... In your case, don't worry about his age or the difference, just think about who he is, or is becoming, who you are and what you both want from the future." (Question 1, May 1985, p. 78)

The agony here arose from an application of expectations (on one's self) that were too severe. The Agony Aunt counselled to relax about the age difference and try to understand the nature and the principle of marriage.

In another example,

Agony: "Why can't I make a commitment to a man? ... But even though I do love him, I just can't do it—not only because I still love Jeff, my old boyfriend, but I also worry about breaking away from my friends and family and moving to another town. Do you think I am scare[d] of being happy?"

Agony Aunt: "I don't see your problem as an inability to make a commitment to a man; I see it as a deep reluctance to be a grown-up ... My advice is to get out on your own for a while and establish a little independence, even though you seem unusually afraid of it." (Question 2, May 1991, p. 52)

Here, the relationship between the woman in agony and norms (about commitment) was shown to be too far apart: she had to grow up and become mature first.

In this context, there were again two forms of resolution. On the one hand, the difficulties with the norms might stem from a lack of maturity (as in the last case). The adviser, in effect, had to recommend "growing up." Alternatively, the woman might be "mature," but the difficulties of her situation required more reflection. Here, the pathway was to deepen one's understanding of the nature and principle of love, marriage and relationship in general, or philosophy of life.

Implementing Resolutions: The Choice of Pathway

As the descriptions and examples of the six types of "agony resolutions" show, within *each* type and across *all* the types there was another dimension of variation: the mode of involvement. This dimension opened out in two ways: in terms of whether the agony woman was advised to be passively or actively involved in solving the problem with her man. In other words, the actual implementation of agony resolution involved a kind of "fork in the road"—There was a choice to be made in terms of how the solution should be pursued or implemented. It was at this juncture that a gender politics was revealed.

The plausibility of either choice and its appropriateness within a real situation indicated different strategies that could minimise the agony woman's agony and maximise her self-interest. Either way, once there was a calculus of self-interest, gender politics began. These two pathways (passive versus active mode of involvement) within each type of agony resolution implied two different kinds of gender politics in heterosexual relations. Therefore, an expanded theoretical typology of "Agony-Resolution Pathways" was developed and grounded in the Agony Column data (see Table 6-2). Twelve types of agony-resolution pathways are presented in Table 6-2. The frequency for each of the types is listed in parentheses.

Table 6-2: Gender Politics: A Typology of Agony-Resolution Pathways

Woman in an agony relationship sees herself as being:

Advisor sees solution as:	**NOT in control of her man (N=110)**		**In control of her man (N=20)**	
	1. Reliant		4. Carefree	
Centred on the woman (N=63)	Help Yourself Rely on yourself to get happiness: He can't let you down. (N=27)	Assert Yourself A rebuff may occur but the relationship might also move to a new plane. (N=30)	Ignore the Negatives Minimise the burdens of his bad habits that cannot change. (N=1)	Enjoy the Positives Focus on the good things. All else can be ignored. (N=5)
	2. Robust		5. Hedging	
Centred on the relationship (N=22)	Accept What's There He may have problems, but they are his, not yours. (N=7)	Quit the Relationship Don't waste your resources on this hopeless man and his promises. (N=15)	Wait and See Reduce efforts to fix this relationship; rely on time to "cure" the problem. (N=1)	Provoke a Response Find out what sort of man he is and what is really there in the relationship. (N=2)
	3. Realist		6. Authentic	
Resting with values and norms (N=42)	Acknowledge Norms Reduce the agony of unrealistic expectations and of daydreams that cannot come true. (N=22)	Work It Out Reorient yourself to the problem and let benefits emerge regardless of the mess. (N=9)	Understand Norms Focus on the internal relation and reduce risks of making silly decisions. (N=9)	Become Mature Urge the woman to become mature, transcending a narrow assessment of the situation. (N=2)

A passive mode of involvement within each cell implies that a "safe card" was being played in dealing with the man, because the future would not be dramatically different from the present—the agony woman still had her man. While the passive pathways (strategies) aimed to reduce the agony, the activist pathways aimed to increase the benefits that could be extricated from the relationship. The agony was not so much reduced as made less significant from a new perspective of what was really important about life for the woman.

Once the Agony Aunt proposed a "pathway," the agony woman and each reader could link the agony-resolution pathway to their own experiences and figure how much risk they would personally endure (or enjoy) on the way to solving a problem. Whether the risk is minimised or extended, a gender politics is developed, since both extremes forced a form of personal calculation about intimate matters to emerge. It was here that the hidden assumptions and deep-seated ironies in gender relations emerged.

Discussion and Conclusion

To conclude this chapter, I discuss a few insights regarding gender relations in the secular West which are generated from this theoretical typology grounded in the Agony Column of the American edition of *Cosmopolitan*.

Women's Assumptions about Men

In all this advice, men clearly were perceived and depicted by the Agony Aunt as not being expected to change or even capable of changing. As a result, this idea is implicated in *all* the different types of agony-resolution pathways in this typology.

The *reliant* woman resolved her agony by looking to herself (Help Yourself) or to what she wanted or did not want (Assert Yourself). This left open the possibility of the man responding to a self-assertion, but it also risked a rebuff. The crucial issue within this type of agony resolution was that the woman focused on herself, was committed to her standards, did not give in and/or was exercising a "right" to assert herself. As a result, her man could take on or not take on her assertion. Similarly, with the *robust* woman, the man did not need to change either. The *robust* woman resolved agony by "toughening up" against an unchanging source of frustration (the man): either she left him or she accepted him as he was. The *realist* woman resolved agony by focusing on the reality of the constraints that applied. Of particular significance here were normative constraints that impinged on relationships. Whether through acceptance of constraints as given, or through compromise ("working it out" together as a couple), the realist was not placing any burden on the man to change by himself. Being *carefree* created no requirements for men to change either. With her focus on delights or deliverance, the *carefree* woman enjoyed what she got and was not burdened by the hassles caused by the man. With *hedging,* change was allowed for, but not "banked upon." The *hedging* woman resolved agony by focusing on further insights—achieved over time or through provocations in the relationship. In this context, the agony woman's feeling toward her man might change "naturally" or reveal aspects of the relationship if provoked, but neither form of hedging implied a sustained attempt to actually change the man. Finally, with *authenticity,* agony was reflected upon and used as a "teacher" of life—the *authentic* woman grew or deepened. Again, the "learner" was the woman, not the man.

Therefore, there is an overall implication from all the resolution pathways in this typology—whichever way the woman travelled, it was she that did the pedalling.

Ironies as Entry Points in Gender Relations

At a deeper level, there are profound ironies involved in women in agony seeking release. An overall irony is that the Agony Aunt's advice to women is based on her own stereotypical perceptions about men. As a result, the conventional gender morality is reproduced and individualism is reinforced through the advice system run by, and for, modern women.

All the advice the Agony Aunt gives as well as the resolution pathways revealed in the Agony Column imply that women can or should achieve personal transformation, figure out optimum strategies and make tough decisions. As a result of men not making changes or not being expected to change, women are the ones who have to do all the work, such as self-help, self-assertion, making tough decisions (to leave the man), being patient (wait and see), acknowledging and compromising relative to gender norms (to put up with the man) or learning to be more mature (to be good) and fit into the gender morality. But since gender relations involve two participants, the more women take on, the less men need to take on.

In part, this assumption toward men (i.e., men cannot change) and the requirements on women (i.e., women have to change) might be because it is women who are writing in, and the female adviser, in having to be "positive," has to focus on what women can do. And since *Cosmopolitan* projects women as being autonomous, professional, young and in charge of their lives, this kind of positive pitch seems the only way to go. But even if this is so, or precisely because this is so, there is a pervasive sensibility being propagated by women themselves: woman can fix things for themselves. Men cannot, or need not, be relied upon. Consequently, there are ironies to be revealed.

One irony is on the level of conditions for men and women. Given such assumptions about men and the advice being supplied, one prospect may be that men can justify being emotionally "lazy," since it is women who end up taking more of the "hardship" on themselves than before. The irony is that modern women are advised, by a modern woman "expert," not only to accept the conventional (stereotypical) gender norms and values, but also to focus exclusively on themselves to fix any problems or issues resulting from that conventional system of morality.

The other irony is that the advice or solution being given in the Agony Column reinforces individualism, even if the problems on relationships, marriage and family are clearly beyond the level of single individuals. Women are advised by an "expert" woman that the individualised woman, in command of her individuality, rather than the web of social relationships in which a woman is engaged, provides the only acknowledged pathway to success.

Engendered Collaboration

The advice given and the range of options the Agony Aunt proposed for the women in agony did not offer men opportunities and resources for change. Yet, men are, after all, meant to be "change agents" rather than "free riders" within the vortex of social forces that impinge on gender. Masculinity itself, along with femininity, are resolutions of social forces, not static features of humans. I would argue that through Agony Columns men can improve problematic relationships. This is an unrealised potential that should be explored much more fully.

In the "Concluding Remarks" in this book, I will explore ways in which men can be constituted as subjects of advisory discourse regarding gender and/or relationship problems so that a new engagement between the genders can be promoted and both genders can jointly "make sense of each other."

NOTES

1. I contacted the editorial office in New York as well as the "Agony Aunt" herself and learned that the "Agony" letters are written, and sent in, by real people.

2. I also discussed with the editors the "selection" criteria I developed about which agony letters to be published.

Part 5:

Chinese Versus Western

Chapter 7

Infidelity

The findings regarding gender relations and issues from the discourse analyses of the Taiwanese and American editions of *Cosmopolitan* presented in Chapter 3 and Chapter 6 respectively introduce the broader comparative studies of Chinese and Western cultural settings presented in this and the next chapter. Through this comparative research, it becomes possible to discern not only if something can be called "Chinese" sexuality, but also, if, in contrast, something can be called "Western" sexuality.

To bring to the surface the nature of these possible cultural differences, this chapter will focus on comparing sexual transgressions, notably, marital infidelity. This is because sociologically, a transgressive behaviour can reveal more than a normative practice does about where boundaries are and what a social arrangement or institution means when boundaries are broken.

Some argue that deviance mirrors and/or revitalises core cultural values (Shaw, 1991). Deviance, therefore, strengthens norms and clarifies boundaries (Durkheim, 1976). Others argue that deviance breaks norms, which sometimes leads to social change (Parsons, 1951). I argue that breaking the "boundaries" is sometimes actually a part of the social change process. The cross-cultural comparison of marital infidelity in contemporary Chinese and Western settings can isolate the cultural specific and/or universal linkage(s) between cultural values on marriage, family and sexuality, (breaking) boundaries and social change.

Affairs can reveal a core part of a culture. Leading historian of sexuality Randolph Trombach emphasises that "sexual behavior is the most highly symbolic activity of any society. To penetrate to the symbolic system implicit in a society's sexual behaviour is therefore to come closest to the heart of its uniqueness."[1] Following up Trombach's statement, Plummer highlights the point that "sexual stories are a major key to this system" (Plummer, 1995, p. 176). The construction of sexuality takes us to the core of a culture, but sexuality may not be contained by the core of that culture. Sex seems always to exceed the specifications of norms.

Every culture has norms and regulations to protect its ideal form of sexuality from variation and excesses. This is why extramarital affairs reveal more about the forms of variation (actually deviation) as well as the nature of this "excess" aspect of sexuality (Murphy, 1971). In other words, extramarital affairs can be seen as a "key" to where the system of marital expectations "leaks" and where possibilities of transgression abound.

Given the argument of the cultural centrality of sexual practices, extramarital affairs in particular, I further want to argue that a cross-cultural comparison of extramarital affairs can produce "cultural shock" in reverse, leading us to reexamine all assumptions and meanings regarding sexuality and normative boundaries taken for granted in each culture.

Extramarital affairs exist cross-culturally, historically and in modern times (Kinsey et al., 1948, 1953; Fisher, 1992; Greeley, 1994). Yet for all their ubiquity and capacity to be sociologically revealing, extramarital affairs have not been researched extensively. There is one obvious reason why extramarital affairs are understudied: collecting valid and reliable data is difficult due to the nature of the transgression.

Yet even a cursory glance at magazines or newspapers reveals that much popular material has been written regarding extramarital affairs. Whatever the frequency of extramarital affairs, it is clearly outnumbered by the frequency with which reports about extramarital affairs are read and/or discussed.

Therefore, this study exploits this proliferation of material by using an unobtrusive approach which treats reports of extramarital affairs as "data," to examine how extramarital affairs are reported and depicted as *real* events in the popular press and how problems of extramarital affairs are dealt with by people who have lived with such events in contemporary Chinese and Western cultural settings.

The purpose of this study is *not* to generalise to a population about people's extramarital attitudes and behaviours. Rather, the aim is to generate insights about the nature and meanings of infidelity. For this purpose, the study of real-life events reported in the media is more relevant than determining the exact figures (if this were even possible) on such sensitive matters. Another important aspect of studying these media reports is that even if individuals may not "live by" or "live through" such events, they can barely avoid "living with" such material, particularly if such material is taken as real.

There are, however, a few surveys and some empirical research in this area (Hunt, 1969, 1974; Reiss et al., 1980; Saunders and Edwards, 1984; Lawson, 1988; Greeley, 1994; Edwards and Booth, 1994; Laumann et al., 1994; Bender and Leone, 1995).[2] Past research done about extramarital affairs in Western societies shows that extramarital affairs may be "functional" in terms of men and women finding more fulfillment in more "flexible" gender roles than they may be able to find in the marital context. Lawson (1988) finds that men can feel constrained by their culturally defined dominant role or strong breadwinner role in marriage, but they have emotions and needs which cannot be structurally met by the given marital and familial relations. In extramarital relations, men can play more flexible roles (by sometimes being a dependent boy needing to be looked after, or by being emotionally vulnerable and receiving gentle nurturing from a woman).

For women, the "flexibility" of an extramarital relationship is more difficult to define but can be related to her sense of "autonomy" and control, which may be lacking in a marital context. Yet, women may still desire a dominant male figure in an extramarital romance as long as this autonomy is not constrained. In other words, this argument implies that in the Western cultural setting, the familial structure and conventional gender roles cause problems within marriage and push married people to seek a more fulfilling relationship outside marriage. In particular, with the "feminisation of love" (for men) and "masculinisation of sex" (for women) in the West (Lawson, 1988), the rates of extramarital affairs have converged for men and women (Richards and Elliott, 1991).

The reasons for women being involved in extramarital affairs have also converged with those of men: sexual freedom and short-term enjoyment for sexuality itself, variety, adventure and the need to feel attractive and desirable (Hunt, 1974; Pietropinto and Simenauer, 1977; Seidman, 1992). It has also been argued that, even if both men and women benefit from engaging in extramarital affairs, men are still in a more "advantageous" position than women in the extramarital context (Lawson, 1988), on top of the fact that men are in a more advantageous position in the marital relationship[3] (Duncombe and Marsden, 1996; Elliott, 1996; Holland et al., 1996).

Are such arguments regarding the "problematic structure" of marriage, the convergence in the propensity to be involved in extramarital affairs and "men always being in an advantageous position in both marital and extramarital relations" valid? This study explores these arguments by examining the way cases of extramarital affairs are presented in print. The advantage of this study is that these extramarital reports are typifications of the process by which a person gets involved in such an affair. These typifications can reveal gender politics in both marital and extramarital settings and the meanings of sexuality for both genders.

This study examines these issues by comparing Chinese and Western reports of extramarital affairs. I have chosen Taiwan to represent a contemporary Chinese setting for this cross-cultural comparison with the secular Western culture because Taiwan can be seen as a baseline for the study of contemporary "orthodox" Chinese culture as discussed in Chapters 4 and 5. These two cultural settings have very different value bases and two contrasting ideals of individualism versus familism. The comparison of extramarital affairs in contemporary Western and Chinese settings can alert scholars and social commentaries to the possibility that changing sexual mores in a Chinese setting need not follow a path similar to that in the West, nor be simply an extension of existing Chinese values. I argue that in a Chinese cultural setting, the sexual constructions (as revealed in extramarital relations) in modern times have their own forms, which are not immediately congruent with the forms developed in the West.

The shift of major feminist concerns from a critique of "women as objectified and exploited in sexual relationships" (Dworkin, 1981; MacKinnon, 1982) to an elaboration of possibilities regarding "women-centred pleasure" (Vance, 1984; Jeffreys, 1990) and "diversity and fluidity in women's sexuality" (Rich, 1980; Stacy, 1991; Robinson, 1993) may not be sufficient to inform the issues on gender politics and sexuality in the contemporary Chinese setting. The crucial issues involved in the validity of these Western ideologies and debates are what the actual object of fidelity is in each society and what the meanings of "love," "sex," "marriage," "family" and "manhood/womanhood" are in each culture/society.

Furthermore, the comparison between the Chinese and Western cultural settings might appear as an artefact of some essentialist construction. While there is diversity with respect to sexual behaviors and familial arrangements within each culture on such dimensions as religion, ethnicity, class, generation, gender and sexual orientation, portrayals of marital transgression in particular are uniquely placed to reveal fundamental differences that go to the core of each culture. This is because the diversity of sexual attitudes and practices does not expand the limited number of ways in each culture in which responses or solutions to marital transgressions are dealt with. In other words, diversity within a culture or "variance" of meanings between cultures actually still hangs on some core "central tendencies" to the extent that in all cultures, men and women "fall in love," make and break commitments, enjoy or avoid sex and engage in sexual activity beyond the bounds of what is acceptable in that society. A number of forces—normative, situational and emotional—resolve themselves into patterns that appear cultural specific and/or universal, which makes cross-cultural comparative research more revealing than research based only on one culture.

The research questions to be posed for this comparative study are: Are extramarital affairs reported to follow common trajectories in each of the cultural settings? Specifically, do these real events follow some "scripts" that define basic patterns of plots, moves and resolution of conflicts? How do reports of extramarital stories exemplify values of fidelity to people in modern times? More generally, what do reports of infidelity reveal about the very nature of fidelity? What do depictions of extramarital affairs reveal more generally about problematical aspects about manhood and womanhood within each culture? Love, sexuality, marriage and family are the basic and universal dimensions of human beings, but to what extent are the meanings of these dimensions cross-culturally universal? To what extent are the meanings of these dimensions culture-specific or unique? Some of these questions can be answered directly by an analysis of the various reports under investigation. Others cannot be so directly answered by the data, but they are suggestive of some cultural dynamics.

Methodology

Data

Data for this study were collected in the mid-1990s. The reported *real* cases of extramarital affairs are the units of analysis. Forty-five Chinese cases of affairs come from reports occurring in Taiwanese newspapers from 1987 to 1994 (including affairs reported in advice columns, commentaries and features). Twenty-seven Western cases of affairs come from a series of interviews with women (who were either "wives" or "third-party" figures in the events of extramarital affairs) reported by Leigh Cato in *Her Version* (1995).

For the Taiwanese data set, reports of extramarital affairs are from newspaper clippings collected by the Women Awakening Foundation (*Funu xinzhi*) in Taiwan. This influential feminist organisation, founded in the early 1980s, has been actively involved with numerous social reforms regarding Taiwanese women's issues. It lobbies to change legislation, publishes documents and books and mobilises women's movements. The foundation's collection of newspaper clippings (including news, columns, commentary and articles) is drawn from nine widely circulated newspapers under many subjects/indexes on women's issues.[4] These newspaper archives are open to all policy-oriented and academic users.

The coverage period of my Taiwanese newspaper data is from 1987 to the first half of 1994. My fieldwork was undertaken in Taiwan in June and July of 1994. The rationale for using 1987 as the starting point is that this is the year that marital law was abandoned. In the political liberalisation which followed, even "tabooed" ideas of the past were exposed to Western and other globally dispersed ideas. The mass media have highlighted the many ways this further societal "liberalisation" and openness have "speeded up" the modification of Chinese people's thinking about, and behaviour toward, sexuality and marriage.

I photocopied all of the clippings under the subject name of "extra-marital affairs" from 1987 to June 1994. Since the unit of analysis in this study is each case of an affair being reported, the first step in "cleaning" these data was to screen all of the reports to see if each contained a reference to a "real affair" and a complete description of the whole process of such an event. Forty-five cases showing the complete process of affairs (from beginning to end) were thus obtained.

The gender of the writer reporting an event influences the way the event is presented. This data set does not contain enough information to definitively identify the gender of the "reporter," because writers (even commentators and authors of features) tend to use gender-neutral pen names. However, theoretically, I would like to argue that most of those reporting such events (and problems) to advice columns are women. Very often the content itself reveals the gender (such as "my husband is having an affair"). Most "advisers" on such so-called women topics are also women. This same conjecture can be applied to the authors of features or commentaries on "soft" topics of marriage and family: they are also more likely to be women.

Using the foundation's newspaper (rather than source materials from a nonfeminist or other more "conventional" or male-dominant organisation) as the Taiwanese "data source" has two advantages for this study. First, since women's issues are their focus, they can be expected to "clip" relevant information more thoroughly. Second, the ideology of the group provides a particularly sensitive "lens" through which relevant clippings might be spotted and selected. Standard news clipping services or newsrooms may not have the necessary "sensitivity" to spot relevant clippings. In addition, news items that might be classified under some other topic by mainstream news clipping services may not then appear under the heading "extramarital affairs." Thus, the foundation's clippings are likely to "catch" most of the news and columns that fall under this heading. Their sensibilities are going to be particularly attuned to the rare "odd" cases that are especially "progressive" (in their terms) or especially patriarchal. In this sense, there is likely to be a bias toward oversampling the extremes. But within this framework of isolating types of affairs, this kind of bias is an improvement from the point of view of the analytical inductions to be developed. The logic of the sampling is therefore "theoretical" rather than enumerative (Turner, 1953; Barton and Lazarsfeld, 1955; Glaser and Strauss, 1967).

The advantages cited above for the Taiwanese data can also be applied to the Western data set in this study. For the Western data, 27 real events of extramarital affairs in Cato's book *Her Version* were reported by women. These women, across all backgrounds (mostly on three continents, namely, North America, Europe and Australia), were interviewed by Cato over the last 10 years.[5] Cato has been married three times. She is concerned with the stories of ex-wives and the "third-party" women in terms of "What does [the story] say about the status of women in our society, despite the advances of feminism in this century?" (p. 236). Regarding other people's lives, Cato writes: "I have found that real life is richer and more complex than most fiction" (p. 1). The reports in her book are real-life events presented by an author who is concerned with women's issues, and thus, they are comparable to the Taiwanese reports on affairs (mainly reported and written by women) taken from the foundation's newspaper clipping collection.

There is, however, a limitation in this Western data set: in all the reports, the husband (or the man) is mainly the "initiator"—the events are reported from the prospective of the "wives" or "third-party" women. (In six cases, the "other woman" herself was also married.) The implication of this limitation will be discussed further when I present the results of my data analysis.

Coding, Analysing Data and Generating Topologies

Through a comparison of affairs in each data set, a number of generic components or elements become visible. For instance, each "affair" has to refer to a married couple and a third party. The participants in the affair bring specific orientations and resources. After reading through all of the reports, I developed a coding scheme regarding extramarital affairs for each data set. The components I coded include location and duration of the affair; demographic features of the first party, the second party and the third party; how the affair happened; the first party's marital condition; the first party's "explanations" for the affair; the third party's "explanations"; who was blamed; where the spouse found out and the outcome of the affair as revealed in each report.

These components are relatively easy to spot and code. I first randomly chose 10 reports to assess intercoder reliability. The other coder and I were consistent in our coding. After coding all the reports in terms of components, two major underlying variables regarding the characteristics of the participants and their situations could be discerned from the coded data.

The intersection of the categories of the two variables determines the types of affairs possible. This set of different types of affairs—realised and unrealised—can be arranged into a theoretical typology. Some of the entries in this typology may not be "realised" in any reports, but their "absence" is as much a matter of investigation as those that do appear.[6]

For each data set, a theoretical typology of four types of extramarital affairs that define players, plots, conditions and outcomes can be generated. To assure the validity of the typologies generated, I plugged all the cases back into the typologies and they did fit into certain types of affairs in these typologies. Comparison and contrast can be made between the two typologies.

Differential Gender Allurements to Infidelity

In most cases in the data, affairs were introduced in terms of the kinds of persons who were involved. Participants can be characterised by their propensity to engage in affairs as depicted in the reports. Specific situations and mechanisms were involved in the whole process. Across all the reported affairs, two underlying variables characterising the motive forces and situations can be discerned from each data set. One variable concerns the characteristics of the woman; the other variable concerns the man's condition. In this section, I shall outline, compare and contrast the two variables which underlie all the affairs between the two cultures.

The Woman Participant: Traditional Versus Modern

This variable concerns the female participant in the affair. The woman was depicted in terms of her self-definitions ("modern" versus "traditional"). In the contemporary Taiwanese setting, people perceive women who are "modern" as being highly educated, career oriented, financially independent, self-determined and not necessarily fixed on marriage as an ultimate goal. Meanwhile, women also use such a definition to define themselves. I call Taiwanese women with this ideology "modern" women, while women without such an ideology I call "traditional."

In a Western setting, two types of women characterised as being "traditional" and "modern" were also depicted in the reports of affairs. Some aspects of the definition of this variable are similar to the Taiwanese ones, but some aspects are different. The "modern" women in the Western reports were depicted as having a career and/or some money and being more "calculating"—for instance, helping a man to set up a business or develop a career. Such women had autonomous minds and strong personalities.

In contrast, the "traditional" women in the Western reports were seen as non-career-oriented in general terms. They were often depicted as "dumb blondes" or even occasionally as a "slut" (particularly by the aggrieved wife). Such a woman offered good sex or comfort for a man who had become bored or marginalised by his wife—according to the reports from the third-party women.

The Man's Condition

This variable concerns the male participant in the affair, particularly his appeal to the woman. In contemporary Taiwanese setting, the conditions of the men who participated in the affairs can be defined according to the kind of support the male participant in the affair was depicted as being able to provide to the female participant. One kind of support involved a man of wealth or high standing, someone who could provide "material" support for the woman. The lure of this man is his standing and command of resources (and respect). The other kind of support was depicted in "spiritually" supportive, rather than materially powerful, terms, with the man providing emotional support, mutual understanding and sharing common interests in a career. Here, the lure is the man's "understanding" of the woman's needs or situation.

As mentioned above, the instigators of affairs in my data set of Western reports are mainly husbands, so the "male participants" here will be referred to as married men. The key variable that marks out the variety among the conditions of these men is the extent of their control over their spouse. In some reports, the men were described as being in control of their domestic situation (or at least were quoted as if they were); their spouse did everything right to be a good wife and mother, but the husband took her for granted. Despite this, the man was depicted as being bored and in need of something more exciting.

In contrast, the condition of having a status of "not controlling the spouse" was depicted as being in a marital relation in which the wife was a career woman, or she was said to be opinionated, demanding or making the husband feel marginalised or tired. The thing missing in such a man's life was centrality or comfort.

In other words, in the Taiwanese setting, a male participant in the affair was tied to what kinds of resources he had and was able to offer, while in the Western setting, the male participant's propensity for an affair was caused by something that was lacking in his marital relation.

Typologies of Marital Infidelity

The two underlying variables discerned in all the reports deal with the two participants in the affairs. Because the two data variables define the gender orientations of both participants in the affairs, it becomes appropriate to cross these two variables in order to generate a set of types of affairs. In other words, these two variables define a typology of the possible modes of encounters. For each data set, a typology of four types of extramarital affairs can be isolated. However, the types are different, particularly given the different conditions that apply to men, for the two cultural settings. Within the typology of affairs emerged in each cultural setting, each type of affair has autonomy of its own. Once the affair starts along the path set for each type, it does not move to another.

Typology of the Chinese Affairs

A typology of extramarital affairs in the Chinese setting which can be generated from these two underlying variables is presented in Table 7-1. The table can be read as follows. Each gender is depicted in terms of a basic orientation in the affair. For men, they can provide either material or emotional support (the vertical variable in the table). For women, they can be defined in terms of traditional or modern self-definitions (the horizontal variable in the table). From this "encounter" come four types of affairs. Each type of affair has a "script" emerged from the Chinese data. In each script there is a specific kind of plot, a key player who "drives" the action, a specific structure and dynamics in the marriage, in the affair and in the triangle, even "words" spoken by each party, and a finale or "conclusion" to the process.

Table 7-1: Typology of Depicted Affairs and Key Players—The Chinese Case

Men depicted as:	Women depicted as: Traditional	Women depicted as: Modern
Materially Supporting "Third Party"	*Saviour*	*Manipulative Women*
Spiritually Supporting "Third Party"	*Unhappy Housewife*	*Soul Mates*

Chinese Type/Script 1: "Traditional Masculine Saviour"

This first type, the "masculine saviour," has the man depicted as materially "powerful" and the third-party woman as "traditional." This affair takes the form of the man using the explanation or excuse of "saving the woman." The reason why such an affair can work is that the woman's traditionalism is said to be a lure (to the man) and a weakness (for the woman). The "powerful" man portrays himself as a saviour. Conversely, the affair can be seen by the man as fitting a traditional setting in terms of enjoying the privilege of having a mistress in the "postconcubine" era.

The affair follows this plot. First, the man had power, money and/or the opportunity to provide "material" support and to be a paternal figure for a "subordinate" (usually in a work context). The subordinate was shown to be young, pretty and often a virgin. Second, the young woman had a poor family background and an innocent disposition. Third, the man offered "excuses" about a weak marriage, a wife being bossy or tough or uncultured. Such accounts were shown as provoking compassion and enticing the young subordinate to "listen." Fourth, divorce was revealed to be a prospect, although no definite deadline was given. Fifth, the young woman felt "honoured" by the attention and rapport and was compassionate about the situation. Together, these provided the context for the women to "fall in love." The prospect of marriage gave the love a purpose and a justification.

The next part concerns the "exposure" of the affair. The women were usually the ones to provoke exposure: either the young woman began to question the deadline for marriage—perhaps due to pregnancy—or the wife found out and demanded a resolution. At this point, we see three kinds of "blame" for the affair: First, the wife blamed the third party for stealing her husband. Second, the husband blamed the wife for not being able to share his work pressures. Third, the third party blamed herself for being stupid enough to trust the man's "promises."

The finale concerns outcomes. First, the wife fought and humiliated the third party or the two women fought. The wife awaited the return of the husband. Second, the husband, in some cases with the assistance of the wife, found a mechanism to get rid of the young person. Normally, the husband explained that his wife did not want a divorce, and he gave the third party money and asked her to leave. Third, the third party felt heartbroken, cheated, humiliated and regretful. Fourth, in some cases, the wife developed mental problems (depression, neurotic behaviour, insecurity, suspicions) after the event.[7] It is significant that in this final stage, the conflict was between the women, rather than between the wife and the husband.

Chinese Type/Script 2: "Soul Mates"

In the second type, "soul mates," the opposite characteristics of "actors" are involved. The man is depicted as not using material "power" as a lure. Instead, he is shown to be genuine, innocent and honest about having a good marriage. The third-party woman is depicted as nontraditional, having a career and not requiring marriage as a prospect.

The outline of the plot is as follows. First, the man had no power or money, but he had the opportunity to be a workmate with an unmarried woman who was mature, intellectual, career oriented and a "modern woman." Second, the man in this affair needed no "excuse." He told the woman that he had a fine marriage, that divorce was not envisaged and that his relationship with his wife was not exciting but was harmonious. Nevertheless, he was interested in the workmate's concerns and aspirations, and he was responsive (say, to her sense of humour). Third, the woman was depicted as seeking romance and as enjoying "spiritual" support from the man. She did not want money and did not care about marriage, nor did she need any excuses or promises from him. The affair occurred for whatever reasons—office politics created embattlements, similar interests flourished or intensive project works brought them together. The affair took on a life of its own. She promised not to break up his marriage. Fourth, there was no future plan, but both enjoyed the romance and treasured the "free spirit"—no feelings of responsibility or duty.

Then, there is the episode which reveals how the wife found out. In the process of resolving this situation, the question of blame comes to the fore. First, the wife blamed the third party. Second, the man might partly blame his wife—he could not share with her most of his intellectual interests and ideas regarding his career. He might also blame the "modern" woman for initiating the affair. Third, the modern woman did not have anyone to blame and could be depicted as uninterested ("easy come, easy go") or as lost ("what does this all mean to me?") or as tragic (the "lot of women").

Finally, there is the episode that reveals the outcomes. First, the wife humiliated or sued the third party. These stories were more likely to have the wife take on more aggressive "retribution roles" than in the first script. Sometimes, the third-party woman had to pay a "fine" to the wife, because the feminist had a career and money. Second, the man found a mechanism by which to quit the relationship. It was not very difficult to quit, because he did not promise her anything in the first place. Third, the third party felt heartbroken and empty and she wonders what this romance meant. Fourth, the wife might be shown as sliding into mental problems (depression, neuroticism, insecurity or suspiciousness) after the event.

Chinese Type/Script 3: "Unhappy Housewife"

The preceding two scripts had the husband engaging in the extramarital affair. This next script concerns the wife who is depicted as the key player who "caused" the affair. The cause was primarily lodged in her "situation" (of unhappiness), rather than in any "drives" she had toward promiscuity or an affair. This was a less common scenario in Taiwan, but its incidence had been increasing, and this has caused a crises for some men.[8] These crises in which the wife had an extramarital affair were much more intolerable for men than the similar crises were for women: "wearing the green hat" (*dailumao*) is most humiliating for a Chinese man.

The plot begins with an unhappy housewife. The husband took her for granted or mistreated her; she was not cared for, or satisfied by, her husband. She felt lonely. She had few opportunities to meet men by herself, although she did meet men who were her husband's friends or workmates. Reports of this type of an affair elaborate scenarios in which another man showed care and concern for the woman. She was shown to be attracted to him and/or even willing to give up this marriage for him. For her, this was more a psychological need than a sexual need.

Then, there was an episode dealing with the husband's reaction when he found out. The husband was shocked and very angry. He felt he had lost face—the worst thing that can happen to a Chinese man. He was emotionally out of control; he might have beaten up the man and/or his wife. Another episode showed the wife as "brave" and blaming the husband for not treating her well in marriage. The finale was that the angry husband sued both the wife and the third party. The husband divorced the wife. The wife wanted to marry the third party, but in a tragic twist, these affairs then had the third-party man not wanting her and leaving her. Her life was ruined. She felt heart-broken and ended up with nothing but a bad reputation.[9]

Chinese Type/Script 4: "Missing Script"

The question arises as to what this type would look like that, with the man depicted as materially "powerful" and the woman depicted as "modern." The type can be tied to a modern woman (regardless of marital status) who is shown as taking advantage of a powerful man to achieve more for herself. In this case, she may be seen as being "manipulative." The gender politics revealed in this type seem very real, but this type is not revealed in any of my newspaper reports.

The plausible explanations for the "absence" of this type may be related to people's perceptions of modern women in Taiwan. Chinese people can imagine a powerful man being able, or willing, to be taken advantage of by a poor woman, because such manipulation still reflects men's masculinity such as where a powerful man looks after a poor woman. Male writers in newspapers, however, may not like to think about this possibility or envision a scenario in which a powerful man could be manipulated by a modern woman. Even if such women were perceived to be intelligent, less feminine, capable and sometimes threatening, they are still women. Female writers might not want to paint such a "negative" image of modern women nor "admit" that such cases exist, because they tend to portray "modern" women (in particular, feminists) as conscientious, projustice and supercapable.

Chinese Trends

Many reported affairs in my data set followed the "saviour' type."[10] The relative frequency of each type of affair in this theoretical typology will not remain constant. The main change in emphasis can be expected to move in a downward direction along the diagonal with the opportunities for personal relationships between the sexes emerging from work. The opportunities for "romance" are growing along with an increased significance of "romance" as an important aspect of relationships.

By contrast, the implied traditionalism of young women "believing" the promises of powerful men can be expected to decline. Either way, one can expect greater interest to focus on the newer form of "soul mates" than on the traditional type ("saviour"). However, with this move there are subsidiary moves. The traditional woman (as housewife or daughter) may succumb to the nonrich men who can provide "spiritual" support. Conversely, the modern woman may make "inroads" into powerful or rich men by "playing them," though this type has yet to find much expression in current materials.

Typology of the Western Affairs

The Western-reported affairs can also be framed within a typology that defines the possible modes of encounter. This typology is presented in Table 7-2. The table can be read as follows. Two variables define this typology. For men, their conditions can be defined in terms of whether they can control their spouse in marriage (the vertical variable in the table). Women can be defined in terms of being "traditional" or "modern" (the horizontal variable in the table). The results of this "encounter" are four types of affairs which reveal various "push-pull" mechanisms in marital and extramarital relations.

Table 7-2: Typology of Depicted Affairs and Key Players— The Western Case

		Women depicted as :	
		Traditional	**Modern**
Men depicted as:	**Controlling Wife**	*Sex Saviour*	*Adventurer*
	Not Controlling Wife	*Comfort Provider*	*Toy Boy/Manipulative Man*

In the Western setting, the four types of affairs presented in Table 7-2 do not have corresponding "scripts" (as those in the Chinese setting). The trajectory of the affairs is less constrained by the social structure and so lacks the structured variety of "scripts" that apply to the Chinese setting. This is consistent with Gagnon and Simon's argument in relation to their approach of studying sexual behaviors via three levels of sexual "scripts"/"scripting" (i.e., cultural scenarios, interpersonal scripts and intrapsychic scripts). They argue that in the secular West (which might be termed as "postparadigmic" societies by them), there are substantially fewer shared meanings and potentially profound disjunctures of meanings between different spheres of life than the so-called paradigmic societies in which "cultural scenarios and a limited repertoire of what appear to be 'ritualised improvisations' may be all that is required for understanding by either participants or observers" (Simon and Gagnon, 2007, p. 31). The contrasts between the two sets of typologies of extramarital affairs isolated from the Taiwanese and Western reports can certainly reflect and highlight the different "cultural scenarios" (i.e., the social norms and values that influence the interpersonal and intrapsychic "scripting" of affairs) between the two cultural settings.

Although no corresponding "script" can be isolated for each type of Western affairs in my data, there is a persistent "theme"—a sexually driven motive and consequence—that comes through, regardless of what types of extramarital affairs are involved.

Western Type 1: "Sex Saviours"

In the first type, "sex saviours," the man was able to control his spouse in a marital relation, and the third-party woman was depicted as "traditional." Control over a spouse made that spouse appear boring and, as a result, made the man feel bored in his marriage, or even in his life, in general. This condition of "feeling bored" pushed the man away. The "pulling" force usually came from a third-party, noncareer woman, who was often stereotyped as a "dumb blonde." She tried many ways to provide good sex to this man, including wearing sexy lingerie, putting on makeup before he woke up, and initiating sex in an unusual setting (for example, inside a phone booth). They were the best lovers for each other. In the reports, these women expressed pride at being able to "rescue" the unhappy man and bring excitement into his life. In this case, the man was the initiator of the affair, but the woman actually played an active role in the relationship by acting as a "sex saviour" for this man whose life lacked excitement.

Western Type 2: "Comfort Provider"

In the second type, "comfort provider," the man was less able to control his wife in marriage and the third-party woman was "traditional." The wife was depicted as career oriented, demanding, tough or perhaps even a perfectionist. The man felt marginal or tired in his marriage. This marginal or tiresome condition pushed him away. The "pull" force tended to come from a young woman or a noncareer traditional woman. Here, the third-party woman could make the marginal man feel central and "in control" by being obliging. Or, she brought the "tired" man a lot of comfort by looking after him, happily doing all the domestic chores, and being available for sex anytime after he came back from work. Being with such a woman, this man could become dominant and/or feel relaxed. In other words, this "traditional" woman was a "comfort provider" for this tired man. Compared to the "sex saviour," the depictions here have the third-party women being more passive and obliging.

Western Type 3: "Toy Boy/Manipulation"

In the third type, "toy boy/manipulation," the man was also depicted (in the accounts of the "third party") as having had difficulty controlling his wife in marriage, but found himself with another woman who was also strong and "modern." This other woman was portrayed as autonomous, assertive, calculating and having a career or money. In this type of "push-pull" situation, the man was pushed away from a demanding or powerful wife and pulled toward another strong and calculating woman. The encounter of these two types of people generated two sorts of relationships revealed in reported affairs. In some cases, the man was said to be "weak," i.e., indecisive, and caught between two strong women. The way of the third-party woman dealing with such an indecisive man was to be persistent and set up strategies to intervene in the man's marital life until his wife could not stand it and chose to give up her marriage. The man was controllable and could be like a "toy" to this strong woman.

In other cases, the man was depicted as being manipulative of a powerful third-party woman's money. The woman would set up a business plan, or even give money to this good-looking big "dreamer" to assist his business ventures. At the same time, the woman was usually aware of, and alert to, the possibility that this man was using her. When this man's business did not take off, the man was suspected of being manipulative and the woman tried to "cut her losses."

Western Type 4: "Adventurer"

In the fourth type, "adventurer," the man has a controllable spouse and feels bored in marriage, and a "modern" woman who is autonomous and competent. The affair constructed between these two people could be very adventurous, such as a one-night stand during a conference, or a "self-contained" romance in terms of the woman not being interested in having a marital commitment and the man not intending to break his marriage. This type of affair does not appear in any of the Western reports in this study. The plausible explanation for this "missing" type may be related to the "selectivity" bias in the Western data set. All the reports included in the book *Her Version* came from interviews with women who had been left and women who had been left for, so all the marriages between a wife and a "stray" husband must have been broken. The "adventurous" type of affair, which doesn't mean to break up a marriage, could not occur in this book, because such an event and the people involved would always have been hidden in the reality.

Western Trends

The majority of the affairs in the data set followed the traditional types of "sex saviour" and "comfort provider." The relative frequency of the four types of affairs in Table 7-2 can also be expected to change. The irreversible trend toward gender egalitarianism would lead more women out of the "traditional" mode (regardless of whether they were a wife or a third-party woman). More men will live in an egalitarian relationship in terms of a "not-controlling spouse." As a result, in an extramarital relationship, fewer women would like to be in a position of only playing a "provider" role—providing sex or comfort to men. More women would like to be able to assert, negotiate and critically assess what she can get in such a relationship. Therefore, the newer form of "toy boy/manipulation" would likely increase.

Major Western Theme: The Centrality of Sexuality to Personal Development

Regardless of the types of extramarital affairs, all the Western reported cases unfolded in the following way. First, the man met the woman. Second, the woman felt that this man was "Mr Right" and the quality of the sex with this man validated this impression. Third, the man made "excuses" about a dead marriage, a boring wife, lack of understanding and not good in bed. Such accounts were shown as provoking compassion and rapport, and enticing the woman to "rescue" him. Fourth, shortly after the affair started, both parties saw the "best sex" or "always ending up in bed" as "we were meant to be together." Fifth, divorce was a prospect.

The next part concerns the "exposure" and the consequences of the affair. Usually the wife found out and felt shocked: she had always trusted her husband. Marriage had been quite normal, even if not exciting. Their sex life was okay, given they had been married for so long. The man in this phase first tried to deny the affair, then got angry. Usually after a few weeks, he moved out without explanation and stayed with the other woman. The wife was heartbroken and felt that she didn't deserve this treatment: she had done everything she could to be a good wife and good mother. She could not help asking, "What did I do wrong?" In some cases, the wife would try to warn the third-party woman how bad this man really was and that he was not trustworthy.

At this point, the third-party woman thought that the wife behaved too nastily and "doing this only pushes us closer." Normally, she felt no guilt about breaking up someone's family, because "if not me, it will be someone else." Instead, she was proud of herself for being able to win this battle, bringing happiness to this man (because his wife failed to do so) and felt lucky to have this wonderful lover.

Regarding the final outcomes, they varied and depended on individual choices (or no choice at all), regardless of what kind of situation caused the affair in the first place. There were two kinds of outcomes for the wives. On the one hand, the wife would hire the meanest lawyer in town and get the best settlement possible. After a while, she recovered from the anger and hurt. She felt that her new life was actually better than before—having freedom, not having to compromise for anyone, being able to have lovers whenever she wanted or chose to, but not bothering to marry again. Some of the wives happily remarried—the new husband was so much nicer and more solid. On the other hand, in some reports, the wife and children were abandoned and never received any maintenance support from the husband. The wife had to struggle to make a living by herself—no more men in her life. She could not afford to hire babysitters or go out to meet men. She did not want men anymore, because men just "fool around."

There were two kinds of outcomes for the new couple. One was that the new couple lived "happily ever after." In particular, given that the cost of the whole affair was so high and the man had to pay a big settlement to his ex-wife and children, they really treasured their relationship and sex had always been and still was so good after paying such a high price. The other outcome was messier. The new couple became "happy," but not "ever after." The man "repeated" his history again by leaving for another woman. At that moment, the "other woman" (from the first time) really "felt for the ex-wife" and the ex-wife felt sorry for this "other woman." These two women built up a bond because of this common "dick-driven" man (as some put it in Cato's book) in their lives. This "other" woman, after being hurt, either had to struggle to run her new life by herself, or she found a new lover with a stronger emphasis on sexual fun due to her disillusionment with having a permanent relationship.

Therefore, in contrast with the three Chinese "scripts"—being dramatised in the culture, and being shared between individuals and among the society in general, the Western-reported affairs reveals no distinct script. The "affairs" in the West were depicted as being more chaotic. An underlying major theme about the centrality of sexually for both men and women exists, however.

Gender Politics and Infidelity

Salvation and Resources

In both typologies, a "saviour" role exists, but the depictions of the "saviour" vary between the two contexts. The contrast reflects the different gender roles in two cultures. In Taiwanese scripts, a "resourceful" married man "rescued" a third-party woman by providing either material or spiritual "support." In contrast, in Western-reported affairs, a third-party woman "rescued" a married man (who was either "bored" or "tired" of his marriage) by providing him good sex or comfort.

On the one hand, this contrast suggests that the role of Western women seemed to be "progressive" from being passive and dependent (on men) to being a strong figure who could rescue a married man from a miserable marriage. Western married men were depicted as "bored," "tired" or "marginal." In contrast, Taiwanese men were portrayed as strong and resourceful, while Taiwanese women were said to be "saved" or needing men's support.

On the other hand, however, this contrast reveals more progressive gender relations in Taiwan than in the West. Although in scripts the "resources" which a Taiwanese woman received from a man normally were the "traditional" material goods, a new type of resource emerged which was spiritual or involved emotional support from a poor man. This man (who could *only* supply spiritual or emotional support) would have never been "qualified" as a person possessing concubines or extra wives as many rich Chinese men had in the past. Today, the progressive modern Taiwanese women have "upgraded" the status of this kind of man as long as the man provided spiritual, intellectual or emotional company. In contrast, reports show the Western woman used "traditional resources" to "rescue" a married man—either being sexy (providing good sex for a bored man) or being obliging (providing "comfort" for a tired man).

Who to Blame

For marital infidelity, the Taiwanese wife tended to wait back home for the husband—everything was tolerable for the wife because she lived *for* the family, beyond any individualistic concern. Who is to blame? In Taiwanese scripts, men were never at fault. The only "fault" revealed in the reports may be the "nature" of men being more promiscuous. Therefore, a man's infidelity would not be as fatal as a woman's to the marital relation or family system. Furthermore, if women assumed that this "man's nature" was universal to all men, this assumption would only put women in a panic. They would feel vulnerable to the real "possibility" of their husbands engaging in extramarital affairs. The only one a woman in such circumstances could blame would be another woman rather than her husband. Therefore, all of the reports depicted women as perceiving other women as threatening—the feminists in particular were shown to be most threatening to the wives.

In contrast, in the Western reports, men were the ones being blamed by their wives. The wife could not accept the treacherous man again, because this was simply portrayed as intolerable for a Western woman from an individualistic perspective. In such circumstances, the wife would normally warn the other woman about how the man really was. Sometimes the two women got together to attack the man for creating the mess or repeating the history. Some reports even described a situation in which both ex-wife and the "other" woman lived together to care for one another. Their emotional bond (or sisterhood) was established due to the common man.

The Loser

In such a battle, who is the loser? In Taiwanese scripts, the ultimate justification was familism. A marriage (actually a family) would normally not be broken by an extramarital affair. As a result, the third-party woman would be the loser. In contrast, all of the Western stories suggest that "good sex" was a necessary and sufficient condition for such a big decision—a married man would leave his wife and children for a new (and good) sexual relationship with less regret. A woman, for the same sexually driven motive, could be depicted and refer to herself as taking another woman's husband without feeling guilty. Extramarital affairs were "justifiable" as long as the new couple was happy and the old marriage was (sexually) dead. In this context, the wife would be the loser.

In addition, the wife's role in the West was depicted as being more vulnerable than a Chinese wife's role. When the wife was controllable, the man talked about himself as being bored. When the wife was not controllable, then the man was depicted as tired. In either case, the wife's role could push the husband away, even if she was a good wife and a good mother. The significant feature of this depiction is that the role of "wife" was seen as fundamentally threatened. In contrast, my data show that the Chinese wife's role as well as her position as a wife was depicted as being more stable regardless of whether the husband had "resources" to offer to other women. Men normally tended not to leave their wives (actually their families) for another woman, as long as their wives played their roles as a good wife and mother. In other words, the Chinese familism secured the wife's role (although the wife might feel threatened by the "other woman").

Discussion

The two typologies developed from the reported extramarital affairs show similarities and differences between the contemporary Chinese and Western cultural settings. Moreover, these differences point to social change dynamics: the incidence/propensities of the structure and contents of certain types of the affairs. Given the irreversible trends toward gender equality in both structural and ideological senses, certain types of extramarital affairs can be theoretically expected to increase while other types of affairs can be expected to decrease. Other "missing" types not seen in my data can be predicted to appear as a result of social change. Beyond these cross-cultural commonalities of pattern and linkage (both empirically and theoretically) between boundary breaking, values reinforcing and social change regarding extramarital affairs, there are specific cultural meanings, mechanisms and politics that merit attention. In particular, differential roles played by values of familism and individualism affect the meaning of love, sex, marriage, family, fidelity and infidelity in each cultural setting. These can now be addressed.

Meanings of Romantic Love and Sexual Ethics

In both cultural settings, romantic love features prominently. In the

Western cultural setting, romantic love is more central and controlling in all the reported affairs. Romantic involvement and sexual validation is the path to happiness, personal development and a sense of identity. Within marriage, the expressive nature is emphasised and sexuality is necessary for intimacy and individual members' well-being. In this circumstance, sexuality is not only permissible but is obligatory (Edwards and Booth, 1994, p. 233). Passion can fade, and consequently, sexual life can wane. This change is often taken as "personal"—being a bad situation or a personal failure. The women in this context see themselves as offering or having offered love. If it disappears, this is an occasion for loss, regret, self-doubt, resignation or anger. Some move on to the next—become alive again—while some become cynical about so-called love from men. Given that the data in my Western reports is restricted to women's narratives, the subjective feelings and meanings of romantic love of Western men cannot be directly discerned. The only "hint" that can be indirectly derived from women's perceptions in these reports is that for men, romance or "love" is mainly sexually driven.

The sexual ethics revealed in the common theme in my Western reports of extramarital affairs is more toward sexual libertarianism (rather than sexual romanticism). Sex is an act of self-expression and pleasure, or a sign of affection or love. Individuals ultimately have autonomy and are free to pursue their wants—as illustrated particularly in the form and content of sexual pleasure, which often started either in a casual relation and/or with the man "repeating history" and sleeping around. This may be due to the "selectivity" bias of my data, which focused on men leaving their wives for other women. In other words, in this data set, all the marriages were broken by extramarital affairs. These were "libertarian" type of behaviours in the first place. The spirit of sexual romanticism would be shown if there were reports about affair participants going back to their own marriage.

In the Chinese cultural setting, to the "straying" married men, the ideal of romantic love might spark the affair, but it does not control it. Rather, a wider set of forces come into play. Romantic passion is seen as momentary and doomed to fade, which is not comparable to the importance of the familism ideal.

Sex is treated as a natural urge. For Chinese men, if the urge overflows its outlets, it means pressure was relieved and some "clean-up" of consequences would be required. The "extra" sexuality also brings Chinese men status—"extra" wealth and power for materially resourceful men, and extra charm for "spiritually" resourceful men. This "deviance" is actually quite "normal," mirroring the traditional value of Chinese male sexuality and one aspect of masculinity. For Chinese wives, the "objective" or culturally defined meaning of sexuality is tied more to familial responsibilities and gender roles, such as procreation (the most important one) and pleasing the spouses. For women as the first or third party in an extramarital affair, the meaning of sexuality is tied more to romantic love and a desire for emotional support than physical satisfaction. In sum, reports of extramarital romance in Taiwan reveal an integration of the Chinese sociocultural legacy and the Western romantic love ideal. However, the concerns, consequences and endings of extramarital affairs remain resolutely Chinese—familism is still the ultimate value for everyone in cases in which a husband goes astray, and the sexual ethnic is still defined only by the fidelity virtue of women.

Meanings of Infidelity

In the legacy of concubinage and prostitution, Chinese men's needs are given wider scope but less significance. At worst, the infidelity of Chinese men is a detour. The husband is expected to return and is normally "welcomed" back home by his wife. The whole affair has provoked shame. Shame is brought onto the husband, the wife and potentially their families. Shame provides a powerful incentive to simply "bury" the affair within, as it were, the garden of familial responsibilities. Therefore, the infidelity of men reinforces conventional values and solidifies marriage boundaries.

The infidelity of Chinese women, on the other hand, is not a detour. It brings permanent damage—divorce. This dire consequence of female infidelity on marriage, on the other hand, reflects the persistence of, and has reinforced, the traditional values of gender roles, female virtues and patriarchal familism. In other words, gender-specific meanings of infidelity are present in the Chinese context, which permeates the "scripting" of all the reports of extramarital affairs.

All the Western-reported affairs reveal that infidelity is less of a detour and more of an intersection. It is fraught with the intensity of all big decisions: which way to turn? The irruptions of extramarital affairs are treated far more as individually centred concerns and consequences. This is why no "scripts" exist among all the reported extramarital affairs in my Western data. Owing to the centrality of sexuality in affair participants' lives and the intolerance of the spouse from his/her individualistic concern, the prospects of return are less clear (than the Chinese ones). However, the common prospect among all such "individualistic" events is that, regardless of who (husband or wife) is the first party or what the outcome of such events is, affairs are less able to be "buried" in the Western context. Breaking the boundary often results in breaking up the marriage and family. In such an eventful process, shame is much reduced while the impact of guilt is attenuated, rationalised and relocated onto many other objects. For example, "She can't give him happiness, but I can!" Again, Western men's subjective feelings of guilt or shame are beyond my data, but in a few cases, the wives or the third-party women mentioned that the men felt somewhat guilty initially, but their guilty feelings did not last very long. Overall, my data show the meanings of infidelity being less gender-specific in the West (than in the Chinese context).

This is consistent with as well as related to the argument that there is a trend of so-called masculinization of sex in the current of changing Western sexual mores which makes the gender gap smaller (Lawson, 1988; Seidman, 1992).

Constructions of Manhood/Womanhood and Gender Politics in Marital/Extramarital Relations

In the Chinese depictions, the force to push people into extramarital relationships is contingent on whether a man has (material or spiritual) resources to be a saviour for a woman who needs material or emotional support in her life in certain circumstances. The way to end such an event is defined by familism and by the roles of husband/father and wife/mother. As long as a married woman plays her wife and mother roles well, the stray husband will not leave her and their children. He would end the affair and come home to play his husband/father roles in the family. After all, family roles (not individuals) are the concern. In other words, the constructions of manhood and womanhood as well as marital and extramarital relations are determined by the Chinese familism and familial roles. As a result of these primary familial roles and duties in the "big picture" of familism, there tends to be less room for playing, or being presented/represented by, gender politics in both marital and extramarital settings (compared to the Western cultural context).

In contrast, in the Western reported extramarital affairs, gender politics is a more significant feature and dynamism in both marital and extramarital relations. Based on the typology of affairs in this chapter (when a married man is the initiator), the force that pushes a married man into a certain type of affair is determined by the gender politics in his marital relations in terms of whether he can control his wife. However, both kinds of power structures in marriage present problems of boredom, fatigue or marginal feelings that cause the man to seek a woman saviour to provide him with some excitement, comfort or sense of centrality. The depictions of Western manhood and womanhood in marriage do present structural problems for both married men and women. For a married man, whether he has power over his wife or not, something is missing in his marriage. For a woman, whether she is playing a traditional or modern role of being a wife and/or a mother, or whether she is controlled by, or controls, her husband in a marital relation, either way could push her husband away.

In this context, neither men nor women have a more "advantageous" position. Married men are depicted as weak, bored, tired and marginal in the marriage, and they need to be rescued by a woman in an extramarital relation, while married women are depicted as playing an impossible role (always the loser) in gender politics. In addition, in an extramarital relation, a man may be rescued by and depend on a traditional woman to fulfil his sexual and emotional needs. Or, a man could manipulate a powerful woman's resources while also constantly being watched by such a woman, who is often calculating. Or a man could be such a woman's toy. This kind of gender politics in these extramarital relations does not indicate a more "advantageous" position for men compared to the position of the women involved.

Of course, a selectivity issue is involved in this study inasmuch as all reports are about married men who initiated the affairs and left their wives and families for another woman. We don't have enough cases in the data set yet to examine the circumstances, dynamism and consequences when a married woman gets involved in such an affair (rather than her husband). However, theoretically, I wish to argue that it is reasonable to imagine similar gender politics and the potential force to push a married woman into an extramarital relationship: either she controls her spouse in marriage but feels bored, or she cannot control her spouse and feels tired and marginal. In other words, the power relation and politics in marital relations could create the same effect on both husbands and wives (given the cultural ideals of ultimately individualistic concerns and the centrality of sex for an individual's sense of self, worth and well-being), which is a structural limitation in marriage and can be an underlying incentive for both genders to engage in extramarital relations.

The potential force or motive can be the same for both genders.[11] But the types of affairs (format, content and gender politics within the extramarital relation) presented/represented when a married woman has an encounter with a man could be quite different from the four types of affairs presented above when a married man is the initiator, due to the different gender roles in the culture. Therefore, the typology generated from reports of a married man being an initiator is partially reversible when a married woman is an initiator in terms of the linkage between a marital condition to the propensity for an extramarital affair.

Therefore, the cross-cultural comparison of the reported extramarital affairs cannot only reveal the boundary, norms and values related to marriage and family systems, which are a core part of a specific culture, but also shows the relevance of the constructions of manhood/womanhood and the meaning of sexuality to marital infidelity in that culture. The Western-specific problematic manhood/womanhood construction and gender politics revealed in marital and extramarital relations can challenge the Western feminist view that "men are always in an advantageous position in any heterosexual relationship." Moreover, in the Chinese culture, men and woman have given familial roles, and the emphasis of familism and familial structure remains significant in the contemporary Taiwanese setting. The arguments about gender relations developed in the West might not be completely applicable in other cultural settings unless we examine what the "roles" are and what the meanings of those roles are in a specific culture. The contentious ideological debates over sexual ethics (in term of romanticism versus libertarianism) in the West also show little relevance to a context of Chinese sexuality. The cross-cultural comparison of reported marital infidelity has generated many insights for the important issues addressed in this study.

Conclusion

In talking, or making exhortations about, the importance of fidelity, the assumption is that it applies to the "other" in a marital relationship: one is to be "faithful" to the spouse. However the preceding study and discussion suggests that a "deconstruction" of fidelity is possible when viewed from the content of the reports of infidelity. In both cultural settings, fidelity goes beyond the spouse: either fidelity extends to the depths of the self (in the West) or it extends to the depth of family responsibility (in Chinese culture). As a result, in the West, affairs threaten the marriage and yet release the "self" to desire new experiences. For both men and women, an affair is an "intersection point" within a biography: whichever turn is taken is fraught with consequences.

By contrast, in the Chinese cultural setting, affairs threaten individuals' esteem, which is bound to the family. Affairs ignite a momentary episode which is driven by the circumstance to revalidate the marriage, and then, with that validation completed, dissolve itself back into an intergenerational stream of familial expectations. The affair for men is more of a "detour." The patience and persuasion of the wronged wife and the wider kin bring the errant behaviour back to the main road. However, for women who have initiated affairs, the road turns out to be, more likely, a dead end.

Therefore, for individuals who are "allowed" to have affairs (i.e., both genders in the Western cultural setting and Chinese married men in my data), authenticity of self (West) versus responsibility of familial roles (Chinese)—these are the real objects of "fidelity" in each culture. In the next chapter, we will trace the "genesis" of such contrast by digging into each of the cultural roots (Christianity and Confucianism) so that the embedded meanings of sex in Chinese and Western cultures can be revealed.

NOTES

1. This quotation about Trombach is from Plummer, 1995, p. 176.

2. Salamon (1984) conducted interviews with "kept women" in London, exploring the rationale and meanings of being a kept woman. However, "kept women" is only one category of extramarital relations involved.

3. Western feminists emphasise that masculinity in the West is defined in terms of aggression and sexual predatoriness, so the dominant sexual ideologies reflect and reinforce the sexual privileges and power of men. This "male-dominated heterosexuality" makes it difficult for women to assert their needs and desires (Elliott, 1996) and constructs heterosexual identity with the "male in the head" (Holland et al., 1996). Some radical feminists even insist that "heterosex *invariably* involves male domination" (Dworkin, 1993). (This Dworkin quotation is from Duncombe and Marsden, 1996, p. 223.)

4. These nine newspapers include: *Zhongguoshibao; Lianhebao; Libao; Zilizaobao; Ziliwanbao; Lianhewanbao; Zhongshiwanbao; Ziyoushibao and Minshengbao*. All of these newspapers are privately owned and normally take more liberal positions than the newspapers owned by the KMT Party. *Zhongguoshibao* and *Lianhebao* have the largest circulation among all of the newspapers in Taiwan (Tien, 1989).

5. This statement is based on my speculation. The author of this book does not inform readers exactly when these interviews were conducted. My speculation comes from this sentence, "The original concept of the book came over 10 years ago when the marriage of one of my closest and dearest friends in Canada broke up ..." (p. 1).

6. This is the argument in the area of "sociology of the lack of knowledge" in which the exclusion of material is a matter of theoretical and empirical interest in the feminist research area (see Jane Haggis quoted in Reinharz, 1992, p. 163).

7. A typical story with such a "script" can be seen in an article entitled "A Third-Party Story" (*Ziliwanbao,* 19 March, 1992).

8. News reported in *Minshengbao,* 4 August, 1989.

9. An example of such a script can be seen in a story in *Lianhebao* (16 August, 1989).

10. I did not count the frequency for each type of affair among the 47 cases included in the data analysis. This is because, as I mentioned above, the selection of these 47 cases from the Taiwanese newspaper clippings on extramarital affairs was based on one criterion, namely, the case must contain a complete report of the whole process of the affair. Reports that mention only part of the process were not selected for analysis. Therefore, methodologically, it is not appropriate to conduct a frequency count for each type of affair out of the 47 cases as selected as such. The main aim in examining these 47 cases is to discern the *possibilities* of types of participants and resulting affairs.

11. Of course, even with the same potential force or motive, the real "force" may normally be stronger for married men than for women when they have young children. Young children would inhibit women more than men.

Chapter 8

Meal Versus Game: The Embedded Meanings of Sex

In the last chapter of this book, I propose and illustrate a cross-cultural sociological approach to research into the embedded meanings of sex in Chinese and Western cultural settings. The "embedded meaning of sex" can more clearly emerge through cross-cultural contrasts, as well as being traced within each of the cultural traditions, regarding definitions and configurations of human nature, sex, self, human relations, marriage, family and the recognition and validation of being a man, a woman or a "decent" human being. This sociological approach is not only "broad" in terms of being "cross-cultural and comparative," but also "deep" in terms of being "genealogical," by digging into the "roots" of both Chinese and Western cultures.

This research aims to answer the question I have posed throughout this book: Is there something which can be called "Chinese sexuality"? Following from this question, further questions can be posed: If yes, what is it? Is it different from sexuality in another culture such as the Western culture? Is there something which can be called "Western sexuality"? If yes, what is it? This approach, therefore, challenges the adequacy of the Kinsey-type approach, which has been widely used in much research into sexual practices in different societies for several decades.

Converging Figures and an Inadequate Kinsey-type Approach

Much research into sexual practices in different countries has reported a ubiquitous trend toward "permissiveness" in response to so-called modernisation. This type of research has been inspired by the original form it took in Kinsey (Kinsey, 1948, 1953) and has been conducted in both Western and Asian countries in the past several decades. A common approach has compared so-called Kinsey rates of specific sexual practices across different societies, and reduced much of the variation of sexual attitudes and behaviours to a "permissiveness" dimension regardless of the society in question. These Kinsey-type studies tend to use the modernisation paradigm to interpret the figures between societies and find a "convergence" in sexual permissiveness in the globalising world. People in a more "modern"/ Westernised context tend to have more liberal or permissive sexual attitudes and behaviours.

In Chapter 4, I critiqued the insensibility of the modernisation paradigm to variations in pathways of changing sexual mores between contemporary Chinese societies due to political economy and colonial experience other than the level of modernisation or "development." This chapter will further critique the insensibility of modernisation paradigm to culture. For example, these Kinsey-type surveys claim that a quiet "sexual revolution" has been happening in various Chinese societies (including Taiwan, Hong Kong and mainland China) in recent decades due to the modernisation process. Yet, compared to the Kinsey figures in Western societies now, the Chinese figures are still quite low. The surveys also claim that sexual mores in 1990s' Chinese societies were actually similar to the 1950s' West, such as having premarital sex primarily in a committed relationship and/or resorting to "shotgun" marriages. Although they were still not as liberal as those of Westerners today, they were similar to those seen in the transition that occurred in the 1950s' West, and they will be loosening more in the future, as evidenced by the fact that the sexual attitudes and behaviours of Chinese people are more open in the 2000s.

This is a simple narrative. Yet, its simplicity betrays a lack of cultural sensitivity. The direct comparison of Kinsey figures across different societies and/or cultures assumes that the sexual behaviours investigated have the same meanings across different cultural settings. It is assumed that everywhere, holding hands is holding hands, kissing is kissing, intercourse is intercourse, an affair is an affair, etc. I will argue that the direct comparison of Kinsey figures is inadequate because while these sexual behaviours may *look* the same, they may not *mean* the same in different cultural settings. In order to make sense of what the Kinsey figures mean, it is important to explore and situate sexual practices on a more fundamental level regarding sex—namely the embedded meaning of sex.

The "embedded meaning of sex" can more clearly emerge through cross-cultural contrasts of different definitions and configurations regarding human nature, sex, self, human relations, marriage, family and the recognition and validation of being a man, a woman or a "decent" human being. Without grounding sex in cross-cultural settings, the embedded meanings of sex would be harder to be made visible because people take for granted that they know what sex means within their own culture. Cross-cultural contrasts show different possibilities, and people in a specific culture have a distinct "home base" regarding how their embedded meaning of sex operates.

This chapter will illustrate a cross-cultural sociological approach to reveal different embedded meanings of sex in two cultural settings—each is based on a major world religion (as defined by Weber).[1] Confucianism in one and Christianity in the other. The illustration will include four major sections. The first section reconceptualises the notion of "sex" by differentiating it into three distinct dimensions (i.e., the purposes of sex, sexual practices and the embedded meanings of sex) and defines "culture" through Weber's world religions with a comparative approach that differs from Weber's comparative methodology.

The second section grounds sex in world religions by tracing and digging into the cultural origins (as defined in the Confucian classics and Christian scriptures), and contrasting core cultural ideals and configurations regarding self, family and individual recognition, validation, completion and transcendence as well as the relevance of sex to these cultural configurations. Different metaphors and embedded meanings of sex emerge from such cross-cultural contrasts: "meal" for "sustenance" in Chinese cultural settings versus "game" for "individual recognition, validation and completion" in Western cultural settings.

The third section elaborates this finding of different embedded meanings of sex with contemporary cultural representations and existing social research data as well as how the same embedded meaning of sex is implicated in men and women in different ways within each of two cultural settings.

The final section discusses significant implications of my research approach and findings.

(Re)conceptualising Sex

Before presenting this cross-cultural sociological research into the embedded meaning of sex, it is appropriate to isolate distinct levels of analysis. I reconceptualise the notion of "sex" in three distinct dimensions.

Sex encompasses a range of human activities and serves multiple functions, regardless of culture. Sex can deliver procreation. It can also offer recreation. And in the case of recreation, it might also be the consummation of a relationship or a service (perhaps for payment). It might also express other emotions: sex can express love; it can express anger. Therefore, the first dimension involves the (multiple) purposes of sex, including procreation, maintenance (urge release), expression (of romantic love,[2] affection, emotional intimacy, commitment, or erotic desires toward someone), recreation (play, pleasure, fun) and exchange for "valuables" (e.g., money, power). These multiple purposes of sex, which have been in evidence in most places and for most of human history, are not the focus of my cross-cultural sociological research into the embedded meanings of sex.

The second dimension concerns sexual attitudes, behaviours and mores that I call "sexual practices." This dimension has been studied by social scientists since the early twentieth century. For example, Unwin (1934) differentiated societies into "uncivilised" versus "civilised" and surveyed 80 "uncivilised" societies and a few "civilised" societies in various historical periods. He found that the "civilised" societies had compulsory sexual regulations that lead to more social energy. Such energy was rationalistic, expansive and productive. The "uncivilised" societies were in states of "lesser energy" (Unwin, 1934, p. xv). In other words, Unwin regarded sexual mores as an "independent variable" that had effected on the level of civilisation of a society.

The more recent and the most famous example has been the so-called Kinsey-type empirical studies mentioned above. Sexual practices are "measurable" in Kinsey's surveys, and they vary between individuals as "dependent variables" according to the social, economic and psychological background factors of individuals. At aggregated levels, sexual practices vary between different social strata, groups, regions or historical times within the same society/cultural setting and across different societies/cultural settings.

Unwin and Kinsey-type studies of sexual practices across societies or cultures seem based on two notions. One is the notion of "development," e.g., sexual regulations lead to "civilisations" (as in Unwin's study); "modernisation" leads to sexual permissiveness (as in Kinsey-type studies). The other notion (or actually assumption) is that similar sexual behaviours have similar transparent meanings, regardless of where they occur.

However, the direct comparison of sexual practices across different cultural settings is not illuminating and even possibly obscuring regardless of whether they were regarded as an "independent variable" (as in Unwin's study or as a "dependent variable" as in Kinsey's study), because the same sexual practices may not have the same embedded meanings. Consequently, it is problematic to claim an association between "development"/"modernisation" and sexual practices across societies or cultures. What these sexual practices signify is tied to a cultural setting. This creates a third dimension in relation to sex.

The third dimension, which I call "the embedded meaning of sex" in a specific culture, is the focus and outcome of a cross-cultural sociological research project I propose here. The embedded meaning of sex could be associated with the purpose(s) of sex, but it is on a different level from the purpose(s): it tends to be (generally) less visible than the (often) obvious purposes. For example, an earlier cross-cultural study of sexual customs and practices found that a guest having sex with his host's wife was a way of showing "hospitality" in the Eskimo context (Gregersen, 1986).[3] This "unconventional" function or purpose of sex is *obvious* to the people in that society, which is a "first-order" subjective account from the locals in Schutz's terminology (Schutz, 1967), or an ethnographic finding from research based on the cultural influence models of sexuality in anthropology (starting around 1920 and remaining influential in contemporary works) using an "emic" approach (Pike, 1967).

The cultural influence models emphasise variations in sexual practices through cross-cultural surveys or in ethnographic accounts of single societies with sexual norms and practices different from those of Euro-Americans. They suggest human sexuality being malleable and capable of assuming different forms as well as critique Kinsey's "counting sexual acts" as ignoring what sexual acts mean to local people (Vance, 2007). However, locals' (obvious) subjective sexual meanings are relevant to but not equal to the notion of the *embedded* meaning of sex that I am presenting in this chapter.

The embedded meaning of sex in a specific culture can more clearly *emerge* through comparative research, particularly via *contrasts* beyond sexual practices and into the wider social structure and deeper cultural configurations which frame humans and define manhood/ womanhood and personhood between different cultural settings.

In other words, if we only study one culture, even from the "emic" approach, to find a "first-order" subjective account from the locals, "the embedded meaning of sex" remains harder to emerge because people in the same culture would likely take for granted what sex "obviously" means in certain situations within that culture (e.g., an Eskimo husband would let his wife have sex with his guest). Or, even if the Kinsey-type approach undertakes comparative studies, their comparison is only on the dimension of sexual practices. The notion of the embedded meaning of sex cannot clearly emerge either because the direct comparison of the "Kinsey figures" assumes that "sex is sex" (so obvious!).

Without the notion and the knowledge of the embedded meaning of sex in a specific culture, it will be difficult to make sense of the "figures" or to make any valid comparison between those figures across different cultures. I will use "the embedded meaning of sex" and "the meaning of sex" interchangeably in this chapter.

Comparing Cultures Defined by World Religions

What is "culture" here? The basis for this cross-cultural variation, I argue, relates to "world religions" as defined by Weber (Bendix, 1973; Gerth and Mills, 1977). World religions are a "religiously determined system of life regulation" (Gerth and Mills, 1977, p. 267), and they frame the meanings of mundane social interaction. World religions provide a "sacred canopy" (Berger, 1966) of meaning over the everyday world. While sex can function in such a mundane fashion, it can unleash intensities and issues beyond the narrow confines of sexual behaviour. Each world religion provides distinctive meanings, models and metaphors of sexual encounters.

Weber focused on contrasting different orientations toward man and God between Confucianism and Puritanism with reference to the meanings of religious worldviews for man's life on earth and how these meanings influence man's conduct, particularly his economic conduct (Bendix, 1973). In my research, using Weber's notion of world religion, I explore specifically how aspects of cultural ideals and configurations in Confucianism and Christianity impact the embedded meanings of sexual conduct in the two traditions as well as in contemporary Chinese and secular Western settings.

It may look oversimplified to categorise the contemporary secular West as a cultural setting based on Christianity and countries in contemporary East Asia as a cultural setting based on Confucianism, given multiculturalism as well as the fact that "culture" and subcultures in each of the regions and subregions have been changing and developing their own paths within the "West" and East Asia. But my approach and argument proposed in this chapter are focused on the most *dominant* cultural tradition as the "root" in each of the major contemporary cultural settings. This "root" is defined by the major ethico-religious traditions in that cultural context. The major ethico-religious traditions are "world-religions" in Weber's use of the term. For example, the influence of Confucianism, one major world religion, as a cultural root is visible in today's East Asia and some countries in Southeast Asia, notably Japan, China, South Korea, Hong Kong, Taiwan and Singapore. Tu Wei-ming (1996) emphasised the Confucian role and "its presence virtually in every aspect of interpersonal relations in East Asian life" (p. 5), although each of these countries has had its own culture evolving in history and presented in its current form. Similarly, the most dominant cultural tradition, or "root," of Western civilisation and today's Western world has been "Christianity," regardless of the fact that Christianity itself has undergone major transformations in its own history as well as being presented diversely in different regions and subregions in the West.

The comparative approach I am proposing here differs from Weber's approach (Smelser, 1976). Weber argued that a relationship exists between Protestant ethics and the spirit of capitalism. His conclusion was based on a comparison between Protestant and other societies based on world religions in which the particular (Protestant) type of ethics was lacking and consequently the spirit of capitalism was not developed. Weber's primary focus was on Protestant societies, and he used the "lacking" (of both the Protestant ethics and capitalism) in other world religions to "back up" his argument regarding the impact of Protestant ethics on capitalism. This approach has limits. As Smelser (1976) points out, "Even if a certain factor—such as extensive internal trade or a monetary system—is positively associated with cases of nondevelopment of capitalism, this does not prove that it is not a necessary condition for the development of capitalism ... Weber's line of reasoning thus established the nonsufficiency but not the nonnecessity of such factors" (Smelser, 1976, p. 13).

Therefore, in the comparative approach illustrated below, I treat the two cultural settings (defined by Confucianism and Christianity) on an *equal* ground: the embedded meaning of sex in each of the two cultural settings cannot emerge except in contrast with the cultural configurations of "the other."

This approach is along the lines of one of the two approaches in "comparative macrosociology," namely "case-orientated" comparative sociology, which treats each nation/culture as a whole historicistic "holism" with its own "complex and unique socio-historical configuration" (Skocpol and Somers, 1980, p. 178). The comparison between "Chinese cultural settings" and "Western cultural settings" may be criticised by poststructuralists as "essentialising" both cultures, but the scope and logic of comparative sociology is far beyond the "essentialism" idea or concern raised by poststructuralists.

In the comparative sociology tradition, each case/culture has its own historical particularities and cultural configurations, but this does not imply that anything is being "essentialised" within any case/culture. "Case" in comparative sociology is a methodological unit, which is unrelated to whether this "case"/culture is being essentialised. Therefore, in my approach, "Chinese cultural settings" and "Western cultural settings," can be looked upon as two cases in comparative macrosociology, because they are holistic entities grounded in their own civilisational traditions defined by world religions, historical particulars and cultural configurations during contemporary processes of modernisation and globalisation.

Grounding Sex in World Religions

The significance of sexual encounters will vary to the extent that world religions have different definitions and configurations regarding human nature, sex, self, human relations, marriage, family and the recognition and validation of being a man, a woman or a "decent" human being. In this section, I will contrast these aspects of cultural ideals in Confucianism and Christianity. Before "grounding" these aspects in the cultural scriptures in the Confucian classics and Christian Bible, I would briefly address one issue regarding whether the masses within these cultural traditions are exposed to, or live by, their cultural ideals. It has been argued that Christianity has a missionary drive to engage and convert (subvert) the popular cultures with which it makes contact. Christianity can then be seen as a mass religion which aims to incorporate everyone.

By contrast, it has been argued that Confucianism was produced primarily as literati doctrines (Bendix, 1973, p. 127). The masses, by implication, would not be "touched" by such doctrines, remaining instead within the popular or folk forms of Taoism and some elements of Buddhism. While Confucianism does not have a "missionary zeal," it did permeate the wider Chinese culture—even of the masses. Confucianism had an influence way beyond its intellectual stratum. It had always been the dominant creed of the Chinese empire. To some extent Confucianism suppressed, tolerated or even absorbed some of the beliefs of the masses which were influenced by Taoism and Buddhism[4] (Bendix, 1973; Gerth and Mills, 1977; Kwok, 1998). In addition, as some have argued, the Great Tradition and Little Traditions were always closely connected in Chinese cultural contexts (Redfield, 1962; Johnson et al., 1985) because of various sociocultural mechanisms, e.g., the role of "market town" for peasants, popular folk songs, drama, plays and stories, as well as memorable and "children friendly" *sanzijing* (Three-Word Scriptures or poems). A comprehensive and competitive imperial civil service examination (started in the Tang Dynasty), which was the primary mechanism for the masses to memorise the required Confucian classics and to pursue upward mobility (under a social prestige hierarchy with officialdom or intellectuals at the top), had impact across the Chinese empire.

Individuals and "Self"

A "Self" Defined by Family Versus an Individualised Self

In Confucianism, although there is the notion of "individuation," the unit of society is the family (rather than individuals) and the focus is on human relations, radiating out from the family. The notion of individuation, as emphasised by the notion of "self-cultivation," is *not* for individuals themselves; instead, it is for the sake of family and human relations. Some phrases presented in the first chapter of *Great Learning* are, "self-cultivation of an individual (*xiushen*) can make his/her family harmonious (*qijia*), and harmonious families can make the whole country manageable (*zhiguo*) which can lead to the conquering of the whole world (*pingtienxia*)."[5] Also, "Harmony in the family can make everything thrive." An individual being able to manage his/her family well has the same importance as if the person pursues a political career to run the country.[6]

The nature of human relations in society is based on the same nature of relations in the family. The principle of familial relations with its hierarchical nature and familial roles is projected into the human relations and social structure in the wider community and society. Confucian social order is constructed on the notion of *lun* (differentiation among role relations), and there are five fundamental relations defined in Confucianism, so-called *wulun*. The five Confucian cardinal relations are: emperor-subordinates, father-son, older brother-younger brother, husband-wife and friend-friend in the society. Principles associated with the five cardinal relations are: between father and son there should be affection; between ruler and subordinates there should be righteousness; between husband and wife there should be attention to their separate functions; between old and young there should be a proper (hierarchical) order and between friends there should be sincerity.[7]

The social norms are determined by the so-called *sangang wuchang* (three principles and five constant virtues). The three principles are: the emperor is the principle of subordinates; the father is the principle of the son; and the husband is the principle of the wife. The five constants of cultivation are: *ren* (benevolence); *yi* (righteousness); *li* (propriety); *zhi* (knowledge/wisdom) and *xin* (sincerity). Four out of these five constant virtues are "virtues" in relations to others.

In this cultural context, the family is the main context in which to understand the nature of the self (Tu, 1996). Individuals (*ren*) are defined and embedded *within* multiple layers of human relations, which produce what I call a "familial self" for individuals. The multiple layers of human relations are based on familism, seniority and harmony as core values. Under these core values, filial piety is the most fundamental and required moral virtue, which can be illustrated by two examples in the *Works of Mencius*. Mencius preached, "*Ren ren qin qi qin, zhang qi zhang, er tien xia tai ping.*" (If each person loves his/her parents and shows the respect for the elderly members in the family, the world will be in peace).[8] Also, "*Wu fu wu chun, shi qing shou ye.*" (A person who cannot acknowledge and respect his/her father or emperor is an animal).[9]

By the Han Dynasty, filial piety had already become institutionalised as a criterion for the selection of persons into officialdom (Kwok, 1998, p. 6). This explains a comment such as this: "Chinese people don't have [Western kind of individualistic] 'selves'!" The "self" here, as a centre of relationships rather than as an isolated individual, is primarily defined in terms of reciprocal duties and moral obligations to others rather than as a self-expanding claim to individual rights, autonomy or transcendence beyond existing social bonds as in the West (King, 1994; Tu, 1996; Kwok, 1998). The direction of the interpersonal transaction is actually toward others (rather than focused on the "self"), just as Confucius says, "*Bu huan ren zhi bu ji zhi, huan bu zhi ren ye*" (I am not afflicted with not being understood by others; instead, I am afflicted with not understanding others) (*Analects* 1:16).

Regarding the self in the West, the individualism prevalent in secular contemporary times actually has its root in Christian traditions in which "individuation" is achieved in opposition to, or beyond, "family." The Judeo-Christian God "disrupts" relations between generations—especially between father and son. Thus, the seemingly bizarre story in Genesis of God's instruction to Abraham to sacrifice his own son and Abraham obeying God's order (although in the end an angel holds back Abraham's arm just before he sacrifices his son)[10] (Genesis 22: 1–2). Here, both filial piety and paternal care are brought under the sway of individual faithfulness to a mighty God figure. Instead of harmony, there is a sacrifice of the family in the name of a God.

Furthermore, in Christianity, the very nature of God defines individuation: the embodiment of the Christian principle in a unique case. The incarnation (of Jesus) is the complete unity of human and divine natures in the fully embodied Word (Gudorf, 1994, p. 11). Consequently, this unique "case" becomes a generalised mechanism in terms of the revelation of God as given through a "Jesus figure." Through this exemplary figure, Christianity is able to talk about "individualised" individuals who separate from familial, tribal and local affinities. In the Bible, Jesus asked His followers to leave their families and follow Him. For example, Luke 18:29–30: "I tell you the truth," Jesus said to them, "no one who has left home or wife or brothers or parents or children for the sake of the kingdom of God will fail to receive many times as much in this age and, in the age to come, eternal life" (New International Version, 2000, p. 144).

Also, the idea of social justice in the contemporary world is rooted in Christian ideas about individuals: "Before God, everyone is equal." "Everyone is God's child." Even Jesus' phrase, "The poor shall inherit the earth" focuses on each poor person as an individual (e.g., the parable of the "Good Samaritan" is about helping each particular person as the need arises), and each poor person has to deal with his/her own salvation. In other words, the unit of Christianity is, primarily and ultimately, individuals who have faith in God (and are in receipt of grace from God) rather than families.

Although individuals belong to, or participate in, various social institutions in kinships, churches and the feudal system in different historical periods, Christianity has had a tendency to revert to the fundamentals of individual faith. The Reformation in the sixteenth century strengthened the individualisation of Christians through their being encouraged to directly connect to and communicate with God. The Protestant reformation drove Christian thinking back to individuals with a zeal that has had wide and long-term consequences for Western society.

Individual Transcendence: This Worldly Versus Other Worldly Orientation

Confucianism has a positive view toward human nature, based on Mencius's doctrine of the goodness of human nature: "*renxing ben shan*" (the basic human nature is kindness).[11] In addition, this good human nature presumes an interrelation between self and others, as expressed in *Four Beginnings* by Mencius. The heart has all four elements of kindness (in relation to others): "*Ce yin zhi xin, ren je you zhi; xiu er zhi xin, ren je you zhi; gong jing zhi xin, ren je you zhi; shi fei zhi xin, ren je you zhi.*" (Humans have the sense of sympathy, of shame, of deference to others and of judging right and wrong).[12]

Confucianism has a "this worldly" orientation (or an "inner worldly" orientation, according to Weber), so the self-cultivation of (familial) relations-defined individuals is *within* social structure—a moral character will fulfil duties and responsibilities with others and bring peace and harmony in and between all five cardinal relations.

Is there a super force beyond humans and social relations in this "worldly" orientation? There is the notion of *tien* (heaven), but *tien* does not mean a "paradise" like heaven or like "a supramundane

God" (in Weber's term). *Tien* is part of the universe or nature; *tien* is big and awesome. There is a *lau tien ye* (an elderly godlike figure) in the "heaven" to watch what humans do on earth. The godlike *lau tien ye,* according to Weber, is "an impersonal spirit of heaven" in contrast to "a supramundane God," a personal Father in heaven, as in Christianity (Bendix, 1973, p. 137). *Tien* (heaven), *di* (earth) and *ren* (humans) all are parts of the *daziran* (big nature or universe), and coexist in balance and harmony. Becoming a *shenren* (sage), the ultimate "reach" of the transcendence of individuals through self-cultivation is to this highest moral and spiritual state—harmony between human relations as well as *tien ren he yi* (unity of humans and heaven, and harmony between humans and the big nature).

Wang Yang-ming, a great Confucian scholar in the Ming Dynasty (1368–1644) said that "the way to sagehood lies within one's own nature" (de Bary, 1970, p. 13). This earlier Confucian idea, *tien ren he yi,* developed into the Neo-Confucian doctrine which sees "the human man [forming] one body with heaven-earth and all things." As stated by de Bary (1970), "For the Neo-Confucian, ... self-transcendence should be attained not by denying one's humanity but affirming it" (de Bary, 1970, p. 15). "Unselfish performance of duty to others was a discipline of ordinary life leading to both self-transcendence and self-fulfilment" (de Bary, 1970, p. 17).

The sanction of an individual's wrongdoings is through the external mechanism of shame (represented by losing face in public), shaming the individual him/herself and the whole family. *Ren bu ke yi wu chi, wu chi zhi chi, wu chi yi* (Humans cannot live without the sense of shame. When a person doesn't have a sense of shame, it is a big shame on him/her) (*Works of Mencius*, Book 7 Jin Xin, Part 1, Chapter 6, p. 616). The worst an individual can do is to bring shame to his/her ancestors, as evidenced by the saying, *Buyao diu zuzong badai de lian* (Don't let your ancestors of the past eight generations lose face).

In contrast, Christianity has a negative view of human nature which says that humans are "defective" (fallen) in relation to God. This "fallen nature" is itself inscribed within the privileging of "free will": within the Creation mythology, it is humans (Adam and Eve) who freely chose to deny an injunction from their God and thus find themselves thrown from the Garden of Eden.

At odds with the Confucian orientation of adjustment to "this world," Christianity has an "other worldly" orientation (termed by Weber). Humans are made in the holy "image" of God, but they are not divine/spiritual/flawless like God. They can work and purify themselves in order to become closer to the image of God as well as to be recognised and validated by God. There is a possibility here for a body/spirit dualism to emerge. Over time and under the influence of Greek thinking, Christianity increasingly developed a dualism in which "flesh" had a propensity for evil. The human body and flesh are not part of the image of a spiritual God. The semidivine human has to overcome his/her flesh and weakness (due to physical needs) so that his/her mind/spirit can be enhanced and transformed.

Individual transcendence is achieved by moving away from the sinful (physical) aspects of human nature and toward the holy/spiritual image of God. The sanction for an individual's bad nature and behaviours (which distance the individual from God) is primarily through the notions of (internal) guilt and sin. Although Christianity teaches Christians to love their neighbours and to be devoted to their communities and churches, the ultimate orientation is "other worldly" in terms of salvation in heaven, the final destination. Even the most primary social institution, i.e., the family formed by marriage or a conjugal bond, did not have a positive connotation in early Christianity and in the Middle Ages—"normal" and safe marital sex was used for curtailing sexual desires: "for it is better to marry than to burn with passion" (1 Corinthians 7:1). Marriage and family were merely "negative" means to achieve the Christian moral end (unlike in Confucianism where the family and familism are the ultimate "positive" ends).

Individual Recognition/Validation and Completion: Familial Roles Versus the Most Significant Other

Under "this worldly" Confucian tradition, the significant others are within the social structure, from living family members (particularly parents) to ancestors (*laozuzong*, old ancestors back thousands of years). The "name" and reputation of an individual starts from within the family (having a harmonious family). In extreme and rare cases, the "good name" can be made for posterity (*ming quei qien shi*, leaving your name in thousands of years of history, which can honour the ancestors). So, all the significant "others" are *within* social structure and history.

The recognition and validation of being a man, a woman or a decent person in general (for everyone) is primarily by fulfilling one's familial roles. The (familial) relations-defined "individuals" do not need to (yearn to) be "recognised" as "individualised" individuals; they are recognised as part of the human network defined by familial relations and roles. Consequently, in terms of "cultural ideals," the "completion" of a man is to continue his family line by having son(s).[13] The "completion" of a woman is to marry into another family to have "permanent position" by being a wife and a mother.[14] But, in terms of "social realities," some men only have daughters and some women never marry. There are "alternative" social arrangements in Chinese societies by which men and women in these nonideal circumstances "complete themselves."[15]

In contrast, in Christianity, a personal supramundane God is the ultimate significant other and heaven is the final destination. The ultimate recognition/validation of being a man, a woman or a decent individual, as well as the ultimate completion of a human, is defined by two aspects of the human-God relation.

One (major) aspect of human nature in Christianity, as discussed earlier, is defined as being "defective" or "fallen." Another is defined as being "incomplete." Some theologians (Bailey, 1959) posit that humans are created in the "image" of God and this "image" of God is "trinitarian" in nature (i.e., God is three relations). Humans are created in "trinitarian relations," and humans cannot exist in solitude. An "alone" individual is "incomplete" in his/her human nature. Furthermore, these theologians stress that God is love. Therefore, humans created in these three relations are yearning to give and receive love (in fellowship) and to achieve mutual fulfilment and completion in the grace of God's love.[16]

These two aspects of human nature as defined in Christianity are on different levels. The fallen aspect of humans motivates a sinful individual human to improve and enhance him/herself toward the "perfect" spiritual image of God. The "incomplete" aspect of humans actually provides (and/or makes individuals yearn for) a loving context (i.e., grace) in which an individual resides when the (defective) individual is working hard to grow toward, or get closer to, God in his/her spiritual journey. This loving context situates an individual human in "relations," both in fellowship and in relation with God. Individual humans are not alone, or at least are not "meant" to be alone.

In summary, every human yearns to become closer to the perfect/divine (image of) God in order to overcome his/her "defective" nature. They also yearn for love and communion with/in God in order to round out their "incomplete" nature. Therefore, the relationship between an individual and God is especially intense and intimate. This special relationship between an individual and God became most direct after the Reformation. "Individuals" (as humans) have a need and yearning to be recognised as decent individuals by, and to be loved and in communion with, this most significant other.

Relevance of Sex: Yin/Yang Balance for Natural Urge Versus Sin/Guilt as Moral Ethics

As mentioned in Chapter 4, there is the famous saying in Confucianism, "*Shi se xing ye*" (Eating food and having sex are in the nature of human beings), defining sexuality more as a natural urge than as a social encounter or a basis for the most crucial aspect of moral ethics defined in Christianity.

In Taoism, "Yin" (female, as a negative force) and "Yang" (male, as a positive force) are complementary and should be holistically united into a balanced natural order in the universe (Lin et al., 1995). Sexual pleasure and satisfaction is therefore appropriate for both sexes. The *Sunujing* (Classics for plain women) describes bed chamber sexual skills and techniques that enable both men and women to be sexually competent and capable of reaching satisfaction. Western poststructuralist feminism argues that such an appetite for sex or sex itself is far from "natural," because many ancient Chinese sex philosophy and bedchamber arts manuals were actually written from a male perspective despite various techniques aimed at giving pleasure to women (Farquhar, 2002). From the level of everyday life, however, this view of sex being a natural part of the cosmic universe has been believed and lived by most Chinese people (even today).

These natural aspects of sex imply not that people could or should have sex all the time. A balance is required between the two elements or forces of Yin and Yang. For while, Yang can *enrich* Yin, and Yin can *exhaust* Yang. The prospect of exhaustion, for men, is related to the view that men have only limited semen (the essence of vitality): although historically, Chinese men were allowed to have multiple legitimate outlets for their ("extra") sexual urge (wife, concubines, courtesans and prostitutes), too many ejaculations could weaken men's energy or even fatally "drain" them (Tseng, 1970; Wen, 1995). In this sense, some women are portrayed in classical novels as "man killers"—due to their capacity for inciting sexual activity (Kang, 1996).

Taoism contains a range of techniques that enable men to reach orgasm without ejaculating (Ruan, 1991).

The more sensible path, though, for health and a good life, is simply to temper the sexual appetite. Therefore, there is a "constraint" on this natural urge—more like the advice that not only will eating too much food make people sick but eating too much "cold" food or "hot" food is also unhealthy. Various taboos in Chinese culture on eating and having sex are all based on the same logic in terms of keeping the balance between "Yin" and "Yang" with the body as well as between the body and nature.[17]

As discussed before, in the traditional Chinese cultural settings, the exercise of sex was not normally associated with a feeling of sin or moral guilt as long as sex was with the right party in the right place (van Gulik, 1974; Hsu, 1983). The violation of the "right party" and/or place was associated with "shame" to the individuals involved and to their family members. Male homosexuality was not ideal (due to it not being with the "right party") but tolerable as long as homosexual men still got married and produced offspring to continue the family line. It was even acceptable in the case of the emperor or in the upper class in historical China (Hinsch, 1990; Lau and Ng, 1989). Lesbianism was less visible than male homosexuality, and it was also tolerated (Ruan et al., 1992; Hinsch, 1990), particularly because it didn't involve the issue of continuing the (patriarchal) family line.

In contrast to this naturalized Yin/Yang balanced view of sex, as defined in Confucian/Taoistic traditions, sex has always been "a big deal" in Christianity and Christians have traditionally "worried the most about sexuality" (Posner, 1992, p. 15). As well as being a major theme in the most dominant discourse in Christianity, to most theologians, sex has had negative connotations and moral implications with the result that "morality is essentially sexual morality" (Uta Ranke-Heinemann, 1990, p. 13, in Nye, 1999, p. 34). "The traditional code of Christian sexual ethics is for understanding both sexuality and morality"

(Gudorf, 1994, p. 1). Robert Nye (1999) provides a good summary of the relevance of sex to ethics and morality in Christianity:

> The early Christians deeply distrusted their sexual impulses because they bound them to the earthly, human sphere. The most devout attempted to purge themselves altogether of desire; the married majority were enjoined to restrict sexual desire to procreate coupling. In the Middle Ages, a revival of Greek medical learning elevated discussions of sexual matters into a topic for theological disputations. The medieval church acknowledged the necessity of pleasure in marital, procreative sex, but forbade all other carnal contact, warning believers in particular about the dangers of loose women. The growth of stronger state authority in the period after 1500 provided religious elites with more power to regulate sexuality closely and greater reason for princes—in the name of public order—to see danger in forms of sexual expression that violated patriarchal and procreative norms (Robert Nye, *Sexuality*, 1999, p. 13).

In early Christianity and Catholicism, due to the "defective" nature of humans based on the body/spirit dualism discussed above, the sex act of the human being can only be justified for the purpose of procreation. Nonprocreative sexual pleasures (e.g., masturbation, adultery, homosexual acts, prostitution, pornography) were regarded as sinful evils. "Sex is, at best, a necessary evil ... when that evil ... is stressed rather than the necessity—to the glorification of celibacy and virginity as holier states than marriage" (Posner, 1992, pp. 15–16).

Even the acceptance of, and the value placed on, marital (procreative) sex in Christianity did not aim to strengthen the conjugal or family bond; instead, the latent function was to provide a safe outlet and prevent individuals from engaging in dangerous sexual temptations and sinful sexual acts. For example, St Paul strove to point out that "marriage was safer than unconsidered celibacy" (Peter Brown,

1988, p. 54, in Nye, 1999, p. 35). In the Middle Ages, the Church finally established the legitimacy of marriage and made the marital relationship the single acceptable one for sexual activity, but the marital bond was still seen as "an imperfect foundation for a reliable regulation of sexuality" (Nye, 1999, p. 40).

The Reformation in the sixteenth century brought changes to the church system, but Protestantism did not challenge the ascetic cast of the traditional spirituality (Gudorf, 1994, p. 208) or challenge its emphasis on sacrificial (physical and material) suffering when pursuing spirituality (Gudorf, 1994, p. 209).

Protestantism and pre-Reformed Christianity (i.e., early Christianity and Catholicism) had a similar view overall toward the family as an institution: they did not value "family" per se because actualising the spirit and principles of Christianity was via individual cultivation and loyalty to God. On this front, the attachment and loyalty to family would have become a rival force distancing an individual from God, distracting his/her devotion from God. This perception can be seen in 1 Corinthians 7:32–35, "I would like you to be free from concern. An unmarried man is concerned about the Lord. But a married man is concerned about the affairs of this world—how he can please his wife—and his interests are divided. An unmarried woman or virgin is concerned about the Lord's affairs. Her aim is to be devoted to the Lord in both body and spirit. But a married woman is concerned about the affairs of this world—how she can please her husband. I am saying this for your own good, not to restrict you, but that you may live in a right way in undivided devotion to the Lord" (New International Version, 2000, p. 291).

However, Protestantism and pre-Reformed Christianity had different views toward celibacy and marriage. While the former valued the idea of companion marriage and the conjugal bond itself over celibacy, the latter valued celibacy more and had a negative view toward marriage (i.e., seeing marriage only as a safe outlet for procreative sex). Luther insisted that marriage was the natural state of life, even for the minister. In Calvinist "domesticated (marital) sexuality, sex is reproduction as well as a way of cherishing and loving the spouse" (Gudorf, 1994, p. 208). In this regard, sexual intimacy in a loving relationship means letting two individuals share their love and enjoy meaningful communion with one other in the grace of God (Nelson, 1978). Therefore, compared to that of early Christianity and Catholicism, Protestantism's sex theology was less severe in terms of not just treating marital sex as a (negative) mechanism for defending nonprocreative sexual temptation (due to the "defective" aspect of human nature) but also strengthening the marital bond as a communion for fulfilling the individual's yearning for love and completion (due to the "incomplete" aspect of human nature).

Meal Versus Game: Different Embedded Meanings of Sex Emerge from Contrasting Chinese and Western Cultural Settings

The Embedded Meaning of Sex in Chinese Cultural Settings: Meal and Sustenance

In summary, the embedded meaning of sex in the Confucian/Taoistic cultural settings can be seen as *sustenance* and the metaphor of sexual encounter can be seen as a *meal* because Confucianism treats sexual appetite as a natural urge. Just as people shouldn't eat too much and should have proper eating manners, so too should people maintain a Yin-Yang balance in sex; too much sex is not healthy. Proper manners for conducting sex are sexual norms, which include the right place (i.e., the bedroom) and the right parties (for a woman, her husband;

for a man, his wife, plus concubines and prostitutes). This has created a lasting cultural legacy.

In the postconcubine era (even today), many young Chinese men's first sexual experiences are with prostitutes and many Chinese men's extramarital affairs remain somewhat tolerated by their spouses and by the wider society (1990 Hong Kong Family Planning Association Report; Chang, 1999). The violation of sexual norms would bring shame to individuals and family members—no sin or guilt would be involved.

The recognition and validation of being a man, being a woman or a decent person in Chinese cultural settings has more to do with a person's familial roles rather than with his/her sexuality. They find that even in modern times, concepts of masculinity and femininity still seem to be anchored primarily in the roles of mother/father and wife/husband (Brownell and Wassertrom, 2002; Barlow, 1994). As evidenced in Chapter 5, highly educated youths in major cities in China, Hong Kong and Taiwan tend to define "self" or "who they are" by their familial roles.

The Embedded Meaning of Sex in Western Cultural Settings: (Social) Games and (Individual) Validation and Completion

Overall, in the Western cultural settings, sex has always been a "big deal." As discussed above, in Christian traditions, sex (essentially all nonprocreative sex acts) was critically tied to the "flawed"/defective part of human nature that needed to be repressed or sublimated in order to bring it closer to the flawless image of God. On the one hand, the human "body" is associated with "earthly nature," which goes against the "holy" mind/spirit, as indicated in "Rules for Holy Living" of Colossians 3:5–6, "Put to death, therefore, whatever belongs to your earthly nature: sexual immorality, impurity, lust, evil desires and greed, which is idolatry. Because of these, the wrath of God is coming" (New International Version, 2000, p. 356).

On the other hand, the human "body" is associated with a "holy temple" where God resides so that a human should not engage in immoral sexual activities that go against the "body" and pollute this temple. In 1 Corinthians 6:13, regarding sexual immorality: "The body is not meant for sexual immorality, but for the Lord, and the Lord for the body." In 1 Corinthians 6:18–20, "Flee from sexual immorality. All other sins a man commits are outside of his body, but he who sins sexually sins against his own body. Do you not know that your body is a temple of the Holy Spirit, who is in you, whom you have received from God? You are not your own; you were bought at a price. Therefore, honour God with your body" (New International Version, 2000, p. 297). As a result, as theologian Christine Gudorf (1994) argues: "Humans are in fear of the body and of sexuality in pursuing spirituality" (Gudorf, 1994, pp. 2–3).

Under this antibody (or a body should be "guarded" at least!) and antisex Christian tradition, it would become reasonable to expect an ironic consequence: an individual, as bodily and sexually human, would have a "doubt" about his/her own self-being. If the body with an "earthly nature" is part of the human self, a human would be unsure about this "self" (which contains the body) and consequently, would have doubts about its mind and spirit (which is also part of the human "self").

Gudorf (1994) addressed the "self" issue in a different way. She argued that "one of our deepest Christian problems is our understanding of self" and how we should understand the self when the Christian tradition and even contemporary theologians have ambivalent and contradictory (both positive and negative) views about "self" (Gudorf, 1994, p. 27). Therefore, a sense of insecurity about "Who I am?" or "Am I okay?" will drive an individual to seek ultimate recognition, approval and validation from God or from someone/somewhere.

In the secular West, if God is considered to be dead (Bruce, 2002), how do individuals access, or obtain, the ultimate recognition? I would argue that sexual intimacy with a most significant other has become a primary mechanism for individuals to get (or to imagine or hope to get) such recognition and validation in terms of "I am (or must be) okay" and/or "I am (or must be) special." This need for "reassuring" recognition seems to be becoming more urgent for individuals today because they may feel more insecure in a competitive capitalistic system and feel fragmented in a postmodern setting full of multiple identities, incoherence, boundary crossing and uncertainties. Furthermore, individuals may not yearn for love and communion with God these days, but they still yearn for love and meaningful communion with other individuals due to the (human) nature of incompleteness.

This nature of feeling "incomplete" has become more salient for individuals, being highly "individualised" (Beck-Gershem, 2002) and consequently extremely alone/lonely in a modern/postmodern setting with traditional institutions weakened or collapsed. Sexual encounters with a new partner can then become/seem more intense and "meaningful": "one half soul finds the other half soul" (which is supposed to be "happily ever after" as the major script in all Hollywood romantic comedies).

Sex in a committed, ongoing relationship sometimes may fade, but it is expected or hoped to be able to be rekindled so that the two persons in the relationship can still feel special and validated by each other. The significant other in an ongoing relationship can still make the individual feel "complete" in terms of "without you, there is a big hole in my life"; "you have made my life whole"; "love is two souls fused together." In such a context, sex has become even a bigger deal than ever.

Therefore, sex has always been associated with the recognition/validation and completion of individuals/selves in the West, being either *extremely negative* needs that must be repressed/sublimated (particularly in the presecular settings as defined in the Christian doctrine) or *extremely positive* needs that must be pursued at all costs (which is evident in the fact that one of the most cited grounds for divorce in modern times is extramarital affairs). Hein (2000), as a clinical psychologist, finds from many of her clients that affairs were actually sexual detours to find "self" or to reconfirm (a weak or inadequate) self. Infidels leaving their marriages for affairees are represented in American films as "fidelity to oneself," which is tolerable to American audiences, despite that in reality, Americans tend not to tolerate their spouses having extramarital affairs because such betrayal from spouses have deeply harmed their self-esteem (Pennington, 2007).

In summary, in contrast to the embedded meaning of sex in Chinese cultural settings, in Christianity-based Western cultural settings, the embedded meaning of sex can be seen as *individual recognition/validation and completion,* and the metaphor of the relation used for obtaining such recognition can be described as a (social) *game*—initially between individuals and their God, and then between individuals themselves (whether or not they are heterosexual or homosexual).

The notion of "game" has several connotations. In this chapter, I use it in the sense of an encounter in which individuals anticipate outcomes, impute intentions to significant others or seek a "win" by being recognised. A more colloquial expression of the "game" metaphor lived by modern Westerners can be seen in a popular TV sitcom episode of *Becker*. The 50-something Dr Becker finally got a date with an attractive 30-something diner owner, Chris. His response to getting the date was "I am so happy today, because I thought I was way past the game. Now I am back on the field." During the date, Chris did not eat much in front of her favourite seafood because she didn't want to give Becker an "unladylike" impression (by eating a lot!). This example clearly portrays how individuals in the secular Western settings are playing and living this "game."

The success of a series of *Mars Versus Venus* bestsellers can indicate that men and women yearn to know the "opponent" on the game field. The rich articulations in these books not only highlight the dynamics between the two players in the game but also map out contingent strategies for all moves and countermoves on the field, particularly in the contexts of the first-time encounter with new partners or in ongoing relationships when things go wrong.

Overall Contrasts and Facades of Convergence in Contemporary Times

Both Chinese and Western cultures may indeed have both elements of "meal" and "game" in sexual activities: Westerners certainly have "natural" urges, and Chinese are not that unlikely to "play games" in dating and feel "special" through intense sexual encounters (as well as using sexual desirability or performance to boost "self," an ego!). But I would argue that, relatively speaking, there is a sharp contrast in the "home base" of embedded meanings of sex in everyday life that can be captured by my metaphors, and this contrast can only be revealed in cross-cultural comparisons. The metaphor of sexual encounters revealed as a "game" in the Western cultural settings is particularly visible in many Western (re)presentations of relationships and extramarital affairs. Similarly, the "meal" logic and "not eating too much" are often revealed in representations and "lived through" by Chinese people in their everyday lives.[18]

In terms of sexual norms defined in Christian traditions, the "purpose of sex" was more salient than the right place and the right parties. The purpose of sex was for procreation rather than for physical pleasure. The violation of the sexual norms involved, at least until very recently, guilt and sin. Numerous depictions exist of people who had strayed and enjoyed sexual pleasure, but then had to be punished. A nice example depicting the presecular past can be taken from the movie

Canterbury Tales, about medieval English peasants: They had "good times" in terms of premarital sex and extramarital sex, but they all went to hell at the end.

A modern-day example is the popular American film *Fatal Attraction* in the 1990s in which the protagonist enjoys the affair but feels guilty toward his wife even before the affair became "fatal." Also, the book *Her Version* (Cato, 1995) includes 55 real-life narratives of extramarital affairs, describing how the first and third parties lived through the experience: feelings of excitement and pleasure at the start but then guilt and hurt soon after. Even in today's so-called postmodern West, "guilt" remains a sanction for sexuality, which is evident in many representations. A 2003 French film, *Sex and Lucinda*, showed all the male and female protagonists suffering lifelong guilt and loss (e.g., the death of a child) as a most severe punishment.

Survey data[19] representing people's attitudes are also consistent with the above-mentioned representations. Data in the *General Social Survey of Adult Americans, 1973–1987*, show no change in approval, with 72.6 percent saying that extramarital sexual relations were "always wrong"; in the late 1980s, disapproval increased, averaging a constant 78.9 percent in 1988–1991 (Smith, 1994, p. 68). Another national random survey of 2,994 American men and women (aged 18 to 59) conducted in 1992 shows that roughly 90 percent of respondents believe that extramarital sex is either "always wrong" or "almost always wrong" (Laumann et al., 1994, p. 22). This attitude is also reflected in the behaviour of Americans: the incidence of extramarital activity is modest, only about 16 percent of married adults (similar between men and women, between different birth cohorts) reported having "extra" sexual partners (Laumann et al., 1994, p. 208). This same survey shows that 54 percent of men and 46.8 percent of women felt guilty after masturbation (Laumann et al., 1994, Table 3.1, p. 82).

America may be deviant in terms of having a more traditional value system than other advanced industrial societies in the West (Inglehart et al., 2004, p. 15), but a 1991 national random survey of 18,876 British people also shows high disapproval toward extramarital sex (78.7 percent men and 84.3 percent women think that adultery is always or mostly wrong (Wellings et al., 1994, p. 249)). Overall, from studies in Europe, Michael et al. (1994) find that people in Britain, France and Finland have sexual life courses that are virtually the same as that of Americans.

Furthermore, while secularisation has taken place in most advanced industrial societies in the West, a cross-national survey of human beliefs and values conducted in 2000 finds that many Westerners continue to believe in sin. Among the proportions of people believing in sin, there is no clear pattern or variation between (historically predominantly) Protestant, Catholic and Orthodox societies.[20] In historically Protestant societies, the percentages of those who believe in sin are as follows: Australia (74 percent), Finland (67 percent), Britain (67 percent), Switzerland (66 percent), New Zealand (66 percent), Germany (41 percent), Netherlands (40 percent), Sweden (26 percent) and Denmark (21 percent). In historically Catholic societies, the percentages are: Ireland (86 percent), Italy (73 percent), Spain (51 percent), France (40 percent); in historically Orthodox societies, Greece (73 percent) and Russia (68 percent) (Inglehart et al., 2004, Table F055_1).

The Christian influence on sexuality in today's secular West is also echoed by Horrocks (1997), a psychotherapist in London: "Christian attitudes toward sex have not just been the subject for debate by intellectual clerics, but have penetrated popular thinking. This is important, for while academic scholars may often ignore Christian thinking, it may still be found alive and well in the market-place, or for that matter, in the bedroom. In my work as a therapist, it is clear that many people are still haunted by feelings of guilt and sin, which are partly identifiable as 'Christian'" (Horrocks, 1997, p. 3).

The contrast between the sanctions in the two cultural settings is revealed in another example. As mentioned above, the management of sex is based on the theory of the Yin/Yang balance in the Chinese setting. The ultimate form of consequence for having too much sex for Chinese men is presented in a concept, and sometimes a real sexual epidemic, called *Suo-Yang* (shrunk Yang), which is peculiar to Chinese in Malaysia, Hong Kong, Singapore, Taiwan and mainland China. This illness, so-called a "sex-related culture-bound syndrome" in cultural psychiatry (Mezzich and Berganza, 1984; Bhugra and de Silva, 1993), is based on the belief that if a man has too much sex and loses too much "Yang," his penis will shrink and withdraw into the abdomen, which would be life-threatening (Bhugra and de Silva, 1993; Wen, 1995).[21] This ultimate "punishment" for having too much sex is not a matter of guilt or sinfulness but is tied only to a health concern. Therefore, there is no suggestion that sex as such is intrinsically "bad" in Confucianism and Taoism (Tseng and Hsu, 1970; Jai, 1995).

Further, I would like to go back to the phenomenon of "converging" sexual mores in this contemporary globalised world. Chinese societies today have been exposed to, and/or "imported," the Western ideas and ideals of romantic love, individualism, democracy and equalitarianism since the early twentieth century in the process of modernisation, Westernisation and globalisation. As presented in previous chapters of this book, these ideas and ideals (perceived as "modern") have added extra colours, flavours, fashions and possibilities to Chinese people's courtship processes and intimate behaviours—from arranged marriages to dating and love matches, with loosening premarital sexual mores and increasing extramarital affairs.

Love stories in Hollywood movies provide a global "script" for romantic and sexual episodes, and "selves" get recognised and validated in these episodes. A Chinese person can be a "Harry" or "Sally" and something particularly magic will happen when Harry meets Sally. Overall, however, beneath all the "Harry-Sally" interactions, regardless of how spicy and colourful such romance may be, a Chinese "self" is still primarily defined by his/her familial roles rather than through sexual encounters (Chang, 1999, 2003). There is no doubt that sexual encounters and romantic exposures will sometimes make the Chinese individual's life better. The embedded meaning of sex, however, is still seen primarily as a natural urge. Even now, the natural urge has incorporated Western ideas (e.g., romance), language (e.g., "I love you") and ways to be expressed (e.g., sexual skills or tips offered by the popular Chinese editions of women's magazines such as *Cosmopolitan*). Sex is just not a "big deal" (for validating man/womanhood/personhood), at least not as big a deal as it is in the Western cultural contexts.

Finally, one may argue that for women, the changing premarital sexual mores (e.g., sex in a committed relationship) and the primary emphasis on "happy family" and playing their familial roles well in Chinese societies today are "converging" or similar to the situation in the West's 1950s. I would argue that the two sets of *practices* may look the same, but the embedded meanings of their practices are not the same. As discussed earlier in this chapter and in previous chapters, even today, the recognition and validation of Chinese people, *both* women and men, remain primarily defined by their familial roles with an emphasis on filial piety (particularly the responsibility to look after elderly parents) in a family with an intergenerational *vertical* orientation which goes beyond an immediate nuclear family (even if many more post-World War II couples are living in a nuclear family than was the case in their parents' generation). The "relations defined" Chinese individuals aim to achieve harmony among all family members, the core criterion to define a "happy (extended) family" (Chang, 2003).

In contrast, in the 1950s' West, the cultural ideal of a "happy family" and the familial roles (mainly defining women)[22] were referred to as a *nuclear* family setting with a *horizontal* orientation of the blissful conjugal bond (Chang, 2003), although in social reality, many housewives were in misery (as represented in popular culture such as a 2003 film

Far From Heaven). The advice given to the 1950s' housewives was focused on *individualistic* "self-help" to overcome misfortune and to achieve individual *perfection* in terms of their desirability and excellence in multiple female roles (mother, lover, cook and wife) in order to have a "happy (nuclear) family" (Ferguson, 1983, p. 52).

Gender Differences in (Heterosexual) Sexual Practices in the Contemporary Chinese and Western Cultural Settings

As argued before, even with situational contingencies, each cultural tradition has a "home base" or primary embedded meaning of sex for individuals, but men and women end up having different sexual attitudes and behaviours (which I call "sexual practices" in this chapter). The patriarchal social system, in both the Chinese and Western cultural settings, has certainly impacted gender roles and gender-role-associated sexual practices for individuals and relationships which have been studied and documented in much research. My analysis below will move the studies of men's and women's sexual practices to a deeper level, to examine in our times how the same embedded meaning of sex is implicated in two genders in different ways within each cultural setting, as well as how different meanings of sex infuse sexual practices of both genders in different ways between the two cultural settings.

Secular West: Sexual Performance Versus Desirability to Gain Individual Recognition/Validation—Sex Is Not What You Do but Who You Are

Here, I only focus on how the aspect of "recognition and validation" regarding the meaning of sex becomes implicated in the sexual practices of contemporary Western men and women. I assume that the aspect of "completion" regarding the meaning of sex gets achieved by men and women in a similar way, i.e., the same "destination"/outcome in terms of each party feeling "completed" and "whole" as a result of the sexual encounter (despite the fact that sexual practices may differ in the two parties).

For Western men, being recognised and validated as a man in a sexual encounter is through (sexual) performance.

Masculinity is largely defined by performance (including sexual performance) in the secular West. For men, performing well sexually includes being active, ready, able or willing to have sex (Seal and Ehrhardt, 2007), "in control" and goal-oriented (e.g., good "scores," and "making her achieve orgasm"). Using the gender role strain perspective, Levant and Brooks (1997) argue that men are socialized into being tough, not showing feelings[23] and achieving by conquering and winning. There are side effects for many men (and for many women as a result). For example, men use sex as a way of getting close or showing love (Zilbergeld, 1992, p. 163) because they have difficulty getting in touch with or expressing their emotions (Hite, 1987).[24]

Male concern for being "in control" may relate to the fact that men are more likely than women to engage in nonrelational sex—experiencing sex primarily as lust without any requirements for relational intimacy or emotional attachment (Levant, 1997). This mode of sex tends to objectify the "objects" of sexual desires and to affirm one's sense of adequacy as a man (Regan and Brooks, 1995). Pornography, prostitution, coerced sex and repeated infidelity or "Don Juanism" (Lusterman, 1997) are examples of nonrelational sex. Furthermore, male concern for "scoring" causes many men to worry about penis size and impotence and whether they "can go all the way."[25] Such a "performance" focus and concern tends to be primarily male-centred, more for the men's sense of masculinity than for satisfying women's needs.

It is argued that Viagra has successfully "fixed" men's impotence but may have hindered the man or the couple from exploring or working on relationship issues, possibly contributing to the impotence (Loe, 2004). The goal of making a woman come to orgasm leads to background anxiety for many men ("Did she really come?") as well as for women ("Should I fake?" "I didn't have an orgasm. What's wrong with me?") (Reiss, 1986; Hite, 1994; McCormick, 1994; Levant and Brooks, 1997).

For Western women, being recognised and validated as a woman comes through being desired, wanted and needed by a man.

Again, the gender role perspective argues that femininity (under patriarchy) requires women to be socialised into being passive, responsive, nurturing, loving and desirable (by men) (McCormick, 1994). More traditional heterosexual script theory posits that men tend to pursue courtship based on a woman's potential sexual desirability (Seal and Ehrhardt, 2007). Accordingly, the self-esteem of a woman is crucially defined by whether she is recognised and desired by a man; her worth is validated by whether she is wanted and loved by a man. Many women feel that good sex makes them feel womanly, desired, liked, needed, wanted, accepted or loved (Hite, 1987; 1994).[26]

Many men perceive many women as being obsessed about love (Hite, 1987) or "loving too much" (Norwood, 1985). This suggests that such women need the constant love of a man to prove themselves as a worthy woman.[27] The man might feel that the love he gives a woman is never enough because she tends to focus on love as a basic means of fulfilment and self-identity, and has a constant need for (more) love, which is actually a desire for (more) reassurance. The woman might feel the man doesn't love her as much as she loves him. Consequently, the man feels that the woman loves too much.

Another side effect of this yearning for recognition is that many women are concerned about whether or not they are sexually attractive and desirable. Thus, they worry about the shape and the size of their bodies and whether they can make their men feel manly enough by showing that they really enjoy sex and/or by having to fake orgasms. The example of women who cannot get out of an abusive or incestual relationship shows in the extreme how some women need to feel "wanted," even if sex itself is "unwanted."

Although the embedded meaning of sex is the same for both genders in terms of individual recognition and validation, all these issues reveal a gender difference that operates at the level of sexual practices.

Furthermore, in the game played between the two genders, while the man tends to be seen as the "initiator" in the seduction process, underneath it normally is the woman who feels responsible for setting up the right context to start the game—she feels that she has to be attractive enough to be desirable. If the man doesn't seem sexually aroused, the woman feels inadequate and tries to make herself more sexy: she wears special sexy clothes and makeup and surrounds herself with candlelight, romantic music, etc. If she does not have, or has to fake, an orgasm, she feels something is wrong with her. This is why, in the secular West, women are often the ones who to go to sex clinics for counselling and to work out their relationships.

Men tend to focus on their sexual problem in a narrowly defined way by getting a quick fix, for example, by taking Viagra to make them perform better for this specific task and be able to "shoot." If a man performs good sex, the woman tends to compliment him by saying, "It was amazing! You just did an amazing job!" In other words, men tend not to treat their own sexual inadequacy as a relationship problem that may reflect on the relationship as a whole and must therefore be solved together with the woman. Men tend to treat the relationship matter as female territory because they see women as being responsible for the daily and long-term routine emotional and sexual maintenance of the relationship.

Chinese: "Feeding" Versus "Being Fed"—Sex Is Not Who You Are but What You Do

In contrast to "sex is not what you do but *who you are*" for secular Westerners, the meaning of sex in Chinese culture primarily tends to be a natural urge/"meal," and the crucial definition and validation for being a man or a woman is related to his/her familial roles. In this context, sex for Chinese is not who you are but *what you do* (related to the duties from familial roles).

Here, the obvious substantive familial roles for men are son, husband and father. The husband's role is to perform adequately sexually and satisfy his wife's sexual needs along with caring for her. This is why Chinese herbal sexual medicine is consumed mostly by middle-aged or older men who worry that their sexual drive and performance may decline through aging, making them inadequate to do their (husband) job properly.

Using the metaphor of "meal" and the understanding of sex as "'sustenance," Chinese husbands and wives are both conscious of each other's sexual "hunger," and feel obligated to "feed" each other adequately. The difference between the feeding of the husband and wife is that the husband is the "cook" who starts the cooking—his penis has to be ready and adequate for making the meal together with the wife. Once the meal is underway, both parties feed each other. In contrast to Western women being responsible for arousing the man enough, the Chinese man is responsible for getting his penis erect and for starting the job (of feeding). This also explains why, in contrast to Western women getting professional help, medical specialists in sexual dysfunction in Taiwan told me that only husbands turn up in their clinics and sometimes arrive secretly without their wives knowing. The men feel worried and shameful that their erection was not adequate enough to do their job of feeding their spouse.

Again, the "performance" problem may seem a common anxiety for both Western and Chinese men, but I argue that the anxiety is only on the level of sexual practices. The embedded meanings behind the "performing," which are on another level, are different between the two cultural settings.

Some Western men consume Viagra to enhance their performance, but this has more to do with the individual's ego according to the individualism-based definition of men being achievers who accomplish (or conquer) in bed, rather than necessarily performing their familial role of "feeding" women properly. But again, when the sexual act fails, both Western men and Chinese men may feel that they performed inadequately, but the former fails as a man and the latter fails as a spouse or boyfriend (boyfriend perceived as a pseudo husband by the woman).

When the sexual act fails, the Western woman feels inadequate—she is not sexually attractive enough, while the Chinese woman puts less significance on the sexual encounter itself and says that sex is not really that important. The most important thing the Chinese woman thinks is that "he cares about me and treats me well" or "we have a harmonious family" (Li, 1996).

If older Chinese women feel their sexual drive declines, this does not bother them—just as one's appetite diminishes naturally over time and one doesn't need to be fed that much. If their husbands can't "feed" them, it is not a big deal. Sex for Chinese people is not who you are but what you do ("feed").

Conclusion

This research has framed and interpreted sex in two contrasting world religions in both classical and contemporary times. Table 8-1 summarises what has emerged about sex in Chinese and Western cultural settings. Methodologically, the findings and insights gained from this research can enable more valid and reliable measures to be constructed and to differentiate and reveal different embedded meanings of sex between Confucian- and Christian-based cultures. I propose an example in Table 8-2 of how the Kinsey-type of sex surveys can be "upgraded" by incorporating a level that influences the embedded meanings of sex. The arguments and findings presented in this chapter have both theoretical and methodological significance as well as practical implications for the future. These will be discussed in the final chapter, "Concluding Remarks."

Table 8-1: Sex in Cross-Cultural Settings

		Chinese	Western
Metaphor		Meal	Game
Embedded Meanings of Sex		Sustenance (Natural urge)	Individual recognition/validation and completion (as a man or a woman)
		Sex is not who you are but what you do *("who you are" is tied to familial roles)*	*Sex is not what you do but who you are*
Sexual Practices			
	Men	Feeding	Sexual performance
	Women	Being fed	Desirability
Sanction		Shame	Guilt

Table 8-2: Rationale for Questionnaire Design for the Embedded Meanings of Sex

Theoretical Constructs	Conceptua-lisation	Operationa-lisation	Direction of Questions		
	Dimensions	**Indicators**		**Implications from Expected Responses**	
Nature of Gender	*Salience*	Nature and extent to which self-descriptions refer to gender	Think of a situation in which you felt authentic and alive. What was it about the situation that created this effect?	**Chinese** Gender not very salient in descriptions	**Western** Gender highlighted in descriptions
	Identity	Richness in describing gender	Describe what being a man/ woman means to you these days	Descriptions based on roles, particularly familial roles	Descriptions based on intimacies and gender politics
	Difference	Nature and extent of gender differences	What are the most important ways in which men and women differ?	Differences articulated in terms of functional roles	Differences expressed as biological and emotional differences (Mars vs. Venus)
	Family Basis	Whether family defines gender identity	How does family provide a basis for being a man, a woman or a person generally?	Family basis extensively quoted	More ambivalence—family as constrainer and carrier of biography
Nature of Sex	*Quality of Sex*	Lists of ingredients for "good sex"	What is it about good sex that makes it good for you?	Healthy	Intense
		Lists of impacts of "good sex"	How does good sex affect you?	Keeps me balanced	Makes me feel special and alive
		Exceeds expectations	What can make sex fall short of your expectations?	Too tired/ bad timing	Too many expectations

		Specifiable account of what a sexual partner brings to an encounter	What is it that your sexual partner can contribute to make sex satisfying?	Sincerity	Surprise
			What is it that your sexual partner can do to make sex unsatisfying?	Insincerity	"Nothing there"
	Extremities in the Quantity of Sex	Too much sex	What happens when there is too much sex?	Unhealthy	Worn out
		No sex	What happens if people have no sex?	Delayed gratification	Personal deprivation
Nature of Norms and Sanctions	*Form of Social Control*	Shame vs. guilt	Think of a situation in which someone has transgressed sexual norms. What are some of the reactions others have expressed to this transg ression?	Shame covers many people and lasts over time	Guilt experienced as an inner torment

NOTES

1. Weber refers to "world religions" as the five religions or "religiously determined systems of life-regulation. The Confucian, Hinduist, Buddhist, Christian and Islamist religious ethics all belong to the category of world religion" (Gerth and Mills, 1977, p. 267).

2. It has been argued that the notion of "romantic love" has only been developed in the West in the past one hundred years or so (Solomon, 1988, p. 55). Other cultures may not have had this term at all before it was imported from the West, but they had other notions such as *qing* in Chinese societies.

3. Gregersen (1986) surveyed and found sexual customs, beliefs and practices tend to cluster geographically and vary among nine "sex cultural areas" (including black Africa, the Middle East, India and Southeast Asia, the Far East, Aboriginal Australia, New Guinea, Polynesia, Aboriginal Americas and Europe/America) (Gregersen, 1986, pp. 97–101).

4. Kwok (1998) reviews the evolving Confucian tradition (with change and persistence) across Chinese history. The influence from Buddhism can be seen from the notion of compassion toward ordinary people and all sentient beings and these two relationships were absent in the cardinal relations emphasised in early Confucianism. The influence of Taoism can be seen from the notion of "the natural self" (in the works of Laozi and Zhuangzi), and the liberation of the self was clearly manifested in literature and philosophy (p. 86). However, de Bary (1970) argues that the Taoistic liberation of self can be called a personal or "private individualism," because it only affirms the individual's freedom from society and his own transcendence value. In contrast, a "public" or "social individualism" affects the status of other individuals or has an effect on basic

political or social institutions (p. 147).

5. Another kind of translation for *pingtienxia* can be "The whole universe can be in peace."

6. Confucius said, "A person with filial piety to parents and love toward siblings can manage his family well. Managing family well can be seen as managing the country. We don't need to become an official in order to run the country." *Confucian Analects*, Book 2, Chapter 21.

7. *The Works of Mencius*, Book 3, Part 1, Chapter 4.

8. Ibid., Book 4, Li Lou, Part 1, Chapter 11.

9. Ibid., Book 3, Teng Wen Gong, Part 2, Chapter 9.

10. The quote: And it came to pass after these things (lit. words), that God tested Abraham and said, "Abraham." And he said, "Here I am." And He said, "Take your son, your only son, the one you love, Isaac, and go into the land of Moriah and offer him there for a burnt offering upon one of the mountains which I will show you" (Genesis 22:1–2).

11. "*... er chong qi ben ran zhi shan*" (the nature of kindness), *The Doctrine of the Mean*, Chapter 1.

    Confucius said, "*Xin xiang jin ye, xi xiang yuan ye*" (Humans have a similar nature, but can become very different through developing different practices or habits), *Confucian Analects*, Book 17, Yang Huo, Chapter 2.

12. *The Works of Mencius*, Book 6, Gao Zi, Part 1, Chapter 6.

13. There is a Confucian saying, "*Buxiao you san, wuhou weida*" (There are three things children do which are unfilial to

parents. Among the three, the most unfilial one is to discontinue the family line).

14. A daughter is seen as only being "temporary" in her natal home and eventually will "belong to another family" (after marrying).

15. For a man without a son but only having a daughter, there are alternative social arrangements to make sure his family line is continued. For example, when his daughters get married, his daughters can have their husbands "marry in" (rather than the daughters "marrying out") and the "married-in" husbands have to change their surnames into the man's family name. For a dead woman who had never married, in some Chinese regions her natal family can organize a "ghost marriage" for her so that she can still have a permanent home (in terms of being worshipped by family members).

16. There are other views about this "incompleteness" of human nature (which do not contradict the Christian view) in Ancient Greek myths as well as in the contemporary theory of psychoanalysis in the West. One example of the former is a play written by Aristophanes, regarding a man and a woman being "the other half" for each other in a "fusion" (Solomon, 1988). One example of the latter is Lacan's argument that a human's desire is due to loss. Such "loss" originated from the infant stage, because infants can never get everything they want, which results in emotionally deprived adults who always desire or yearn for an emotional connection with other(s) (Horrocks, 1997).

17. In the Chinese diet, "cold" food refers to the "Yin" (negative) element while "hot" food refers to the "Yang" (positive) element. Certain types of food are categorised as "cold" or "hot" food. Eating too much cold or hot food will cause certain

kinds of diseases. The balance between "cold" and "hot" elements in the diet is crucial for health.

18. Even mainland China has experienced cultural transformations in the past five decades. The most important intervention was that the state tried to replace Confucianism by Maoism from 1949 to 1978. However, certain parts of the traditional/"feudal" beliefs, values and practices die hard. One of the legacies is the area of the Confucian/Taoistic sexual beliefs, such that even today many Chinese men in China (and in other Chinese societies or societies influenced by Confucianism and Taoism) still believe that certain tablets made of Chinese herbs or parts of animal bodies can boost men's sexual drive and the endurance of erection. The demand and the market for these "traditional" medications have survived for thousands of years.

19. See Smith, T. (1994), "Attitudes toward Sexual Permissiveness: Trends, Correlates, and Behavioral Connections." In Rossi, A. (ed.) *Sexuality across the Life Course*. Chicago: University of Chicago Press. pp. 63–98.

20. Inglehart et al. (2004) argue that there are tremendous cultural differences between Protestant and Catholic societies, but for the most part, they do not reflect the direct influence of religious institutions today. Certain values persist as part of the cultural heritage of the given societies (Inglehart et al., 2004, pp. 14–18).

21. *"Suo-Yang"* has been seen akin to the Dhat Syndrome in India and its Sri Lankan variant (Bhugra and de Silva, 1993, p. 246).

22. In the 1950s' West, men were primarily defined by their individual personalised cultural goals such as work achievement

(Ferguson, 1983, p. 65).

23. An example of quotes from *The Hite Report* (1994): "Men in groups I know are hostile, edgy, and like to show that they don't have feelings—feelings of tenderness, caring or friendship (except under the rule of bonding), or pain, be it emotional or physical" (p. 243).

24. Hite comments on men in *The Hite Report on Men and Male Sexuality*: "by 'penetrating' a woman vaginally 'giving her my come,' they are showing her their love" (Hite, 1994, p. 276). Hite also highlights that "Many men feel that having sex *in itself* serves as communication" (Hite, 1987, p. 20).

25. An example of quotes from *The Hite Report* (1994): "My friends in high school called another guy a sissy when he said he was afraid to ask his girl to go all the way" (p. 237).

26. Here are some examples of quotes from *The Hite Report on the Family* (1994): "I started dating at 13. I was flattered; I wasn't used to be liked" (p. 108). "Older boys noticed me and it made my life worth living" (p. 108). Examples of quotes from *The Hite Report: Women and Love* (1987), "I love being in love ... I feel more confident when I am in love. It gives me a good feeling. I feel pretty inside" (p. 158). "... with him I regained much of the self-confidence I had lost with my husband. I also regained the belief in my desirability as a woman and in my own femininity" (p. 164). "Actually, there is nothing like those special little moments of flattery that a man can give you, making you feel adored, that you are the most desirable, the most beautiful ... but just to make you feel really needed and wanted" (p. 192). Although the quantitative data presented in Hite's reports were criticised as being nonrandom or not statistically representative, the quotes I extract here are qualitative data, used to reveal the meaning

and dynamics of a romantic relationship felt by women. The principle of a random sample is not required for qualitative research methodology.

27. In *The Hite Report: Women and Love* (1987), a failed relationship or problematic marriage made some women feel: "I felt unworthy," "I was nothing," (p. 24) or "disregarded as a person" (p. 61).

Concluding Remarks

All the research and findings presented in this book have theoretical and methodological significance as well as practical implications for the future.

Theoretical Significance

Challenging the conventional modernisation argument, the theoretical insight I have developed here is consistent with the argument proposed in a paradigm known as "multiple modernities," which is emerging from comparative civilisational analysis (notably Eisenstadt, 2000, 2003).

The conventional modernisation argument had developed a significant momentum in academia between the late 1950s and 1970s (e.g., Lerner, 1958; Parsons, 1960, 1966, 1971; Rostow, 1960; McClelland, 1961; Levy, 1966; Inkeles and Smith, 1974), and had been applied to those societies in Asia and other parts of the world undergoing rapid processes of modernisation and social change in the closing decades of the twentieth century. This linear and developmental paradigm (with stages from the traditional societies to developed ones) tends to equate modernisation to Westernisation with a consequential convergence of socioeconomic development and cultures in industrial societies. In other words, "modernity" means Western modernity, beginning in the West, particularly based on the ideal of the

Enlightenment in the eighteenth century, and spreads to other parts of the world.

I would conceptualise this Enlightenment project of Western modernity with three different layers from outer surface into inner core. The first layer concerns the development of modern infrastructure primarily through industrialisation, urbanisation, migration and the expansion of education. The second layer concerns the political and economic project of modernity, i.e., the modernisation of political and economic institutions toward democracy and the market economy. The third layer is the so-called cultural project of modernity, based on reasons and rationality (particularly instrumental rationality) as well as social justice, equalitarianism, individual autonomy, reflexivity and rights in a civil society.

In the Western cultural contexts, while the Enlightenment project of modernity has reached their primary goals, there are also major negative consequences—nature and human conditions are having more (rather than fewer) problems, notably the ecological exhaustion and worsening income gaps and wars. Such conditions are critiqued by Habermas (1987) as the unfinished project of modernity or incomplete modernity (d'Entrèves and Benhabib, 1997), and in the postmodernists' lament over the end, or actually the death, of modernity due to the decline of social institutions, e.g., the state, church and family, and the loss of coherent values—as in Weber's thesis that "value rationality" has given way to "instrumental rationality" (Weber, 1993; Kalberg, 2005).

In the past decades, in non-Western contexts, a global "modern" condition has been emerging from the first-layer project of modernity, the development of infrastructure, in parts of the world in the rapid process of modernisation and globalisation. Some of the negative by-products of industrialisation and urbanisation (e.g., the ecological damage and widening gap between the rich and the poor) have also started to appear in other parts of the world. However, in these societies, the projects of modernity have not reached, or will not necessarily reach, their limits, because the institutional and cultural projects of modernity are different from those in the West.

For the second-layer modernisation—the institutional project of modernity—variations have emerged in the particular forms of the democratic system and capitalist market economy in parts of the world. Such variations on the institutional level of modernity are actually determined by the third layer, the cultural project of modernity, which is grounded in specific historical and civilisational contexts.

The cultural project of modernity in contemporary non-Western cultural contexts tends to be a hybrid of global/Western and local/traditional ideas and ideals. My past research has found that this mix of cultural elements has an outer surface and inner core. The global/Western ideas operate on the surface, and as they are appropriated they tend to be filtered or reworked as a new means to achieving old Chinese ends that make up the inner core of the culture, e.g., children buying top brands for parents as a new way to express filial piety, or using Western skills to get good jobs while remaining committed to caring for the whole family, across generations.

I argue, therefore, that the first two layers of modernity define the core global condition of "becoming modern," but underneath, the meanings of being modern are determined by the core of the third layer, i.e., the cultural assumption of humans, the premises of human relations and the relation between the individual and authority, and the configurations of family and manhood/womanhood/ personhood. The "convergence" between societies, which the conventional modernisation argument refers to, has been, in fact, primarily on the first layer and on the *surface* of the second and/or the third layers of modernity.

Two major scholarly arguments were posed in the 1990s to interpret the distinct developments of political economy in the world. One is "the end of history" with ultimate convergence (into Western modernity), argued by Francis Fukuyama in 1992 when Eastern European communism was collapsing. The other is "the clash of civilisations," argued by Samuel Huntington in 1996 when Islamic fundamentalism was appearing anti-Western and gaining in global significance.

While the "convergence" argument has been challenged by the later arguments of the "clash of civilisations," both Fukuyama and Huntington (along with other scholars) have been conscious of "alternative modernity," i.e., the existence of modernities other than Western modernity. All of them, however, seem to assume that the Western modernity is the dominant or "mainstream" form of modernity, while non-Western societies may converge, clash or deviate from this mainstream modernity under modernisation and globalisation.

Parallel to these debates, a paradigm of multiple modernities has been emerging since the 1990s (Eisenstadt, 1986, 2000, 2003; Aranason, 1997; Hefner, 1998; Tu, 2000; Roniger and Waisman, 2002; Sachsenmaier, 2002; Sachsenmeyer and Riedel, 2002; Kaya, 2003, 2004; Taylor, 2004; Kamali, 2006; Lau, 2006; Lee, 2006). To critique it further, the multiple modernities paradigm uses comparative civilisation analysis to identify varieties of modernities (even within "Western" modernity) and different elements, modes and pathways to becoming modern which are grounded in specific civilisations and long-standing historical experiences.

This paradigm treats modernity as a *civilisation*, starting from Western Europe in the eighteenth and nineteenth centuries, spreading to North America, and other parts of the world. This civilisation has different forms, contents and meanings, all grounded in different cultural traditions defined by Weber's world religions (Weber, 1948), or Eisenstadt's Axial civilisations or non-Axial civilisations (such as Japan) (Eisenstadt, 1986). Even within the Western Christian civilisation, different modernities have emerged between Western Europe, continental Europe, the United States of America and Latin America.

In non-Western parts of the world, multiple modernities have also been emerging, notably Confucian modernity and Islamic modernity. Within each of these modernities are variations between different societies, even when these societies are rooted in the same civilisation.

The major "substance" of this multiple modernities paradigm has been built on research into the development of forms of democratic polities and capitalist economies in various societies between civilisations. My research on change and persistence in sexual mores and familism in contemporary Chinese societies has certainly provided relevance, support and enrichment to this paradigm. After all, sexual mores and family values are the core aspect of any civilisation, and it is important that we know what "modernity" means in terms of sexuality, family and manhood/womanhood in people's everyday life within a specific historical and civilisational context.

Due to modernisation, *different* pathways to premarital sexual liberalisation emerged in urban China, Hong Kong and Taiwan prior to the mid-1990s. This intersocietal and intracultural variation can critique the focus on linearity and convergence of the conventional modernisation theory. Furthermore, since the mid-1990s, the premarital sexual mores of young Chinese may look like they are converging to the Western trends, but the underlying meanings are different. Consequently, there is not yet a "real" sexual revolution in these Chinese societies as long as premarital sex occurs primarily in a committed and long-term relationship, and young Chinese are still defining themselves primarily by familial roles and living through familism in their everyday lives. The loosening of premarital sexual mores has not been "clashing" with the ever-present Confucian familism.

The Chinese "modernisation" in sex, love and family is not the same as that in the postsexual revolution West. This is an illuminating demonstration of how core elements of the Confucian tradition are integrated with aspects of Western modernity (i.e., romantic love and consumerism derived from capitalism), and how these core values in tradition have defined and continued in Chinese modernity. In addition to democracy and capitalism, the notion of "multiple modernities" can now be extended to the areas of sex, family and manhood and womanhood.

Methodological Significance

Regarding the methodological significance, the arguments and insights presented in this book are grounded in most appropriate data and various research strategies for the specific research questions posed for different projects. Each additional project raises further research questions, involves more comparisons and consequently develops deeper interpretations. Insights get elaborated and strengthened by being tested through more comparison and particularly more contrast. The challenge, of course, lies in finding the contrasts which generate the largest set of differences, which, in turn, provoke reflection and the production of theory.

As the book has developed, the contrasts have widened in scope—from within a Chinese society, to between Chinese societies and extended to between Chinese and Western societies. Through each expansion, insights from earlier contrasts have subsisted in the texture of the interpretations developed. It merits review to outline how this progressive and iterative comparative sociology operates.

All social structures and behaviours live in the actions of individuals. Actions leave their trace in memories, which colour attitudes and frame perceptions. Accordingly, the life course offers a rich stream of data from which much about social structure can be gleaned. This book begins with life-course transitions, particularly into the realms of the first sexual encounter. In that context, as demonstrated by the event-history analysis with time-specific modelling in Chapter 1, it was imperative to disentangle three distinct sources of changes: age, cohort and period.

Age offers a proxy of the aging process. The contrast between ages offers insights into impacts of aging on some behaviour. "Cohort" actually captures the "defining marks" of biographical experience. Thus, a cohort can experience specific events (of a period as it turns out) and be marked by that. For example, the "baby boomers" define the cohort of people who grew up in the 1960s' West and tend to wear jeans (and long hair for men), care about social justice issues and hold a particular political (ideological) view throughout their entire lives. "Period," by contrast, looks at biography from the surrounding context of historical process. Thus, the key events of a time (for example, the Paris student revolts in 1968 or the events of Tiananmen Square in 1989) leave marks on each cohort that witnessed or lived through them.

As the chapters unfold in the early part of this book, the emphasis moves from age and cohort toward period. These, in turn, require qualitative data to inform the nuances of culture reeling from or enacting responses to specific events or aspects of sociocultural changes (as presented by the focus group data in Chapter 2 and discourse analysis in Chapter 3). "Period," in turn, alters the focus from individual behaviours to aggregated "pathways"—this is on the level of society and beyond the level of individuals. As presented in Chapter 4, different pathways of changing sexual mores exist in different contemporary Chinese societies due to political economy, colonial experiences and historical changes in the recent past.

Furthermore, as presented in Chapter 5, in looking at young Chinese who are urbanised, educated and exposed to avant-garde Western culture (such as growing up in major Chinese cities and/or by studying overseas), any operation of Chinese cultural influences that remain can be expected to be even stronger with the rest of the populations in contemporary Chinese societies. In Chapters 4 and 5, I have had to move from what seemed to be core Chinese values and encircle their operation with contrasts across history and specific societies in order to capture the nuances of historical, political and colonial forces on Chinese culture.

As I widened the scope of comparisons developed within and between Chinese societies, some core aspects of Chinese culture became visible that define Chineseness. In order to vouchsafe the insights, more comparison is required—this time between cultures. Since much of the discussion involved the impact of Western influences, it became critical to turn the comparative gaze upon Western orientations and approaches to relationship and intimacy issues. In order to set a benchmark of comparison, it was appropriate to carry out analysis of media content that captures these issues as well as construct typologies of "agony resolution" when the woman in agony perceives that she is or is not in control of her man, so that a specific focus of solution (shifting between individual, relationship and social norms) would be advised accordingly. To this end, the study of advice column entries in the American edition of *Cosmopolitan* in Chapter 6—within a similar context as used for the Taiwanese edition of *Cosmopolitan* (in Chapter 3) provides such a benchmark. It also offers a background context and content which can then provide an introduction to a comparison of Chinese and Western cultural legacies regarding sex in Chapters 7 and 8.

The comparison of Chinese and Western infidelity in Chapter 7 proves illuminating by studying transgressive behaviours. For in these behaviours, the inner strength and insecurities of a culture become more visible. In everyday life, the culture can almost become invisible in a taken-for-granted set of understandings that sociological scrutiny can witness but not interrogate. With transgressions, the social structure and the culture become self-disclosing.

Methodologically, the typology constructions in Chapters 6 and 7 have different significance. In Chapter 6, the typologies are constructed to reveal a "normative" level in terms of ultimate concerns and solutions that are recommended in advice columns in the West, and those in Chapter 7 focus on the "structure" level in terms of the prospects, possibilities and dynamics of different types of affairs when certain types of women encounter men under certain conditions.

Once these levels were elaborated, I traced the roots of both cultures and did a reading of core Chinese and Western texts (notably the Confucian classics and the Christian Bible). As demonstrated in Chapter 8, there are contrasts between familial relations which defined individuals through a primary emphasis on a never-ending continuity of family lines across generations in the Chinese cultural setting and an "individuated" individual with primary emphasis on the relationship between the individual and God (or a significant other) in the Western cultural setting. Indeed, at this highest level of comparison, the differences are truly stark: Chinese familism defines an empire as so many lagoons of familial and village commitments that aggregate into a quiet ocean of imperially sanctioned Confucianism. In the West, the corresponding comparative metaphor is more akin to many rivers of "calling" creating confluences of irrupting interpretations of values that speak directly to individual consciences, libido, calculations and destiny.

Methodology needs not be seen as some arid discipline of dissecting cultural or social content with the implication that what gives life to the material is somehow drained of its vitality. Rather, methodological rigor involves finding contrasts that surprise and provoke—rather than simply producing arid categories of contrast. It looks for the most animated aspects to study, and sexuality provides an entry for this journey as well as leading the journey of discovery into different pathways between societies within the same culture and into different (albeit buried) meanings that become visible when comparing different cultures.

Practical Implications for the Future

Regarding practical implications, I have developed the notion of a "wisdom bank"—a repository of "solutions" to recurrent problems that beset the human condition to overcome the fact that no individual culture has managed to solve all or most of these recurrent problems. A "transcultural wisdom bank" can broaden the views of people, giving them a larger range of *possibilities* about important issues in everyday life, major values, social institutions and processes. People will not only understand "other" cultures better, but more important, they will understand themselves better. Without cross-cultural comparisons, it is hard to cross taken-for-granted boundaries, definitions and stereotypes. With respect to this approach into cross-cultural research of the embedded meanings of sex, a "wisdom bank" about the metaphors of sex, meanings of sex, sexual norms and sanctions, the relationships between sex, love, marriage and family and self becomes possible.

I will now give two examples of how the insights generated from my cross-cultural research and the transcultural wisdom bank can enable us to review and deal with issues in gender, sex and relationships in a different way or with different possibilities. This first example is an enhancement of the pathways of "agony resolutions" identified in Chapter 6—how to innovatively design an advisory system in the West in which both men and women can be constituted as subjects. The second example is an elaboration of the implication regarding the embedded meanings of sex revealed in Chapter 8 and how these insights can be utilised to reexamine and reframe the problems in sex and relationships in contemporary Western and Chinese cultural settings.

As discussed in Chapter 6, in Western popular magazines, advisory columns are highly feminised with women in agony writing in problems and "Agony Aunts" providing advice. In this respect, advice columns do not have to be feminised. Men's involvement in advice columns actually has had a long tradition in the area of medical discourse, which is permeated with masculine voices. Now the challenge of advisory systems in popular magazines is how to motivate, encourage and integrate men into the discourse which is associated with gender and/or relationship problems. If a problematic relationship caused agony in a woman, the man in that relationship can be expected to have problems as well, simply because a relationship involves two participants with joint responsibility, and both individuals could/should be advised to work together. In addition to "Agony Aunts," "Agony Uncles" could/should be drawn in to offer advice, which will not only sound more relevant and convincing to men in agony or male readers in general but also likely make female readers keen to read (to know how to get tips from an "Uncle" to deal with her man!). To this end, the issue is less about raising consciousness (of men) than it is transforming consciousness (of both genders)—in a specific popular culture medium in our daily lives that can provide new ways for the genders to express themselves as well as to jointly "make sense of each other."

Table 1: Gender Politics Realigned: A Typology of Agony-Resolution Pathways

A woman in an agony relationship sees herself as being:

Advisor sees solution as:	The Writer is the:	NOT in control of her man (N=110)		In control of her man (N=20)	
		1. Reliant		4. Carefree	
		Help Yourself	Assert Yourself	Ignore the Negatives	Enjoy the Positives
	Woman in Agony	"I hate my marriage .... I have lost the art of being me ... I feel rotten in life and guilty about knowing I don't want any of it ..."	"Men I meet are used to having sex much sooner than I am. Is my sex standard too high?"	"My boyfriend is suicidal. Do I leave him? I am afraid he will commit suicide if I leave him."	"Sex in my marriage has been a disaster. I have fallen in love with another man. I need practical advice."
Centred on the woman	Agony Aunt	Do something unorthodox and courageous ...	Stick to your standards and only seek those men who share the same standards as you.	Don't let him blackmail you and victimise you. He should depend on himself.	Enjoy your affair while it lasts. Maybe also share that tender secret with your husband.
	Agony Uncle	Give her space. Surprise her too. But engage her bad feelings.	Show you can wait, in wonder. Describe what you desire.	You're down; seek professional help. Don't lean on her.	Wake up to your wife! Ask about her day. Let her talk. Praise her.
		2. Robust		5. Hedging	
		Accept What's There	Quit the Relationship	Wait and See	Provoke a Response
	Woman in Agony	"My boyfriend says he isn't ready for marriage. I don't know what is holding him back."	"My husband shattered me by leaving. My life is in ruins. I cry and my self-respect is nonexistent."	"My boyfriend is divorcing his wife. He is very caring, but I am not. Breaking up will hurt him, and I will lose the wonderful support of this nice man."	"I am falling in love with my boyfriend's best friend. I am feeling guilty."

Centred on the relationship	**Agony Aunt**	Weren't you listening? He is not ready yet …	Get tough with yourself and him. Stay away from this immature and irresponsible man. Ask lawyers to make him pay.	Your feelings may become clearer as time goes on. If no change later, break the relationship with your boyfriend	Try to see what is really there with the boyfriend. Indicate the lack of real feelings and communicate with him.
	Agony Uncle	Explain yourself, but be honest. Don't fudge the issues.	What's done is done. Now show care and responsibility.	Show you care, even if you feel hurt. Get the divorce finished.	Set some standards with your friends about "closeness." Mark out territory.
		3. Realist		6. Authentic	
		<u>Acknowledge Norms</u>	<u>Work It Out</u>	<u>Understand Norms</u>	<u>Become Mature</u>
	Woman in Agony	"Am I being unreasonable about his children after his divorce? His children are more important than me. I am bitchy about his kids."	"We have a good marriage except for the problem of premature ejaculation. We both said it doesn't matter, but it does matter!"	"He is kind and good—but is that enough for marriage? He pressures me: I want to make the right decision."	"Why can't I make a commitment to a man? I can't commit to anyone. Also, I worry about breaking from home …"
Resting with values and norms	**Agony Aunt**	When you are in love with a man who has had children, there is part of him you cannot share.	Couple should first acknowledge their problem—not deny it. Then consult books, doctor etc. …	Gratitude is a bad reason to marry.	This shows a deep reluctance to be a grown-up. Get out on your own and establish independence first.
	Agony Uncle	Draw boundaries—your kids are not hers.	Time does matter. Share feelings and try it twice.	Pressure gets you nowhere. Find someone else: it's a market.	She can't make commitments, so enjoy what's there or leave.

To give an indication of how such social renovation might proceed and how men might participate within the practice of "agony-resolution" so that there are ways in which new subjects of discourse (of Agony Columns) could be constituted, I have constructed for each of the 12 types of advice (presented in Table 6-2 in Chapter 6) that might go to the man in the relationship, as presented in Table 1 below. I have done this as a heuristic device: to see what the content of the advice that could have been given to the man might have looked like.

Theoretically, there are certainly agony-resolution pathways that can be proposed for the man who the woman perceives as having caused her agony (if he were viewed as a partner/agent in change). Table 1 lists both the Agony Aunt's advice for the woman and the advice that could have been given to the man, given the theoretical logic of each type. As it can be seen, the advice to the man appears "sensible," which can show that there are possibilities for both genders to deal with problematic relations together, even in a society having individualism as a core value.

Furthermore, the interesting feature to infer from this constructed advice for men is that the main change in the advice given to the man *within* each type is that the mode of involvement is *reversed*. When the suggested pathway to one gender is an active mode, the advice suggested to the other gender seems in a passive mode (see Table 1). This complementarity regarding the modes of involvement suggests the way or a logic that the two genders can jointly resolve problems. The very construction of advice—having an Agony Aunt as well as an Uncle—focuses on relationships rather than individuals. The complementarity becomes functional rather than simply political. The resolution pathways suggest "turn taking" (as in a dance) rather than simply a posture (of righteous indignation).

It may be that men are less likely to read such columns, but this could very well be due to the bias such columns have. The presence of an "Uncle" on board would likely attract male readers. Even if there is so-called male aversion to writing in and reading advice columns, it doesn't mean women cannot convey ideas and issues to men. For advice columns in popular men's magazines, the arrangement of having both an Agony Aunt and Uncle could make advice look more balanced and female readers may write in as well. The point is that advice columns can be even-handed with respect to each gender.

Finally, the implication that men can be subjects of advice is particularly an implication of Western gender relations, because within a "game" (as discussed in Chapter 8), men and women might equally want to voice their specific opinions, either as advisors or individuals in relationship agony. By contrast, in Chinese societies, the external reference of familial roles or what a family requires would provide a stronger (or stable) matrix of interpretations regarding expectations, so having men or women give advice would not vary so much or create the same impact as this recommendation does in the West.

It ought to be an objective of men's movements in the West to achieve parity in information flows in such arenas as advice columns. Both genders can contribute and benefit. The ideal form of an advice column would encourage cross-gender understanding and collaboration. Women and men would write in about problems, Agony Aunts as well as Agony Uncles would reply to the specific person *and* include advice to the "other party" in the agony relationship. Readers may find this entertaining: Agony Aunts and Uncles could even "debate" key issues. This would open the dialogue and enhance the collaborative nature of gender. It would also enable quite humorous forms of dialogue to develop, making "light" of serious matters. In this way, both genders bring recreation to roles that have, under individualism, become too prone to producing agonies rather than ecstasies.

The book will conclude with my second example of a transcultural wisdom bank which can be valuable, particularly in the (problematic) area of sex. Quite a few contemporary theologians (e.g., Bailey, Nelson, Goudorf and Countryman) have tried to figure out Christian "solutions" to sex and relationship problems in the secular West. They focus their attack on the old "solution" in Christian tradition, i.e., "demonising" sex, as being out of date. Since "demonising sex" was based on body/mind dualism, these theologians try to break this dualism by advocating a new "solution" that I call "legitimising sex" (including legitimising homosexuality). The examples of the main arguments behind such "legitimising" are: divinity and human sexuality are together in God's creation (Nelson, 1978; Gudorf, 1994); sexuality is part of God's creation and gospel (Bailey, 1959); Jesus is an exemplar of grounding spirituality in embodiment (Nelson, 1978); "all creations (including sexuality) offer the possibility of mediating God to us" (Gudorf, 1994, p. 23); bodily experience can reveal the divine, and the experience of bodily pleasure is important in creating the ability to trust and love others, including God; and sex should not become "over the top" in life as sexual libertarians do, because sex is still under the reign of God (Countryman, 1989).

This new "legitimising" orientation is certainly a significant step for humans to embrace sexuality positively as well as to bring justice to diverse forms of sexuality. However, can "legitimising sex" really solve sex and relationship problems on a more fundamental level (i.e., the embedded meaning of sex)—problems these theologians overlook by narrowly looking at the issues in their own cultural tradition?

From the cross-cultural sociological approach into the embedded meanings of sex presented here, I would argue that in the secular West the issue of "recognition" is more crucial and fundamental to understanding the predicaments in self, marriage, family and relationships than the focus on, and the solution of, "legitimising sex." Does the recognition as a man or a woman ultimately have to come from the most significant other in a relationship? Does the focus of the family have to focus so exclusively on the conjugal bond, that is, on "the" relationship? Other cultures reveal other possibilities.

In Chinese societies, as discussed before, the contemporary influence of modern individualism notwithstanding, the ultimate recognition and validation for being a man or a woman—or indeed, a decent person in general—is gained primarily from playing well the familial roles in a *family*, not just in a relationship or marriage. An individual may not have a relationship or marriage, but all have a family. The focus and definition of "family" goes beyond a narrow horizontal conjugal bond or "the relationship," extending in the vertical intergenerational direction. In Chinese families, the conjugal bond is released from the strains many studies document because marital partners do not require from each other constant emotional/sexual intimacy and recognition.

In contrast, the focus of the Western "nuclear" family system, whether heterosexual or homosexual, is the horizontal conjugal bond, and this bond is expected to be always strong, intense and reassuring to the ego of each partner. Inevitably, with a horizontal focus, the need for recognition and intimacy puts the relationship under stress. Individuals in secular Western cultures are vulnerable: "failing in a relationship" feels almost like "failing as a person," and the harsh reality is that failing in a relationship can happen more than once during a person's lifetime. On this front, Chinese people are fortunate because personal validation is lodged within a structure (that is, the family) that is much less likely to fail compared to a single conjugal bond. In short, solving the problems in contemporary marriage and family in the West may require new perspectives, and cultures other than Western secularism offer insights, wisdom and possibilities. Individualism, after all, has limits. On another front, Chinese couples' long-term routine of "homemade meals" (healthy but sometimes not as tasty or exciting as restaurants meals) could certainly be spiced up by each party in the couple adding more "self" into the meal, rather than staying with the solution of "eating out."

In other words, this comparative sociological research for studying sexuality in a non-Western versus a Western cultural setting can offer some "reverse critiques" of Western ideas and practices about sex. It may be that Kinsey-type reports should be rewritten—even for the West.

Epilogue

This book marks my sociological journey in understanding sexuality as an arena: configurations and contrasts about human nature, self-identity, human relations, roles, love, marriage, family, life-course transitions and manhood/womanhood over time and between Chinese and Western cultural settings. To close this book, I have chosen a few poems I wrote in 2004 to 2006 as another representation of the themes and issues explored in this book. I am not only a sociologist who studies people in society, but I'm a psychotherapist who works with people suffering from mental distress and emotional pain as well. However, I am also a human being who, as do others, lives and deals with those issues which I have been studying and who, together with my clients, struggles with challenges in life as part of the human condition. These poems can certainly reflect that!

Reverse

Once upon a time
In Michigan
Filled with white snow and jingle bells
I was invited to join my friends for Christmas
But my little boy would rather not follow me
He did not want to miss out on his Santa.

Ten years on
In Melbourne
Filled with gold sunshine and beach joys
My adult son's friends invited him for X'mas and he invited me
Surprised and touched I went along
I did not want to miss out on my son's attention.

He is back and he is taking me along
Although I am not an old mother yet.

Vest

This cream-coloured vest

Looks soft,
Comfortable in any movement you may still have;
Looks cosy,
Keeping you warm in the park in the chilly spring;
Looks creamy,
Stimulating appetite for your favourite cheesecake; and of course

Looks special,
Reminding us how special it is—

> you have me, your only daughter,
> who chose this vest for you,
> but I have been away more than twenty years
> and in your drowsy days you still missed me;
>
> I have you, my mum
> who has been paralysed for three years
> but in my dreams you are still making dumplings
> and onion pancakes!

Mask

It is the only place I can no longer wear a mask.
I never intend to wear them,
But the roles we play create those masks for us—
When I am a mother,
When I am a wife,
When I am a friend,
And, of course, when I am a performer.

It is the only place I can no longer wear a mask
When I am meeting myself.
This self does not know—
What she is for,
Who she is,
Or what is the meaning of her life.

When I meet this self in this place, I do not know
If she understands what I am talking about,
If she agrees with what I am talking about,
Or if she likes what I am talking about,
And we both may lose direction and be unaware
Where this will lead us.

There is no mask and the risk of getting lost, yet
It is the only place I can find myself,
Recharge myself—
A new self will be born.

Brick Wall

Nowadays people say that
Many places are like brick walls
In the name of bureaucratic efficiency,
Many people are also like brick walls
In the name of maintaining rational control.

I fight against a brick wall—
    With a sore throat
    But my loudest voice cannot get through the wall
    The wall must be soundproof.
            Or
I run alongside a brick wall—
    With a broken heart
    But my tears cannot permeate through the wall
    The wall must be double bricked.

I am told,
"You actually constructed the brick walls!"
Did I?
Maybe I did.

Without constructing the brick wall myself
I cannot bravely bang my head against it
To test my enthusiasm for that which I care.

Without constructing the brick wall myself
I cannot boldly communicate with my raw feelings
To test the love I have for someone.

Me and the brick walls
Coexist
    No room for negotiation
    No line to be crossed
    Head bleeding
    Heart breaking
            But
From those brick walls
I begin to learn who I am.

Desire

Is desire a beautiful force driving my life journey?
Yes, but—
Desire also reminds me that
        something is missing,
        somewhere I never arrive,
        someone is with me only in fantasy.
After all,
Is desire an ugly force driving me crazy?

Pop

Vibrant beats,
Swinging hips,
Funky instructor,
Youthful participants,
On a shining floor.

A radiant energy drew me into this hip-pop-funk class.
I didn't recognise me,
  a middle-aged hip with a sore back,
  struggling to balance through steps supposed to be funky,
  and ending up standing up tall,
  pain free.
Was it real?

A radiant air drew me into a "love-song-devoted" on the radio,
I didn't recognise me,
  a serious academic with a preoccupied head,
  fighting for concentration through noisy music,
  and ending up feeling like a "red-blooded woman,"
  alive.
Wasn't it surreal?

People say that
Pop is only low art,
  signifying evil and crassness—
  consumed by raw flesh,
  indulged by alienated souls, and
  produced by greed under global capitalism.

But

Isn't it also true that
Pop is actually high art,
  unifying minds and bodies—
  recharging stressed muscles,
  warming cold hearts, and
  energizing kindred souls across the globe?

Face

A face in a TV interview,
like a stranger's face,
No, like my mother's face at forty
when she was tired but confident.
A face that surprises me,
looking familiar but unreal,
I cannot quite recognise her!
Is it me?

A face in a worn TV tape,
like an old friend's face,
No, like my face at twenty
when she was carefree but unsure.
A face that attracts me,
looking familiar but remote,
I cannot quite recognise her!
Was it me?

Two faces,
like two images,
yet more like two phases in my life,
I cannot recognize them but
I have lived through them!

Both faces are me!—
Isn't it nice?

Do faces matter after all?

Reunion

Fannie,
one of my classmates in a Taipei school,
is now tracking us all down, and
a big-30 reunion will be in California and Taipei.

She found me with Google.

A top student and leader in that class,
I end up becoming the weakest link,
the only one located "down under."
I have to miss the big day.

"Why are you there?"
Am I in Port Arthur?—
none of those girls can "drop by" on their way.
I feel displaced and grounded in Melbourne,
even as a most liveable city in the world.

Why do I even care?
Old girls are only names—
dormant in brain cells for three decades;
suddenly these cells let the names out
into real people in my world.

Are we getting old?
Starting to treasure childhood memories and
classmates barely known,
from nowhere and everywhere,
as a truly special world.

I must be getting old!
Having been away from my homeland and
adventurous for two decades,
I had never imagined one day I would trace my "roots"
via an old-girl world.

Grave and Roots

He took us back to his hometown, my father,
an old man of 82 returned to the China
from which he had fled when he was 26.

He showed me our Chinese "roots," my father
located within his reclaimed ancestral hall;
and there we worshiped all our ancestors.

He passed on his familial duty to me, his daughter
to share our heritage with all my brothers
and to continue that duty of ancestral worship.

He believes that this "grave" trip
has fulfilled his ultimate familial duty and
his children, misplaced in Taiwan, now know from where they
came.

He has not thought about
how his daughter would "pass on" these "roots"
to her son who has been "misplaced" in several places in the West.

It is not his problem but mine—
After I die, should I join the ancestors in China?
Or should I accompany my brothers in Taiwan?

Perhaps I should construct "roots" for my son
and his children by establishing
an ancestral hall in Melbourne.

After all, it seems to me that
a truncated family line is better than no family line, and
implanted "roots" are better than no roots.

Bibliography

A Man. (1997). Nüren de wancheng (The completion of women). *Kemengbodan,* March, 28.

Arnason, J. (1997). *Social theory and Japanese experiences: The dual civilisation.* London: Kegan Paul International.

Bailey, D. S. (1959). *The man-woman relation in Christian thought.* London: Longmans, Green and Co Ltd.

Baker, H. (1984). *Chinese family and kinship.* New York: Columbia University Press.

Bakes, S. C. (1994). Zhongwo chuangdi zhudaoquan de xiandai yu-fushu (When he wants you to take charge in bed), translated by Hou Yanqing. *Kemengbodan,* July 104–08.

Barclay, G. (1954). *Colonial development and population in Taiwan.* New Jersey: Princeton University Press.

Barlow, T. (1994). Body, subject and power in China. In A. Zito & T. Barlow (Eds.), *Theorising woman: Funu, guojia, jiating (Chinese woman, Chinese state, Chinese family)* (pp. 253–90). Chicago: The University of Chicago Press.

Barreaca, R. 1995. Tianmi de fuchou (Sweet revenge), translated by Zheng Qilun. *Kemengbodan,* December, 148–49.

Barton, A. H., & Lazarsfeld, P. F. (1955). *Some functions of qualitative analysis in social research.* Reprinted from Frankfurte, Beitrage Zur Soziologie, Band 1.

Beck-Gernsheim, E. (2002). *Reinventing the family: In search of new lifestyles.* Cambridge: Polity Press.

Bender, D., & Leone, B. (Eds.). (1995). *Sexual values: Opposing viewpoints*. California: Greenhaven Press.

Bendix, R. (1973). *Max Weber: An intellectual portrait*. Thetford, Norfolk: Lowe & Brydone (Printers) Ltd.

Berger, P. (1966). *Invitation to sociology: A humanistic perspective*. Harmondsworth: Penguin.

Bhugra, D., & de Silva, P. (1993). Sexual dysfunction across cultures. *International Review of Psychiatry* 5:243–52.

Brownell, S., & Wassertrom, J. (2002). Theorising femininities and masculinities. In Brownell. & J. Wassertrom, *Chinese femininities, Chinese masculinities: A reader,* (pp. 1–42). California: University of California Press.

Bruce, S. (2002). *God is dead: Secularisation in the West*. Malden, MA: Blackwell Publishing.

Buckley, R. (1997). *Hong Kong: The road to 1997*. Cambridge and New York: Cambridge University Press.

Cai, H. M. (1995a). Li Zi de meili bu shefang (When love is concerned, Li Zi is unlike other young people). *Kemengbodan,* December, 94–7.

——— (1995b). Ta bu cha, ta shi wo de qingmi airen (Mr Perfect is not your only choice). *Kemengbodan,* December, 80–2.

——— (1996). Zouxiang baiwan nianxin de hanglie (How to get a real raise). *Kemengbodan*, September, 132–35.

Cai, H. M., Huang, Y. X., Ye, D. R., & Wu, P. W. (1996). Shen nüren jiaoren nanyi kangju (Cosmo girls are talking about allure). *Kemengbodan,* September, 122–29.

Caldwell, J. C. (1982). *Theory of fertility decline*. London and New York: Academic Press.

Cato, L. (1995). *Her version*. Victoria: Australia Penguin Books.

Cernada, G. P., Chang, M. C. , Lin, H. S., & Sun, T. H. (1986). Adolescent sexuality and family planning awareness, knowledge, attitudes and behaviour: Taiwan. *Asian Studies Committee Occasional Papers Series* 12. International Area Studies Programs, University of Massachusetts at Amherst, 1–45.

Chan, D. (1986). The culture of Hong Kong: A myth or reality? In A.

Y. H. Kwan & D. Chan (Eds.), *Hong Kong Society: A Reader* (pp. 209–29). Hong Kong: Writer's & Publisher's Cooperative.

Chang, J. S. (2005). Sexual revolution in Chinese societies—Are young people becoming less Chinese? Refereed proceedings of the Australian and New Zealand Sociological Association Conference 2005: Community, Place and Change. 11 pp.

——— (2003). Encumbered womanhood. *The Drawing Board: An Australian Review of Public Affairs*, 21 May.

——— (1999). Scripting extramarital affairs: Marital mores, gender politics and infidelity in Taiwanese newspaper stories. *Modern China* 25(1):69–99.

——— (1996). What do education and work mean?—Education, non-familial work/living Experiences and premarital sex for women in Taiwan. *Journal of Comparative Family Studies* 27:13–40.

Chang, J. S, Tsang, K. T. , Lui, P. K. , & Lin, J. H. (1997). Premarital sexual mores in Taiwan and Hong Kong: Two pathways to permissiveness. *Journal of African and Asian Studies* 32(3/4):265–85.

Chiao, C. (1969). Female chastity in Chinese culture. (unpublished)

Chu, G., & Ju, Y. (1993). *The Great Wall in ruins: Communication and cultural change in China*. Albany: State University of New York Press.

Chun, A. (1994). From nationalism to nationalising: Cultural imagination and state formation in postwar Taiwan. *The Australian Journal of Chinese Affairs,* January, 31:49–69.

Cohen, M. L. (1976). *House united, house divided: The Chinese family in Taiwan*. New York: Columbia University Press.

Countryman, W. (1989). *Dirt, greed and sex: Sexual ethics in the New Testament and their implications for Today*. London: SCM Press Ltd.

Croll, E. (1981). *The politics of marriage in contemporary China*. New York: Cambridge University Press.

Damm, J. (2005). Same sex desire and society in Taiwan, 1970–1987. *China Quarterly* 181:67–81.

Davis, D., & Harrell, S. (Eds.). (1993). *Chinese families in the post-Mao era*. Berkeley, Los Angeles and London: University of California Press.

Darby, P. (Ed.). (1997). *At the edge of international relations: Postcolonialism, gender, and dependency*. London: Pinter.

Davidson, J. (1995). Nanren bu xian zuoai de shige liyou (Ten reasons men say no to sex), translated by Zheng Qilun. *Kemengbodan,* December, 140–44.

de Bary, Wm. T. (1970). *Self and society in Ming thought.* New York: Columbia University Press.

d'Entrèves, M. P., & Benhabib, S. (Eds.). (1997). *Habermas and the unfinished project of modernity: Critical essays on the philosophical discourse of modernity*. Cambridge, MA: MIT Press.

Dianne. (1995). Xiao nanren dang hong (Give love a chance, give him a chance), translated by Zheng Chunwen. *Kemengbodan,* December, 73–5.

Duncombe, J., & Marsden, D. (1996). Whose orgasm is this anyway? Sex work in long-term heterosexual couple relationships. In J. Weeks & J. Holland (Eds.), *Sexual cultures: Communities, values and intimacy* (pp. 220–38). London: MacMillan Press Ltd.

Durkheim, E. (1976). *The elementary forms of the religious life.* London: Allen and Unwin.

Dworkin, A. (1981). *Pornorgraphy: Men possessing women*. London: The Women's Press.

Editor. (1993). Zixin De Nüren Cai Mei (Confident women are the most beautiful). *Kemengbodan,* September, 8.

——— (1994). Huo de yiran zizai (Women can have a self in life). *Kemengbodan,* July, 10.

Edwards, J. N., & Booth, A. (1994). Sexuality, marriage, and well-Being: The middle Years. In A. S. Rossi (Ed.), *Sexuality across the life course* (pp. 233–59). Chicago: University of Chicago Press.

Eisenstadt, S. (2003). *Comparative civilisations and multiple modernities*. Leiden: Brill.

Eisenstadt, S. (2000). Multiple modernities. In S. Eisenstadt (Ed.), *Multiple Modernities. Daedalus* 129:1–30.

Eisenstadt, S. (Ed.). (1986). *The origins and diversity of Axial age civilizations*. Albany: State University of New York Press.

Elder, G. H. (1979). Historical changes in life patterns and personality. In P. B. Baltes & O. G. Brim (Eds.), *Life-span development and behaviour* 2:118–61. New York: Academic Press.

Elliott, F. (1996). *Gender, family and society*. London: MacMillan Press Ltd.

Elvin, M. (1984). Female virtue and the state in China. *Past and Present* 104:111–52.

Evans, H. (1997). *Women and sexuality in China*. Oxford: Polity Press.

Falangxisi. (1993). Ta guo de shi qingfujie (Mistress's Valentine's day). *Kemengbodan,* September, 252–5.

——— (1994). Sadan de shizhe (Satan's messenger). *Kemengbodan,* July, 169–71.

Fan, M. S., Hong, J. H. , Ng, M. L. , Lee, L. K. C., Lui, P. K., & Choy, Y. H. (1995). Western influences on Chinese sexuality: Insights from a comparison of the sexual behaviour and attitudes of Shanghai and Hong Kong freshmen at universities. *Journal of Sex Education and Therapy* 21(3):158–66.

Farquhar, J. (2002). *Appetites: Food and xex in postsocialist China*. Durham & London: Duke University Press.

Farrer, J. (2002). *Opening up: Youth sex culture and market reform in Shanghai*. Chicago: University of Chicago Press.

Ferguson, M. (1983). *Forever feminine: Women's magazines and the cult of femininity*. London: Heinemann Educational Books Ltd.

Fetterman, D. M. (1989). *Ethnology: Step by step*. New York: Sage Publications.

Fisher, H. E. (1992). *Anatomy of love: The natural history of monogamy, adultery, and divorce*. New York and London: W. W. Norton and Company.

Ford, J., Voli, P. K., & Casey, S. (1998). Gender role portrayals in Japanese advertising: A magazine content analysis. *Journal of Advertising* 27(1):113–25.

Freedman, M. (1970). Rites and duties, or Chinese marriage. In M. Freedman (Ed.), *The study of Chinese society* (pp. 255–72). Stanford, California: Stanford University Press.

Friedan, B. (1963). *The feminine mystique*. New York: Dell Publishing.

Fukuyama, F. (1992). *The end of history and the last man*. New York: Free Press.

Gagnon, J. H., & Simon, J. (1973). *Sexual conduct: The social origins of human sexuality*. Chicago: Aldine.

Gao, S. (1994). Wo de qingrenmen (All my lovers ...). *Kemengbodan,* July, 122–3.

Geng, W. X. (1991). Dangdai daxuesheng hunqian xing xingwei yanjiu ji xing jiaoyu shexiang (Research into the premarital sexual activities of students today and tentative ideas about sex education). Huadong Normal University, Shanghai. (unpublished)

Gerth, H. H., & Mills, C. W. (Eds.). (1977). *From Max Weber: Essays in sociology*. London, Henley and Boston: Routledge & Kegan Paul.

Giddens, A. (1991). *Modernity and self-identity*. Cambridge: Polity Press.

Giddens, A. (1990). *The consequences of modernity*. Cambridge: Polity Press.

Glaser, B., & Strauss, A. (1967). *The discovery of grounded theory: Strategies for qualitative research*. Chicago: Aldine.

Gongwubuke de miantan EQ (Complete guide: how to ace the interview, make them say "We want you"). (1997). *Kemengbodan,* March, 96–102.

Goode, W. J. (1982). *The Family*. Eaglewood Cliff, New Jersey: Prentice-Hall.

——— (1970). *World revolution and family patterns*. New York: The Free Press.

Greeley, A. (1994). Marital infidelity. *Society* 31(4):9–14.

Greenhalgh, S., & Winckler, E. (2005). *Governing China's population: From Leninist to neoliberal biopolitics*. Stanford, California: Stanford University Press.

Greenhalgh, S. (1985). Sexual stratification in East Asia. *Population and Development Review* 11(2):265–314.

Gregersen, E. (1986). Human sexuality in cross-cultural perspective. In B. Donn & K. K. Hillsdale (Eds.), *Alternative Approach to the Study of Sexual Behaviour* (pp. 87–102). New Jersey: Lawrence Erlbaum Associates Publishers.

Gudorf, C. (1994). *Body, sex and pleasure*. Cleveland, Ohio: The Pilgrim Press.

Gulik, R. H. (1974). *Sexual life in ancient China,* Leiden: E. J. Brill.

Habermas, J. (1987). *The philosophical discourse of modernity.* Cambridge: Polity.

Halpern, H. (1994). Cong chikuan danlian di miqing zhong fusheng (Getting on with your life after love addiction), translated by Yanqing Hou. *Kemengbodan,* July, 114–5.

Hannerz, U. (1990). Cosmopolitans and locals in world culture. In M. Featherstone (Ed.), *Global culture* (pp. 237–51). London: Sage.

Hareven, T. K. (1982). *Family time and industrial time.* New York: Cambridge.

Hefner, R. (1998). Multiple modernities: Christianity, Islam, and Hinduism in a globalising age. *Annual Review of Anthropology* 27:83–104.

Hein, H. (2000). *Sexual detours: Infidelity and intimacy at the crossroads*. New York: St Martin's Press.

Hill, N. (1994). Yushuizhihuan shi de gangga yiwai (When sex goes hilariously wrong), translated by Yanqing Hou. *Kemengbodan,* July, 118–20.

Hinsch, B. (1990). *Passions of the cut sleeve: The male homosexual tradition in China*. Berkeley: University of California Press.

Hite, S. (1994). *The Hite report on the family: Growing up under patriarchy.* New York: Grove Press.

Hite, S. (1987). *The Hite report: Women and love.* New York: Alfred A. Knopf, Inc.

Holland, J., Ramazanoglu, C., Sharpe, S. & Thomson, R. (1996). Reputations: Journeying into gendered power relations. In J.

Weeks & J. Holland (Eds.), *Sexual cultures: Communities, values and intimacy* (pp. 239–60). London: MacMillan Press Ltd.

Holmgren, J. (1984). The economic foundations of virtue: Widow-remarriage in early and modern China. *The Australian Journal of Chinese Affairs* 13:1–27.

Hong Kong Family Studies Association, *Youth Sexuality Studies*. http://www.famplan.org.hk

Honig, E. (2003). Socialist sex: The Cultural Revolution revisited. *Modern China* 29(2):143–75.

Honig, E., & Hershatter, G. (1988). *Personal voices*. Stanford, CA: Stanford University Press.

Hooper, B. (1985). *Youth in China*. Ringwood, Victoria: Penguin Books Australia.

Horrocks, R. (1997). *An introduction to the study of sexuality.* Houndmills, Basingstoke, Hampshire: Macmillan Press Ltd.

Hsu, F. L. K. (1983). *Rugged individualism reconsidered.* Knoxville: The University of Tennessee Press.

Hu, T. L. (1982). *Xifu Guo Men (Daughters-in-law stepping over the threshold)*. Taipei: Shibao Wenhua Publication, Inc.

Huang, Y. (1996). Zhang xiaoxian ba lian'ai tan de geng liti (What a love player). *Kemengbodan,* September, 148.

Hunt, M. (1974). *Sexual behaviour in the 1970s.* New York: Dell Publishing.

Hunt, M. (1969). *The affairs: A portrait of extramarital love in contemporary America*. New York: World Publishing.

Huntington, S. P. (1996). *The clash of civilisations and the remaking of world order.* New York: Simon & Schuster.

Inkeles, A., & Smith, D. (1974). *Becoming modern: Individual change in six developing countries.* Cambridge, MA: Harvard University Press.

Inglehart, R., Basanez, M., Diez-Medrano, J., Halman, L. & Luijx, R. (Eds.). (2004). *Human beliefs and values: A cross-cultural sourcebook based on the 1999–2002 values surveys.* Mexico: Siglo XXI Editores.

Ip, H. Y. (2003). Fashioning appearances: Feminine beauty in Chinese communist revolutionary culture. *Modern China* 29(3):329–61.

Jacoby, S. (1993). Xinghuanyu de shashou—nüxing de chuangdi zhi you (Pleasure poisoners: things women fear in bed), Amanda (trans.). *Kemengbodan*, September, 93–6.

Jai, B. R. (1995). Zhongguo renxingguang chutan (An exploratory study of Chinese sexuality). *Thoughts and Words* (*Si Yu Yan*) 33(3):27–76.

Janghorbani, M., Lam, T. H., & The Youth Sexuality Study Task Force. (2003). Sexual media use by young adults in Hong Kong: Prevalence and associated factors. *Archives of Sexual Behaviours* 32(6):545–53.

Jeffreys, E. (Ed.). (2006). *Sex and sexuality in China*. London and New York: Routledge.

Jeffreys, S. (1990). *Anticlimax: A feminist perspective on the sexual revolution*. London: The Women's Press.

Jiang, H. S. (1994). Yinfazu de xing'ai misi (The myth of elderly sex life). *Kemengbodan,* July, 40.

Johnson, D., Nathan, A. J. & Rawski, E. S. (Eds.). (1985). *Popular culture in late Imperial China*. Berkeley: University of California Press.

Kalberg, S. (Ed.). (2005). *Max Weber: Readings and commentary on modernity.* Malden, MA: Blackwell Publishing.

Kamali, M. (2006). *Multiple Modernities, civil society and Islam: The case of Iran and Turkey.* Liverpool University Press.

Kang, C. K. (1996). *Chongshen fengyue jian: Xing yu zhongguo gudian wenxue (Aspects of sexuality and literature in Ancient China).* Taipei: Maitian Publisher.

Kaya, I. (2004). Modernity, openness, interpretation: A perspective on multiple modernities. *Social Science Information* 43(1):35–57.

Kaya, I. (2003). *Social theory and late modernities.* Liverpool: Liverpool University Press.

King, Y. C. (1994). Kuan-hsi and network building: A sociological interpretation. In Wei-ming Tu (Ed.), *The living three: The changing meaning of being Chinese today,* (pp. 109–26). Stanford, CA: Stanford University Press.

Kinsey, A., Pomeroy, W. & Martin, C. (1948). *Sexual behaviour in the human male*. Philadelphia: W. B. Saunders.

Kinsey, A., Pomeroy, W., & Martin, C. (1953). *Sexual Behaviour in the human female*. Philadelphia: W. B. Saunders.

Kirca, S. (2001). Turkish women's magazines: The popular meets the political. *Women's Studies International Forum* 24(3–4):457–68.

Kleinman, S. (1993). Ruhe chengwei yige chenggong de nü zhuguan (Becoming the kind of boss you'd like to work with), Wu Wenqi (trans.). *Kemengbodan,* September, 108–11.

Kramer, M. (1994). Aiqing bian youqing? (Let's not be friends), William Farris (trans.). *Kemengbodan,* July, 14.

Kung, L. (1983). *Factory women in Taiwan*. Ann Arbor, MI: University of Michigan Research Press.

Kwok, D. W. Y. (1998). On the rites and rights of being human. In de Bary, Wm T., & Tu, W. (Eds.), *Confucianism and Human Rights* (pp. 83–93). New York: Columbia University Press.

Lai, P. (1994). *Nüxing zazhi yu nüxing jiazhi xiangguanxing de fenxi (Analysis of the association between woman's magazines and changes in women's values)*. MA thesis, National Chengchih University, Taiwan. (unpublished)

Lang, O. (1968). *Chinese family and society*. Conn.: Archon Books.

Lau, K. W. (Ed.). (2006). *Cinemas and popular media in transcultural East Asia*. Temple University Press.

Lau, M. P., & Ng, M. L. (1989). Homosexuality in Chinese culture. *Culture, Medicine and Psychiatry* 13:465–88.

Lau, S. K. (1987). *Society and politics in Hong Kong*. Hong Kong: The Chinese University Press.

Lau, S. K. (1981). Chinese familism in an urban-industrial setting: The case of Hong Kong. *Journal of Marriage and Family* 43(4):977–92.

Lau, S. K., & Kuan, H. C. (1991). *The ethos of the Hong Kong Chinese*. Hong Kong: The Chinese University Press.

Laumann, E., Gagnon, J., Michael, T., & Michaels, S. (1994). *The social organization of sexuality: Sexual practices in the United States*. Chicago and London: The University of Chicago Press.

Lawson, A. (1988). *Adultery: An analysis of love and betrayal*. New York: Basic.

Lee, R. (1993). *Doing research on sensitive topics*. New York: Sage Publications.

Lee, R. L. M. (2006). Reinventing modernity: Reflexive modernisation vs liquid modernity vs multiple modernities. *European Journal of Social Theory* 9(3):355–68.

Lerner, D. (1958). *The passing of traditional society: Modernising the Middle East*. Glencoe, IL: Free Press.

Leung, L. Y. M. (1996). *The local meets the global: A study of upmarket women's magazines in Hong Kong: The case of Cosmopolitan*. PhD dissertation. Sussex University. (unpublished)

Levant, R. (1997). Nonrelational sexuality in men. In R. Levant & G. Brooks (Eds.), *Men and sex: New psychological perspectives* (pp. 9–27). New York: John Wiley & Sons.

Levant, R., & Brooks, G. (1997). Men and the problem of nonrelational sex. In R. Levant & G. Brooks (Eds.), *Men and Sex: New Psychological Perspectives*,(pp. 1–8). New York: John Wiley & Sons, Inc.

Levy, M. (1966). *Modernization and the structure of societies: A setting for international affairs*. Princeton, NJ: Princeton University Press.

Li, Z. (2000). Guangzhou qingshaonian xing wenti diaocha (Investigation on adolescent sex-related issues in Guanzhou). *Zhongguo Shehui Baojian Qikang (Chinese Journal of Social Health)* 21:105.

Li, L., & Yan, H. W. (1996). Abstract. Taiwan qingshaonian xing xingwei yanjiu zhi huigu (Review of studies on adolescent sexual behaviours in Taiwan). *Taiwan Xingxue Xuekang (Taiwan Sex Research Journal)* 2(2):48.

Li, Y. H. (1991). *Zhongguo Ren De Xingai Yu Hunyin (Sex, love and marriage of the Chinese)*. Zhengzhou: Henan Renming Publisher.

——— (1996). Zhongguo Nuxing De Xing Yu Ai (*Sex and love of Chinese women)*. Hong Kong: Oxford University Press.

Li, A. (1994). Xingsaorao vs xinggaochao (sexual harassment vs. sexual orgasm). *Kemengbodan,* July, 36–8.

——— (1995). Shei shi zui kongbu de nüren? (The most horrible women: the other woman). *Kemengbodan,* December, 40.

——— (1996). Bukeyi Luanmo (Don't touch). *Kemengbodan,* September, 10.

Lin, H. S., & Lin, S. H. (1996). Taiwan diqu gaozhong gaozhi ji wuzhuan zaixiao nan nu xuesheng xing zhishi taidu yu xingwei xiankuang ji bianqian (A study of sex knowledge, attitudes and behaviours among students in high school, vocational school and junior college in Taiwan). (unpublished)

Lin, T. Y., Tseng, W. S., & Yeh, E. K. (1995). *Chinese societies and mental health*. Hong Kong: Oxford University Press.

Liu, D. L., Ng, M. L., Zhou, L. P. & Haeberle, E. J. (1992). *Zhongguo Dangdai Xingwenhua: Zhongguo Lianwanli Xingwenming Diaocha Baogao (Sex culture in modern China: A report of 20,000-case nationwide "sex civilisation" survey)*. Shanghai: Joint Publishing.

Liu, K. (2004). *Globalization and cultural trends in China*. Honolulu: University of Hawai'i Press.

Livingston, R. (1994). Yu yu xiongzhang de nanti (Broccoli and burgers), Kai Li (trans.). *Kemengbodan*, July, 20.

Loe, N. (2004). *The rise of viagra*. New York: New York University Press.

Lu, H. X. (1989). Taiwan funü chengzhang tuanti: nüxing yishi de benti bianzou (Images of women's self-growth groups in Taiwan: a cultural process of women searching for autonomy). In Y. Ma (Ed.), *Dangjin Funü Juese Yu Dingwei (The role and position of women today)* (pp. 269–92). Taipei: Guoji Chongta She.

Lu, T. L. (1995). *Misogyny, cultural nihilism & oppositional politics: Contemporary Chinese experimental fiction*. Stanford, CA: Stanford University Press.

Lu, X. F. (1992). Lu Xiaofeng—tueiquei wuguangshise (Lu Xiaofeng:

yearning for peace in life). *Kemengbodan,* July, 112–4.

Lusterman, D. (1997). Repetitive infidelity, womanising, and Don Juanism. In R. Levant & G. Brooks (Eds.), *Men and sex: New psychological perspectives* (pp. 94–9). New York: John Wiley & Sons, Inc.

Lyle, K. (1983). Planned birth in Tianjin. *China Quarterly* 83:551–67.

MacKinnon, C. (1982). Feminism, Marxism, method and the state: An agenda for theory. *Signs* 7(3):515–44.

Malinowski, B. (1937). *Sex and repression in savage society*. London: Kegan Paul, Trench, Trubner.

——— (1929). *The sexual life of savages in north-western Melanesia: An ethnographic account of courtship, marriage and family life among the natives of Trobriand Islands, British New Guinea.* New York: Halcyon House.

Mannheim, K. 1952. The Problem of Generations. In *Essays in the Sociology of Knowledge,* edited by K. Mannheim, 276–322. London: Routledge, Keagan and Paul.

Martinelli, A. (2005). *Global modernization: Rethinking the project of modernity*. London, Thousand Oaks and New Delhi: Sage.

McClelland, D. (1961). *Achieving society.* Princeton, NJ: Van Nostrand.

McCormick, N. (1994). *Sexual salvation: Affirming women's wexual rights and pleasures*. Westport, CT: Praeger.

McRobbie, A. (1997). More! New sexualities in girls' and women's magazines. In A. McRobbie (Ed.), *Back to reality? Social experience and cultural studies* (pp. 190–209). New York: Manchester University Press: distributed by St Martin's Press.

McRobbie, A. (1994). *Postmodernism and popular culture*. London: Routledge.

McRobbie, A. (1991). *Feminism and youth culture: From Jackie to just seventeen.* Basingstoke: Macmillan.

Mead, M. (1935). *Sex and temperament in three primitive societies.* London: Routledge & Kegan Paul Ltd.

Meade. (1992). Xin qingmi fangshi, oral sex (Oral sex: the new intimacy), Zhang Shiying (trans.). *Kemengbodan,* July, 100–07.

Merli, G., & Hertog, S. (2004). Modelling the course of the HIV/AIDS epidemic in China: An application of a bio-behavioural macro-simulation model of the spread of HIV/AIDS. (unpublished)

Mezzich, J., & Berganza, C. (Eds.). (1984). *Culture and psychopathology.* New York: Columbia University Press.

Michael, R., Gagnon, J., Laumann, E., & Kolata, G. (1994). How many sexual partners do Americans have? In J. Henslin (Ed.), *Life in Society* (2005) (pp. 235–43). Boston, New York and San Francisco: Pearson.

Mills, N. (1994). Yuhuochongsheng de Dennis Quaid (Born again, Dannis Quaid). Kai Li (trans.). *Kemengbodan,* July, 136–38.

Modell, J., Furstenberg, F. F. Jr., & Strong, D. (1978). The timing of marriage in the transition to adulthood: Continuity and change. *American Journal of Sociology* 84:S120–50.

Murphy, R. (1971). *The dialectics of social life: Alarms and excursions in anthropological theory*. London: George Allen & Unwin Ltd.

Natalia. (1992). Ni hen ai ta, ta que bu ai ni (You like him a lot, he likes you a little). M. G. Huang (trans.). *Kemengbodan,* July, 80–3.

Nelson, J. B. (1978). *Embodiment: An approach to sexuality and Christian theology.* Minneapolis: Augsburg Publishing House.

Newman, J. (1992). Shimao hangye: gongguan (Thinking of a career switch? Try PR), L. Y. Han (trans.). *Kemengbodan,* July: 84–9.

Ng, M. L. E., & Ma, J. L. C. (2001). Supplemental countries on the world wide web: Hong Kong. In R. Francoeur (Ed.), *The international encyclopedia of sexuality,* Vol. IV. New York and London: Continuum. (http://www.SexQuest.com/IES4/

Norwood, R. (1985). *Women who love too much*. New York: Pocket Books.

Nye, R. (Ed.). (1999). *Sexuality.* New York: Oxford University Press.

Ogburn, W. F., & Nimkoff, M. F. (1976). *Technology and the changing family.* Westport: Greenwood Press.

Ogburn, W. F., & Tibbits, C. (1933). The family and its functions.

In *Recent Social Trends in the United States,* Vol. 1. New York: McGraw-Hill.

Parish, W., & Whyte, M. (1978). *Village and family in contemporary China*. Chicago: University of Chicago Press.

Parsons, T. (1971). *The system of modern societies.* Englewood Cliffs, NJ: Prentice-Hall.

Parsons, T. (1966). *Societies: Evolutionary and comparative perspectives.* Englewood Cliffs, NJ: Prentice-Hall.

Parsons, T. (1960). *Structure and process in modern societies.* Glencoe, IL: Free Press.

Parsons, T. (1951). *The social system.* London: Routledge & K. Paul.

Pearson, V., & Leung, B. K. P. (Eds.). (1995). *Women in Hong Kong.* Hong Kong: Oxford University Press.

Pegg, L. (1986). *Family law in Hong Kong*. Singapore: Butterworths.

Pennington, J. (2007). *The history of sex in American film*. Westport, Connecticut & London: Praeger.

Pietropinto, A. (1995). Rang nanren kemu ni (The dream girl). Peng Xiaohan (trans.). *Kemengbodan,* December, 138–39.

Pietropinto, A., & Simenauer, J. (1977). *Beyond the male myth: What women want to know about men's sexuality.* New York: Times Books.

Pike, K. (1967). *Language in relation to a unified theory of the structure of human behaviour*. The Hague: Mouton.

Plumer, K. (1995). *Telling sexual stories*. London: Routeledge.

Porter, D. (Ed.). (1992). *Between men and feminism*. London: Routledge.

Posner, R. (1992). *Sex and reason*. Cambridge, MA: Harvard University Press.

Punch, K. (2005). *Introduction to social research: Quantitative and qualitative approaches*. London and Thousand Oaks, CA: Sage.

Qian, X., Tang, S. L. & Garner, P. (2004). Unintended pregnancy and induced abortion among unmarried women in China. *Health Services Research* 4:1 (published online 2004 January 22. Doi:10.1186/1472-6963-4-1).

Qiao, Q. (1995). Nanrenwei de cuiqing xiaoguo (Take a smell and stick with him). *Kemengbodan,* December, 156–57.

——— (1997). Wanquan biyun xinzhi (All new information about contraception). *Kemengbodan,* March, 105–07.

Redfield, R. (1962). *Human nature and the study of society,* Vol. 1. Chicago: University of Chicago Press.

Regan, H., & Brooks, G. (1995). *Out of women's experience: Creating Relational Leadership.* Thousand Oaks, CA: Corwin Press.

Reinharz, S. (1992). *Feminist methods in social research.* New York: Oxford University Press.

Reiss, I. (1986). *Journey into sexuality: An exploratory voyage.* Englewood Cliffs, NJ: Prentice-Hall.

Reiss, I., Anderson, R. E. & Sponaugle, G. C. (1980). A multivariate model of the determinants of extramarital sexual permissiveness. *Journal of Marriage and the Family* 42:395–411.

Rich, A. (1980). Compulsory heterosexuality and lesbian existence. *Signs* 5(4):631–60.

Richards, M., & Elliott, J. (1991). Sex and marriage in the 1960s and 1970s. In D. Clark (Ed.), *Marriage, domestic life and social change: Writings for Jacqueline Burgoyne,* (pp. 1944–48). London: Routledge.

Riley, M. W. (1976). Age strata in social Systems. In R. Binstock & E. Shanas (Eds.), *Handbook of aging and the social sciences* (pp. 189–217). New York: Van Nostrand Reinhold Co.

Riley, N. (1989). *Gender and generation in modern Beijing.* PhD dissertation. Johns Hopkins University. (unpublished)

Rindfuss, R., & Morgan, P. (1983). Marriage, sex, and the first birth interval: The quiet revolution in Asia. *Population and Development Review* 9(2):259–78.

Robinson, V. (1993). Heterosexuality: Beginnings and connections. In S. Wilkinson & C. Kitzinger (Eds.), *Heterosexuality: A Feminism & Psychology Reader* (pp. 80–2). London: Sage.

Roniger, L., & Waisman, C. (Eds.). (2002). *Globality and multiple modernities: Comparative north American and Latin American perspectives*. Sussex Academic Press.

Rosenberger, N. (1995). Antiphonal performances? Japanese women's magazines and women's Voices. In L. Skov & B. Moeran (eds.), *Women, media, and consumption in Japan* (pp. 143–69). Richmond, Surrey: Curzon Press.

Rostow, W. (1960). *The stages of economic growth, a non-communist manifesto*. Cambridge (England): Cambridge University Press.

Ruan, F. F. (1991). *Sex in China: Studies in sexology in Chinese culture*. New York and London: Plenum Press.

Ruan, F. F., & Lau, M. P. (1999). China. In R. Francoeur (Ed.). *The international encyclopedia of sexuality*, Vol. I:344–99. New York and London: Continuum.

Ruan, F. F., & Bullough, V. (1992). Lesbianism in China. *Archives of Sexual Behaviour* 21(3):217–25.

Rubinstein, M. (1999). Taiwan: A new history. New York: M. E. Sharpe.

Rutherford, P. (2007). *A world made sexy: Freud to Madonna*. Toronto: University of Toronto Press.

Ryder, N. B. (1965). The cohort as a concept in the study of social change. *American Sociological Review* 30:843–61.

Sachsenmaier, D. (2002). *Reflections on multiple modernities*. Leiden: Brill Academic Publishers.

Sachenmeyer, D., & Riedel, J. (Eds.). (2002). *Rethinking multiple modernities, Europe, China and other civilisations,* Lieden: Brill Academic Publishers.

Sakamoto, K. (1999). Reading Japanese women's magazines: The construction of new identities in the 1970s and 1980s. *Media, Culture, and Society* 21(2):173–93.

Salaff, J. (1981). *Working daughters of Hong Kong: Filial piety or power in the family?* Cambridge & New York: Cambridge University Press.

Salamon, E. (1984). *The kept woman: Mistresses in the '80s*. London: Orbis Publishing.

Saunders, J. M., & Edwards, J. N. (1984). Extramarital wexuality: A predictive model of permissive attitudes. *Journal of Marriage and the Family* 46(4):825–35.

Schutz, A. (1967). *The phenomeonology of social world.* Evanston, IL: Northwestern University Press.

Seal, D. W., & Ehrhardt, A. A. (2007). Masculinity and urban man. In R. Parker & P. Aggleton (Eds.), *Culture, society and sexuality: A reader* (2nd edition) (pp. 375–96). Oxon and New York: Routledge.

Segell, M. (1993). Kelin yisiweite—duoqing miantian de lengxue yinghan (Clint Eastwood: The man behind the myth). Xiao Lu (trans.). *Kemengbodan*, September, 186–90.

Seneca, T. (1996). *The history of women's magazines: Magazines as virtual communities.* Internet publishing. <http://is.gseis.ucla.edu/impact/f93/students/tracy/tracy_hist.html>.

Shaw, T. (1991). Taiwan: Gangsters or good guys? In Freilich, M., Reybeck, D., & Savishinsky, J. (Eds.), *Deviance: Anthropological perspectives* (pp. 173–90). New York: Bergin & Garvey.

Sheridan, S. (1995). Reading the *Women's Weekly*: Feminism, femininity and popular culture. In B. Caine & R. Pringle (Eds.), *Transitions: New Australian feminisms* (pp. 88–101). St Leonards. NSW: Allen & Unwin, Australia.

Shevelow, K. (1989). *Women and print culture: The construction of femininity in the early periodical.* London: Routledge.

Siedman, S. (1992). *Embattled eros: Sexual politics and ethics in contemporary America.* New York: Routledge.

Simon, W., & Gagnon, J. H. (2007). Sexual scripts. In R. Parker, and P. Aggleton (Eds.), *Culture, society and sexuality: A reader* (2nd edition) (pp. 31–40). Oxon and New York: Routledge.

Simonds, W. (1994). *Women and self-help culture: Reading between the lines.* New Brunswick, New Jersey: Rutgers University Press.

Skocpol, T., & Somers, M. (1980). The uses of comparative history in macrosocial inquiry. *Comparative Studies in Society and History*, April, 22 (2):174–97.

Smelser, N. (1976). *Comparative methods in the social sciences.*

Englewood Cliffs, NJ: Prentice-Hall, Inc.

Smith, L. (1995). Shenyang de waiyu ling ren niannian bu wang? (The most memorable affair?) Yanqing Hou (trans.). *Kemengbodan,* December, 10.

Smith, R. (1993). Jinye, ni yao sex de 25 da liyou (Twenty-five reasons to make love tonight). Amanda (trans.). *Kemengbodan,* September, 98.

Smith, T. (1994). Attitudes toward sexual permissiveness: Trends, correlates, and behavioural connections. In A. Rossi (Ed.), *Sexuality across the Life Course* (pp. 63–98). Chicago: University of Chicago Press.

Smith, V. (1996). Meiyou tingbuliao de ai (The story of my obsession). Yu Xuan (trans.). *Kemengbodan,* September, 118–20.

Snowden, L. (1996). Shei shuo ni zhi neng yongyou yige qingren? (Who says you have to have just one lover?). Shuang Wu (trans.). *Kemengbodan*, September, 96–7.

Solomon, R. (1988). *About love: Reinventing romance for our times.* New York: Simon and Schuster.

Stacy, J. (1991). Promoting normality: Section 28 and the regulation of sexuality. In S. Franklin, C. Lury & J. Stacey (Eds.), *Off Centre: Feminism and cultural studies,* (pp. 284–304). Hammersmith, London, UK; New York, NY, USA: Harper Collins Academic.

Steward, D. W., & Shamdasani, P. N. (1990). *Focus groups: Theory and practice.* Chicago: Sage Publications.

Stuart, A. (1990). Feminism: Dead or alive? In J. Rutherford (Ed.), *Identity: Community, culture, difference* (pp. 28–43). London: Lawrence and Wishart.

Strauss, A., & Corbin, J. (1990). *Basics of qualitative research: Grounded theory procedures and techniques*. London and New Delhi: Sage Publications.

Strauss, A., & Corbin, J. (Eds.). (1997). *Grounded theory in practice.* Thousand Oaks: Sage Publications.

Taiwan–Fukien Demographic Fact Book, Ministry of the Interior, Republic of China.

Taylor, C. (2004). *Modern social imaginaries*. Durham: Duke University Press.

The story of Taiwan: East and west, transition and modern. http://www.gio.gov.tw/info/taiwan-story/culture/edown/3-3.htm, accessed 2 March, 2004.

Thornton, A. (2005). *Reading history sideways: The fallacy and enduring impact of the developmental paradigm on family life*. Chicago and London: University of Chicago Press.

Thornton, A., Chang, J. S., & Lin, H. S. (1994). From arranged marriage toward love match: The transformation of marriage arrangements in Taiwan. In A. Thornton, A., & H. S. Lin (Eds.), *Social Change and Family in Taiwan* (pp. 148–77). Chicago: University of Chicago Press.

Thornton, A., & Fricke, T. (1987). Social change and the family: Comparative perspectives from the West, China, and South Asia. *Sociological Forum* 2(4):746–49.

Thornton, A., & Lin, H. S. (Eds.). (1994). *Social change and the family in Taiwan*. Chicago: University of Chicago Press.

Tien, H. M. (1989). *The great transition: Political and social change in the Republic of China*. Stanford, CA: Hoover Institution Press, Stanford University.

Tsai, Y. M., & Yi, C. C. (1997). Persistence and change in Chinese family values: The Taiwanese case. In L. Y. Chang, Y. H. Lu, and F. C. Wang (Eds.), *Taiwanese Society in the 1990s. Taiwan Social Change Survey Symposium Series II (Part 2)* (pp. 123–70). Institute of Sociology, Academia Sinica, Taiwan.

Tsang, K. T. (1990). Xianggang ren de xingguangnian yu xuanjiao wenhua (The sexual concepts of Hong Kong people and missionary culture). In S. H. Wen, K. T. Tseng, & M. L. Ng (Eds.), *Xing Yu Deyu (Sex and moral education)*. Hong Kong: Joint Publishing.

Tsang, K. T. (1986). Sexuality: the Chinese and the Judeo-Christian traditions in Hong Kong. *Bulletin of the Hong Kong Psychological Society* 19/20:19–28.

Tseng, W. S., & Hsu, J. (1970). Chinese culture, personality formation and mental illness. *International Journal of Social Psychiatry* 16:5–14.

Tu, W. M. (2000). Implications of the rise of "Confucian" east Asia. *Daedalus* 129(1):195–218.

Tu, W. M. (Ed.). (1996). *Confucian tradition in east Asian modernity: Moral education and economic culture in Japan and the Four Mini-Dragons.* Cambridge, MA: Harvard University Press.

Turner, R. (1953). The quest for universals in sociological research. *American Sociological Review* 18:604–11.

Unwin, J. D. (1934). *Sex and cultures.* Oxford: Oxford University Press.

van Gulik, R. (1974). *Sexual life in Ancient China.* Leiden: E. J. Brill.

Vance, C. (2007). Anthropology rediscovers sexuality: A theoretical comment. In R. Parker, and P. Aggleton (Eds.), *Culture, society and sexuality: A reader* (2nd edition). Oxon and New York: Routledge.

Vance, C. (Ed.). (1984). *Pleasure and danger: Exploring female sexuality*. London: Routledge & Kegan Paul.

Walters, M. (1994). *Globalisation.* London and New York: Routledge.

Wan, Y. (1995a). Jiaqi lian'ai jike zhenghouqun (Hunger for romance—holiday syndrome). *Kemengbodan*, December, 14.

——— (1995b). Jizheng yedanye lianren (Hurry up to get yourself a lover before Christmas). *Kemengbodan*, December, 130–32.

——— (1995c). Ruguo haoyou de laogong xiyin ni (Help! Your best friend's man is making a pass at you). *Kemengbodan,* December, 146–47.

Wang, B., & Davidson, P. (2006). Sex, lies and videos in rural China: A qualitative study of women's sexual debut and risky sexual behaviour. *Journal of Sex Research* 43:227-35.

Wang, L. Y. (1997). *Jiexi Xingbie Quanli Xia De Shenti Qingyu—Yi Funü Xinxiang Weili (A discoursive analysis of women's body and sexuality under patriarchal power: The case of the women's advice columns in Taiwan's newspapers).* MA thesis, World College,

Taiwan. (unpublished)
Weber, M. (1993). (c1962). *Basic concepts in sociology,* translated and with an introduction by H. P. Secher. Secaucus, NJ: Carol Publishing Group.
Weber, M. (1948). The social psychology of the world religions. In H. H. Gerth & C. Wright Mills (Eds.), *From Max Weber: essays in sociology.* London: Routledge.
Wellings, K., Field, J., Johnson, A. & Wadsworth, J. (1994). *Sexual behaviour in Britain: The national survey of sexual attitudes and lifestyles.* London: Penguin Books.
Wen, J. K. (1995). Sexual beliefs and problems in contemporary Taiwan. In T. Y. Lin et al. (Eds.), *Chinese societies and mental health.* Hong Kong: Oxford University Press.
Whyte, M. (1990). Changes in mate choice in Chengdu. In D. Davis & E. Vogel (Eds.), *Chinese society on the eve of Tiananmen* (pp. 181–214). Cambridge: Harvard University Press.
Winship, J. (1987). *Inside women's magazines.* London and New York: Pandora.
Wolf, M. (1984). Marriage, family, and the state in contemporary China. In M. Young (Ed.), *Courtship, love, and marriage in contemporary China. Pacific Affairs* 1984 (summer): 213–36.
Wolf, M. (1972). *Women and the family in rural Taiwan.* Stanford: Stanford University Press.
Wu, R. Q. (1997). Youxiu de disanzhe (Being a competent other woman). *Kemengbodan*, March, 26.
Wu, W. Q. (1993). Cuowu—Jinbu de qiji (Mistakes give opportunities to improve). *Kemengbodan*, September, 26.
Wu, Y. M. (1994). Fenshou de yishu (Hello ... and good-bye soon). *Kemengbodan*, July, 124–5.
Xie, L. C., Hu, X. T., Yin, L. , Zhong, Y. L. & Zhang, N. X. (2003). Sheng gang Shaonian xing jiankang bijiao yanjiu (A comparative study of adolescents' sex health in Shenzhen and Hong Kong). *Zhongguo Chuji Weisheng Baojian (China Primary Public Health)* 17(1):44–7.

Xu, X. H., & Whyte, M. (1990). Love matches and arranged marriages in China. *Journal of Marriage and the Family* 52(3):709–22.

Yan, H. W., Lin, Y. C. & Chang, L. C. (1998). Qingshaonian hungqian xing xingwei ji qi qushi zhi tantao (The exploration of the trend of adolescents' sexual behaviours). *Taiwan xingxue xuekang (Sex Research Journal)* 4(2):1–14.

Yan, Y. X. (2003). *Private life under socialism: Love, Intimacy, and family change in a Chinese village, 1949–1999*. Stanford: Stanford University Press.

Yang, M. (1965). *A Chinese village: Taitou, Shantung province*. Columbia University Press.

Yang, Z. J. (1997). *Taiwan Baozhi Meiti Suo Chengxian Zhi Nüxing Jiaose Bianqian (Changes in women's roles in the representations of Taiwanese newspapers)*. MA thesis, Chinese Cultural University, Taiwan. (unpublished)

Ye, D. R. (1995). Shenme yang de nüren gan ai qiong xiaozi (When you earn more than he does). *Kemengbodan*, December, 84–8.

——— (1996). Ruhe rang nanren yuxian yusi (What's on his mind about oral sex). *Kemengbodan*, September, 90–2.

——— (1997). Nüren zai 20, 30, 40 sui xuyao shenme yang de xingshenghuo (What do women want in their sexual life at the age of 20, 30, 40?) . *Kemengbodan*, March, 120–4.

Yu, P., & Zhao, W. X. (2004). Yunnan sheng dexuesheng xing guangnian, xing daode he xing xingwei de diaocha fengxi (A survey analysis of sexual attitude, sexual morality and sexual behaviour among university students in Yunnan Province). Yunnan Shifang Daxue Xuebao (Yunnan Normal University Bulletin) 36(2):111–16.

Yue, H., Dong, G. H., Dai, M. J., Zhang, X. M. & Jing, R. W. (2004). Jaingsu sheng weihun yuling funu xing xingwei, rencheng ji rengong liucan xiankuang diaocha (A survey of sexual behaviour, pregnancy and induced abortion among unmarried women in childbearing ages in Jiangsu Province). *Zhongguo Jihua Shengyuxue Zazhi (China Family Planning* magazine) 101(3):150–53.

Yuen, S. P., Law, P. L. & Ho, Y. Y. (2004). *Marriage, gender, and sex in a contemporary Chinese village*. F. Y. Yu (trans.). Armonk, NY, and London, England: M. E. Sharpe.

Zha, B., & Geng, W. (1992). Sexuality in urban China. *The Australian Journal of Chinese Affairs* 28:1–20.

Zhang, J. H. (1993). Zhao Yu—yunhan chuantong de xinshidai nü jingying ren (A traditional woman but a modern manager). *Kemengbodan,* September, 192–93.

Zhang, M. J. (1992). Liuxing yu shenghuo (Fashioned self). *Kemengbodan,* July, 6.

Zhong, Y. Q. (1993). Xianren zhang zhi lian (In love with a married man: it's hell!). *Kemengbodan*, September, 22–4.

Zhou, Y. Y. (1991). *Jiedu Meijiezhong de Nüxing Yishi (Decoding the gender ideology in print media)*. MA thesis, National Chengchih University, Taiwan. (unpublished).

Zhou, X. (1989). Virginity and premarital sex in contemporary China. *Feminist Studies* 15(2):279–88.

Zilbergeld, B. (1992). *The new male sexuality: The truth about men, sex and pleasure*. New York: Bantam Books.

Index

CPSIA information can be obtained at www.ICGtesting.com
Printed in the USA
BVOW012120200911
271653BV00002B/1/P

9 781432 768218